P9-DGU-350

Discovering Your City

Bringing light to the Task of Community Transformation

Includes an
Urban Analysis
Reference Appendix

By
Bob Waymire & Carl Townsend

Published by:
LIGHT International
PO Box 368,
Etna, CA 96027
Phone: 530.467.5373
www.discoveryourcity.com

Printed in the United States of America

ISBN   0-9675342-0-8

This publication is available through:
* *www.discoveryourcity.com*
* *Amazon.com*
* *LIGHT International (quantity orders-address above)*
  Note: *Orders by U.S. bookstores and wholesalers, please
  contact LIGHT International*

If you are interested in other materials related to the subject and
contents of this book, such as: CD containing color maps, related
publications (books, articles, papers, handbooks, etc.) visit:
www.discoveryourcity.com

Cover:
        Map: Global Mapping International (www.gmi.org)
        Design: Debbie Evans

"Thanks be to God who always leads us in His triumph in Christ..."

2 Cor. 2:14

CONTENTS

Appendices

Preface
(Bob Waymire)

Realistically, writing this book goes back twenty years. It was then I began visiting the countries and the cities of the world on a regular basis.

The purpose of those visits was twofold. One was to make an objective evaluation (involving research and analysis) of the status of the Body of Christ in those nations and cities: to determine where the Church was and was not, where the Church was growing and if not, why? Who the Church was working amongst, and to determine the vision, goals and plans of the corporate Church in each location.

A second and corrolary purpose for those visits was to assist the Body of Christ in the many nations in developing national strategy initiatives for mobilizing the whole Body of Christ. The goal was to reach the whole nation so there would be gatherings of believers in every place and within reach of every person, penetrating society with Christ's love, truth, joy and power, and seeing whole societies transformed.

This all began while I was with Overseas Crusades, working and traveling with Jim Montgomery, then OC's director of Research and Strategy. Jim had recently returned from the Philippines where he had developed the national-level Christ The Only Way movement, the forerunner of the DAWN strategy. In the early 80's he left OC to start DAWN Ministries, and I left to start Global Mapping, and subsequently, LIGHT International.

Although our particular roles vary, the commonly-held vision and overall goals have remained pretty much the same. The vision sees "the knowledge of the glory of the Lord covering the earth as the waters cover the sea" in the form of victorious Christians invading and transforming every segment of society to align with the righteousness of our Lord.

i

Discovering Your City

The next significant milestone regarding this book resulted from a series of *Discover Your City* seminars in the U.S. that began in 1995. Under Mission America's sponsorship, DAWN Ministries, Sentinel Group, Strategic Resources Ministry and LIGHT International teamed up to hold these seminars. The purpose was to expose and challenge key leaders and laity to see their city "covered with the knowledge of the glory of the Lord as the waters cover the sea," and to expose them to key tools and strategies to help facilitate the process.

After holding the first three of these seminars (Houston, St. Louis, Minneapolis), and after Jack Dennison and I visited leaders in several other cities, three things became apparent. First, we saw God was raising up many key leaders with a burden to work with the rest of the Body in their cities to see them thoroughly reached and transformed. Second, although there were many tactical ministries and events, there was a need for an overall city-reaching strategy for mobilizing the whole Church to reach the whole city. And third, there was an acute need for tools to guide and assist the Body of Christ in the city to obtain a thorough assessment and analysis of the societies and workings of the city, and of the Church, the potential Harvest Force. Hence this book.

This book could be considered as containing two volumes. One of narrative, and the other of technical data and how-to's. In fact the appendices make up half the book. The intent is to provide as much detailed helps and samples as is practicable under one cover. There is more help available via CD and also from *"www.discoveryourcity.com."*

There are several people who have made a contribution to this book one way or another. Acknowledgement is due to Paul Cedar and John Quam of Mission America for their encouragement early on. My thanks to Jim Montgomery goes back nearly 30 years. I would be remiss if I did not acknowledge the input Jim has had into my life and also into this book. Mike Steele of DAWN is a very special ministry partner, exhorter, and refiner. My friend George Otis Jr., and his writings have impacted not only this book, but also my perspective on much of Christian life and ministry over recent years. To Jack Dennison goes a very special appreciation, for it was with Jack that I initially visited many of

Preface

the cities and discovered this kind of tool was needed. We spent many an evening in motel rooms and homes refining various aspects of city reaching goals and strategies. His gifts of expression have blessed me on numerous occassions. Jack's expertise in city-reaching strategy is only exceeded by his compassion for souls.

I have a special place in my heart for Carl Townsend, my partner in this venture, and close friend. Carl has taken some of the toughest trials this life can dish out, and hangs in there with grace and love. He will never know how positively his life has impacted mine. What an interesting and pleasureful journey this has been doing this book together. His expertise in authoring technical documents was of immeasurable contribution. His basic faith in God's love and power-unconquerable.

There were several others, such as Pete Morrill and Scott MacGray, who read the manuscript and gave insightful feedback.

I want to thank Mike Wourms and Christian Services Network for much of the final editing, cover design and printing. Mike is a couplet of congeniality and expertise, and persevered through a time of illness to get the job done.

Most of all I want to thank Judi, my precious bride, closest friend and loving helpmate. In addition to her perpetual encouragement, she has proofread hundreds of pages time an time again. Her patience and insights never cease to amaze me. Our son, David, helped at various times and in various ways, his aptitudes helpful, and his attitude a real blessing.

Then there is the foundation of prayer support of the many who have held us up faithfully over the years, especially these last two years. May our Lord continue to meet your every need as you so faithfully serve Him.

The final and ultimate acknowledgement and thanks goes to our Lord Jesus Christ. Without Him there would be no life!

Preface

(Carl Townsend)

Bob Waymire and I crossed paths over the years at various missions-related conferences, but it was in 1989 that we began to apply some of the principles in this book to a city – my own city, Portland Oregon.

Getting the Harvest Field data was easy enough, as it already existed. Claritas, one of the top demographic data providers in the country, provided this to us at a very low cost. Harvest Force data, however, was another story. We didn't have an accurate Church directory, much less know how large the Christian army was in Portland. It was much like us going into a war and not knowing the size of our troops, how well they were trained, and where they were located. When the Billy Graham team led a crusade here a few years later, we could track the growth of the Church after the crusade, as we had a benchmark reference to start from.

The transformation process in the city is much more than simply church growth. All of the city initiative leaders are realizing that the job isn't done until a wide spectrum of the Church in the city is mobilized in the process of being continually transformed: spiritually, economically, politically and socially. What is particularly interesting is that for the first time in history we have fairly adequate tools and guidelines for measuring progress in these areas.

I owe a lot to Bob Waymire for his vision in seeing that churches and missions have adequate tools for determining the distribution and effectiveness of the Church, and to aid in the job of reaching every people group with the whole gospel.

There are many others to whom we both owe acknowledgement for the part they've had in forming this work. In Portland, Dr. Joe Aldrich, Terry Dirks and Dennis Blevins have been leaders in bringing pastors together in unity for the task. Jack Dennison consistently challenges

Preface

me. George Otis, Jr. has led us in the area of citywide transformation, and in the research he has undertaken in identifying the often subtle responsible factors.

We also wish to thank Loren Muhlius at Global Mapping International in Colorado Springs for the map formatting support, and the others at GMI for their support.

Discovering Your City

Introduction

Many writers and researchers who have explored America's Church have all come to an astonishing conclusion. Mike Regele (co-founder and president of Percept Group, Inc.), writing in the *Death of the Church*, states, *"In the face of the current wave of change, the church in America has two options. Either it will go about its business as usual--and be swallowed up by obsolescence and die by default. Or the church will choose to die--and thus find life."*[1] George Barna, founder and president of Barna Research Group, says *"I've concluded that within the next few years America will experience one of two outcomes: either massive spiritual revival or total moral anarchy."*[2]

W. Charles Arn of Church Growth, Inc. observes that in all of the 3141 counties of this country there is not a single county in which church growth exceeded the general population growth during the entire decade of the eighties.[3] People are just moving around between churches that are becoming less relevant to their lives. George Barna reports a startling 68% of born again Christians no longer believe in absolute truth.[4] Not only has America's churched population been decreasing, but the effectiveness of the Church needs to be questionned.

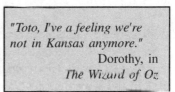

"Toto, I've a feeling we're not in Kansas anymore."
Dorothy, in
The Wizard of Oz

Dr. Bill Bennett, former U.S. Secretary of Education, says that during the recent years (1960 - 1997) when the population increased just 48%, there has been:

- A 467% increase in violent crimes
- More than a 461% increase in out-of-wedlock births
- A doubling of the divorce rate
- More than a 200% increase in children living in single parent homes

- More than doubling of the teen suicide rates
- Almost a ten-fold increase in the number of cohabiting couples
- An abortion increase from 744,060 in 1973 to 1,365,700 in 1996

At the same time, Bennett says that church membership, as a percentage of the population, has been almost constant.[5]

The Church in America has been, at least seemingly, increasingly ineffective as a transformation agent. It has not held its own in the face of the onslaught of secularism and materialism that has swept this country over the past half century. The task of the Church has not changed. From Genesis to Revelation we see that God is continually creating and redeeming lost man to Himself. With the Great Commission, we are challenged by the risen Christ to take this Gospel to every person of every nation [*ethnos,* or people groups] and to make them disciples.

There is little doubt that a major revisioning of the Church's methods and strategies is necessary. The task remains in America for the Church to take and model the living gospel to each person.

> *"When she (the Church) no longer had power she dug in for safety and sought to conserve her gains."*
>
> A.W. Tozer
> *Paths to Power*

With some very notable exceptions, most of the activities involved in by the Body of Christ do not produce new converts to authentic Christianity. In the United States there are more seminars on more subjects than ever. There are more united prayer efforts in more cities than ever (this is good.) Although a good percentage of the evangelical churches around the nation are enjoying some measure of growth, much of it is *not* through conversions.

There seems to be widespread recognition the Church is facing many problems. However, there does not seem to be in motion very many fruitful remedies to these problems. The changes that have occurred in society and in the Church over the past three or four decades that have negatively impacted the growth of the Church have either been so subtle as to not have been recognized, or they have been recognized, but the Church has had an ongoing case of paralysis--often wanting to change but unable to do so.

George Barna, George Gallup, and several others have been pointing out an increasing cultural distance between the Church and three generations. The assimilation of the Boomers, Busters and Generation "X" into gatherings of believers is noticably slow and spotty all across the nation. Any real, effective revival in evangelism is so rare, when it does happen it stands out as a rare phenomenon. Modesto and Jacksonville are cases in point. In an age where 68% of Americans believe there is no such thing as absolute truth, *traditional* evangelism strategies of using biblical references are no longer as effective. In fact,

> *The death knell of Western civilization is perhaps being sounded unless we can find a new sense of mission, purpose and reason for being - in short, new images of the future that speak to us in rich terms of human renewal and are appropriate to the problems and opportunities of our historical period.*
>
> Robert Bundy
> *Images of the Future*

Barna says his research has shown only 10-15% of today's churches are effective in the area of evangelism.[4]

The Church must listen, hear and understand the voices of current generations. It is quite obvious that new creative, contextualized wineskins are sorely needed. These need to be led by people who understand the felt needs of those to whom they are ministering.

It is also obvious some changes are needed in leadership either through new perspectives and functions, via replacement and spiritual renewal. New apostles and apostolic teams, anointed visionaries laying foundations for a variety of new movements are emerging, and needed in greater number to challenge, equip and lead the Body in evangelism and church multiplication, especially across social and cultural barriers. These apostles (visionary foundation-laying mobilizers) can help initiate Body-wide, city-wide initiatives of evangelism and church planting. Mobilizing movements such as DAWN,[6] CitiReach[7], and AD2000 and Beyond[8] utilize, even require, the apostolic gifting for effective mobilization of the Body.

The Body needs to be challenged to face and remedy its lethargy. Pastors should not limit their vision to their own churches, or limit their meetings with other pastors and leaders to only prayer and fellowship. They should be considering and determining how, collectively and symbiotically, they can impact the city or area. This often takes an outside catalyst or facilitator.

The Paradox

If our observations cover only the negative or problematic aspects in which the Chuch finds herself, we stand in danger of both perpetuating the problems and deceiving ourselves. Even though there are a variety of diseases plaguing and threatening the Body, this is an incredible time in the history of the world and the Church.

Paradoxically, most Christian leaders today are saying we are living in unprecedented days with regards to both the Church and the world. Never before has there been such widespread effort by the Church to reach the unreached peoples of the world. In the midst of all the chaos and persecution in many nations of the world, we see the Church making good strides in establishing beachheads in formerly unreached peoples, although the number of those paying the high price of martyrdom is increasing painfully.

Appearing perhaps as a "small cloud the size of a man's hand" (1 Kings 18:44) is the beginning of a marvelous movement of the Holy Spirit in the area of Body life. Over the past three decades we have been witnessing worldwide the exciting phenomenon of unprecedented cooperation among denominations, parachurch groups and individual pastors and churches from a variety of denominations and persuasions. At the national level, many denominations and Christian organizations are working together as never before. Global and continent-level gatherings of Church leaders have exploded over the past three decades.

There are wonderful celebrations by victorious Christians taking place all over the land. Much of it is in the context of united prayer and fasting. There are fires of revival here and there, with many conversions. There are some good, but limited, models of new wineskins. The house church, small group and cell movements are slowly progressing. Even though all of these good things are still spotty, nevertheless they are indicative of the life and faith that exists in the land.

Many alliances, coalitions and united movements such as Promise Keepers, Prayer Summits, Mission America and the Lighthouse Movement are bringing multitudes of both laypeople and leaders together, resulting in renewed lives and churches. Dick Eastman, president of Every Home for Christ, refers to this time in history as the *"dream hour"* for the Church. This is the time in history for which prophet, priest and people have long awaited.

> *The shift from industry to communications is taking place in one generation, and we are living through the turmoil caused by this extraordinary rapid change.*
>
> Robert Theobald,
> *Beyond Despair*

When we consider the *behind the scenes* goal of the Great Commission as being the Body and Bride of Christ, this beginning groundswell of cooperation and collaboration is highly significant. God is building His Church and the gates of Hell will not prevail (stand) against Her (Matt. 16:18).

Yes, the Bridegroom is preparing and developing His Bride. The implication for the Church today is it will take the whole Body, functioning as a body, to build the Body, to take the whole Gospel to the whole city. However, this will not automatically occur. But we can expect to be found working more symbiotically and synergistically than ever before.

In this special time in history, information and communication have made a quantum leap, especially in the past two decades. The amount of information at one's fingertips is staggering. The ability to communicate massive and diverse amounts of data quickly and persuasivley is becoming as common place as the use of the telephone and radio. The available tools are being used by the world to make huge profits, and to tamper with and influence the minds of all who venture to receive the information. The global Church also is benefiting from these tools as they become widely used in more and more nations and cities. But much more needs to be done.

Discovering Your City

The Barna Research Group reports that today 4% of teenagers look on-line for religious or spiritual experiences. But 16% say that in three years they expect to do so. The statistic was higher for teens currently involved in church, and four times higher for black teens.[4] This shift to the information age paradigm is taking place quickly in one generation and includes near zero-cost e-mail, chat rooms, as well as interactive movies and games.

The world has rapidly become urbanized. Nearly 80% of the Western World's population now lives in cities, with the Developing Nations (Third World) approaching 50%. In the U.S., there are 212 media market centers comprising some 96% of the nation's population. These cities are like countries themselves in their ethnic, socio-cultural, economic, religious and political diversities. Strategically speaking, there will need to be at least 212 unique city-reaching projects with their own leadership, assessment, processes and methodologies. This applies as well to the other countries and cities of the world.

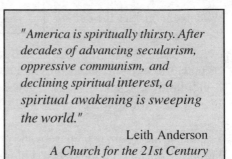

"America is spiritually thirsty. After decades of advancing secularism, oppressive communism, and declining spiritual interest, a spiritual awakening is sweeping the world."

Leith Anderson
A Church for the 21st Century

Yes, this is an incredible time in the history of the world and the Church. Quantum leaps in technology, communication and transportation have shrunk the world, and the impact has been astonishing. Just in the past three decades we have seen significant positive and negative results from this explosion. J. Christy Wilson claims we have already entered the Fourth Great Awakening. He believes this is the final awakening because in it God can complete His plan for discipling the nations. In the face of these changing times, new thinking, new perspectives and approaches are in order.

New Paradigms: Revolutionary Thinking and Action

New paradigms must replace many of the old. We'll take a quick look at some of the basic paradigm shifts needed and/or presently underway that will play crucial roles in the elements of city and nation-reaching addressed in this book. Jack Dennison of CitiReach also provides a list (see figure I-1) of several new paradigm shifts emerging and/or required for successful city-reaching in the days ahead.

A Paradigm

"A particular shared set of assumptions, beliefs, mindset, or viewpoint about reality or how things are. It is a set of rules and regulations that defines boundaries, and tells what to do to be successful within those boundaries" (Joel Barker in *Discovering the Future: the Business of Paradigms*). In other words, a *paradigm* is a world view, a model, a perspective and practice which includes identifiable and describable boundaries. "It's just the way we been a doin' things."

Contextualized Viewpoint

Revolutionary new paradigms are inevitable if the Church is to become a significant agent for transformation of individual lives and elements of society in the cities and towns of this nation. This applies to the way we do Church, to the way the Church perceives and carries forth its mission, and to how the Church functions in relation to itself. That is, how will the Body of Christ function as a body to build the Body?

There are many people today who are innovators of new, broad-based paradigms and movements that embody these paradigms. Many of these are apostles and prophets who have a farflung influence like Ray Bakke, Jim Montgomery, George Otis Jr., Luis Bush, Bill Bright, Thomas Wang, Roger Forster, Lyn Green, Ralph Winter, Dick Eastman, Peter Wagner, Ross Campbell, Loren Cunningham, Lorry Lutz and many others.

There are innovators of new paradigms here in the USA that are active advocates of revolutionary change towards revitalizing the Church. We would do well to learn from them. Included are men and women like Paul Cedar who leads Mission America, Jack Dennison and Jim Herrington of CitiReach, Mike Steele of Dawn Ministries, George Barna, John Perkins, Ted Haggard, Aubrey Malphurs, and Bill Hybels who are having positive influences in leading the Church in America out of its lethargy and impotency.

Closure Versus Growth

The old paradigm focused on *growth*. "Church growth" became a popular term and even a movement (1965-1985). Research and analysis focused primarily on the rates, methods and factors of growth of denominations and local churches. The fundamental criteria was growth-driven. The goal --growth oriented. The frame of reference was "How

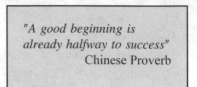

"A good beginning is already halfway to success"
Chinese Proverb

fast were we growing?" and "How can we do better?" We compared the now with the past. The extent of the pastor's responsibility and focus was limited to his own flock, although he might venture so far as targeting his whole neighborhood to reach with the Gospel. The primary focus was on getting the crops to produce more so the harvest would be larger. This growth continues to be essential.

The new paradigm focuses on *completing the task*, or *closure*. "Closure" in this context relates to completing the task of reaching the city, not to any strict eschatological context. The frame of reference is "Where we are in view of where we should be." The primary focus is on the task yet to be done. Research and analysis tracks what is being done, and keeps the picture of "what is yet to be done" before the Church, and tracks and evaluates progress to that end.

Reaching the city applies to reaching an ongoing dynamic state that is being continually sustained. New generations are being born every minute. Populations and society are never static, but always changing. Research and analysis have a whole city focus. The criteria is completion driven. The goal--completion oriented.

A goal becoming more commonly held by many country and citywide initiatives is essentially, *"To see Jesus Christ incarnate, through His Body the Church, ministering in His love, care, truth, joy and power impacting every segment of society, through gatherings of believers within practical and cultural distance of every person in every class and kind of society."* The focus is on getting the total harvest in for each successive season or generation. (More regarding this goal in the next chapter.)

City Church Versus Local Church

The old paradigm places the *local church* at the center of the picture. The pastors' attention was confined to nurturing their own flocks and equipping their own saints for service. Equipping and growth of their congregations were the goals. Fellowship with other pastors was only for that reason, fellowship. Local churches functioned primarily in isolation from others in the city. Few had combined ministries or shared goals with other churches.

In the new paradigm, the city Church *and* the corporate city are both in focus. There are many congregations, but they make up one Church. We recognize it is the responsibility of the whole Church to reach every segment of society, people group and person in the city. Networking and cooperative partnerships are the order of the day. The pastors of the various churches, and the denominational and parachurch leaders, see themselves as part of a larger relational team.

When those living in the city, the city leaders and the bureaucrats see this corporate identity and oneness, they'll have a totally new perception of the Church and perhaps Christianity. They will know we are Christians by our love for one another....preferring one another.. ..serving one another...serving the community. Has society in your city ever seen this fleshed out? Perhaps not....and there's a reason, isn't there? What is the reason in your city?

Inherent in this goal is the measurable criteria that will guide the major portion of our research and analysis, strategy and plans. Goals are especially meaningful and powerful when coupled with information that describes the task yet to be done.

There is a growing realization it will take the synergy of the whole Body to reach the whole city with the transforming love and redemptive power of Christ. The new paradigm doesn't discount the local church and growth. It puts them into more of a Biblical role and purpose.

The fundamental strategy then becomes mobilizing the whole Body to reach the whole city with the whole Gospel.

Old and New Paradigms for the Church in the City
by Jack Dennison, CitiReach, 1999

OLD PARADIGM	NEW PARADIGM
Local Church	Church in the City
Isolation	Collaboration
Leadership Team (Eph. 4 -- Pastors/Teachers)	Leadership Team (Eph. 4-- Apostles/Prophets)
Great Commission is a task to be pursued	Great Commission is a goal to be completed
Contribute -- with no end in sight	Complete -- with clear end in sight
Epistles interpreted from local church perspective	Epistles interpreted from Church in the City perspective
Unity is a theological reality	Unity is a functional reality
Doctrine divides	Vision and values unite
Target audience: our kind of people	Target audience: all kinds of people
Definition of Church is place and time	Definition of Church is "gathering of believers"
Industrial age paradigm	Information age paradigm
Hierarchical control structures	Apostolic order based on spiritual gifts

Figure I-1

Ted Haggard, a pastor in Colorado Springs, tells how difficult it is to cross this gap using the traditional church paradigm. If 10% of his city is in life-giving churches on Sunday morning, to increase this to 15% in a year through his church working alone in the city would take an increased attendance in his church of 15,000 people - quite unrealistic. By working with the other 200 life-giving churches in the city, however, it is possible to increase the attendance at all these churches by 15,000.

The conclusion here is quite simple: the goal is to reach and see transformed every ethnic, socio-cultural, generational and economic group in the city with the wholistic gospel in this generation. We must see the Church functioning as a city Church with a strong vision for completing the Great Commission as quickly as possible. Nothing else will work. This is beginning to happen in some cities.

In Salem, Oregon the majority of churches took out a single advertisement in their area, entitling it "The Church in Salem," listing the churches without their denominational identity. In another city a large megachurch picked up the salary of an inner-city pastor when Promise Keepers could no longer support him. The larger churches with their extensive resources have a responsibility of "raising the water level," as Haggard puts it, for the entire city. These are steps in the right direction, but there's a long way to go to see the Church in America making significant impacts at the whole-city level.

However, there are several citywide initiatives beginning to make good strides, including: Houston, Phoenix, Kansas City, Hampton Roads (VA), Portland and Corvallis (OR), and Spokane and Seattle (WN), for example.

The Need for Insightful Analysis

In view of all the aforementioned, it should be obvious the Church both in its parts and as a whole has been extremely neglectful in self evaluation based upon strategically developed criteria. It has been equally lax in its assessment and understanding of the target audiences, especially the past three generations. However, the hand-sized cloud of change is on the horizon. The recent groundswell of cooperative efforts, led in many areas and ways by the united prayer movements, are beginning to take shape in the form of promising citywide, cooperative initiatives intent on impacting every segment of society, seeing them saturated with dynamic, outreaching gatherings of believers.

A prerequisite for success will be obtaining and maintaining an accurate, up-to-date understanding of both the Harvest Force and the Harvest Field. Never again should the Church be caught unprepared because it did not have available the facts it needed to point out the problems and guide to the solutions. A prerequisite for success is getting the right information into the right form and into the right hands at the right time. This is one of the basic purposes of this book.

Summary

The Church faces major challenges. Yet, as the saying goes, "The future is as bright as the promises of God." The Church finds itself in a paradox. On one hand, we see it fraught with ills and facing mighty external challenges. On the other hand, these are exciting days as we begin to see the Body of Christ uniting as never before under its Head. The Church is positioning to experience God's anointing, power and blessing as never before. Yet, the Church only receives a blessing when it is obedient to the heavenly vision and calling. In this generation it must effect significant revolution and transformation of cities and towns and nations the world over.

A variety of new wineskins are needed everywhere. Business as usual will just bring results as usual. A change is needed in the way we do Church. We don't want to misapply Proverbs 22:28, "Do not move an ancient boundary set up by your forefathers."

The lack of having the right information in the right form in the right hands at the right time has been partly responsible for the fact that the gap between the churched and the un-churched has gone undetected and/or unremedied. In the future it is imperative the Church takes whatever action is necessary to assure it has the data/facts/light it needs to guide, facilitate and evaluate the progress of the Church.

There is the urgent need for the Body of Christ to function as a body to build the Body, the very Bride of Christ. A revolution is needed in the perspective of Church leaders, and in their commitment to become a part of a servant team that functions symbiotically in reaching the whole city, and every element of the city, with the living Gospel. When the "make disciples" task is progressing towards this end, the result will be a transforming trend toward aligning the city with the righteousness of God.

About the Contents of this Book

The fundamental purpose of this book is to provide guidance and help in "discovering your city" so you have the accurate, up-to-date picture necessary for effecting biblically-based transformation of both the city, and the Church in the city. It highlights the vital and strategic role of information in mobilizing the Body of Christ for reaching the whole city with the whole Gospel. It provides guidance and tools needed for identifying what types and kinds of data should be gathered and then takes you, step by step, through the gathering, analysis and communication processes.

It is not the *cure-all* or the *once-and-for-all* answer in the area of city research and information. Hopefully, you will find this book provides the assistance needed to move from where you currently are to a fully operational citywide strategy and community transformation initiative.

It has been compiled to be a valuable ready reference tool for those involved in city-discovery and city-reaching. Found in its appendices is a "reference library" treating much of the details pertaining to obtaining and maintaining an accurate, up-to-date picture of the city and the Church. Included are: *detailed data dictionaries and tables for Harvest Force and Harvest Field data; sample forms, tables, maps, and graphs; growth rate formulas and graphs; helps for surveys and interviews; glossary, bibliography, plus other materials.*

Additionally, there are expanded associated resources available on CD of the same title as this book, or, by accessing the Web page: *www.discoveryourcity.org.* Many of these additional resources are in color (such as maps and graphs) and readily down-loadable.

What's Next

In the next chapter we will look at the prerequisites and processes for mobilizing the Church, paying particular attention to the role of information in that process.

Endnotes:
1. Regele, Mike. *Death of the Church*
2. Barna, George. *The Second Coming of the Church.* Ventura: Regal Books

3. Arn, W. Charles. *Leadership Journal*, Spring, 1996, p. 75
4. Barna, George. *What Effective Churches Have Discovered: Insights on Ministry in the Late Nineties.*
5   Bennett, Bill. *Index on Cultural Indicators.*
6. Dawn Ministries (*Disciple A Whole Nation*) mobilizes the national Church in countries around the world for saturation church planting. Founded by Jim Montgomery who developed the strategy while in the Philippines with Overseas Crusades. Mike Steele is currently North American Regional Coordinator for Dawn Ministries, and a cities coordinator with CitiReach.
7. CitiReach International was begun in 1999 by Jack Dennison who serves as president. Dennison, who has been a pastor, seminary professor, and North American Regional Coordinator for Dawn Ministries, spun off from Dawn to begin this new catalyst organization. The ministry focus of CitiReach is mobilizing the whole Church to reach the whole city with the whole Gospel. Jack is fondly called "an apostle to the Church in America." His recently released book, *City-Reaching: On The Road to Community Transformation* (Pasadena, William Carey Library, 1999) promises to be a timely and powerful influence in establishing a new and sorely needed city-transforming paradigm. See *www.citireach.com*.
8. AD2000 and Beyond Movement. A global networking and mobilizing movement with focus on: a) establishing beachheads for the Gospel in Unreached Peoples; b) development of National Strategy Initiatives for saturation church-planting and evangelism.
9. Haggard, Ted. *Primary Purpose: Making It Hard for People to Go To Hell From Your City,* Orlando: Creation House, 1995

Chapter 1: Mobilization and Information

It is both exciting and a blessing when we see a broad spectrum of the Body of Christ in a nation working cooperatively to achieve commonly held Biblical vision and goals. We know the Church is rightly on the move when we see new congregations of believers emerging in areas and among peoples where previously there were none. We know the Church is healthy when both new and existing congregations are enjoying a good measure of conversion growth and are vigorously reaching out to the lost. We know the Church is being effective light and salt when we see transformations occurring in society aligning with God's righteousness.

The Heavenly Vision

When we see these things occurring, we know God is in the process of fulfilling the startling vision He gave through His prophet Habakkuk.

> *"The earth **shall** be filled with the knowledge of the glory of the Lord as the waters cover the sea."* Habakkuk 2:14

When God gives the vision and says it shall be fulfilled, He reveals to us what is involved in the fulfillment. Throughout scripture, He gives us several principles and measurable goals applicable to the fulfillment. He also provides ample illustrations of the type of men and women He will use to fill the earth with His glory.

> *"What could be worse than being born without sight? Being born with sight but no vision."*
> Helen Keller

Nehemiah is an excellent example of this type of person. As an illustration, consider the following:

> *Now it came about when I heard these words (regarding*

> *the sorry plight of Jerusalem and the Jewish remnant) I sat down and wept and mourned for days; and I was fasting and praying before the God of heaven...confessing the sins of the sons of Israel...I and my father's house have sinned.*
> *Nehemiah 1:4,6*

Later we will look at the results of this prayer. For now note that many others had this same information, but as far as we know, it was only Nehemiah who had God's vision and responded in this manner. Remember the spy story in Numbers 13? All twelve spies had the same information, but only two focused on God's vision instead of on the giants. No matter what else we might consider in this book in the way of vision, goals, strategies, tactics and plans, their relative worth is questionable unless the right people are involved in the right way.

Vision and Prayer

Prayer is an essential component in discerning God's vision for the city and building common goals around it. God, in His omniscience and wisdom, can see the end from the beginning, and knows the best paths to take to reach His intended destinations for His Body.

Nehemiah was a man of God and a man of prayer. He knew God had the perfect plan, and this was couched in love, forgiveness and power. Every time a problem arises, Nehemiah is praying. He's consistently accessing God's Web Page, and the passwords are a repentant heart, faith, praise, worship, humility and brokenness. Nehemiah's prayers were answered because the desires of his heart agreed with God's will.

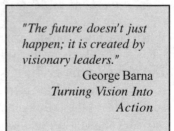

"The future doesn't just happen; it is created by visionary leaders."
George Barna
Turning Vision Into Action

It should be noted at this point, in the new city-reaching paradigm we're looking at, another vitally important perspective needs to be considered. *Each person involved* needs to embody the expressed qualities manifested in Nehemiah's life, especially in respect to prayer and faith. This is especially true for pastors, other leaders and intercessors. To reach the potential for seeing significant transformation in the city, there will need to be a close relationship among these groups, e.g. loving, preferring, encouraging and admonishing one another in love, while holding in common: vision, information and goals.

In many cities, it is through prayer, gatherings that pastors first begin to gain a collective city Church vision and realize the necessity of new paradigms in reaching their city. Through prayer area leaders can come

> *"Soon after the completion of Disney World, someone said, "Isn't it too bad that Walt Disney didn't live to see this!" Mike Vance, creative director of Disney Studios, replied. 'He did see it - that's why it's here.'"*
>
> Aubrey Malphurs
> *Developing a Vision for Ministry in the 21st Century*

together and begin to build a city vision that crosses ethnic, gender, economic, socio-cultural and denominational boundaries.

Where there is no common vision, everyone "does what is right in his own eyes." This can also be said for goals, which should be the normal outgrowth of vision. The goals you establish should, when reached, fulfill the vision. If the Church in the city is not collectively pursuing and pushing toward achieving commonly-held goals, then it will never see the vision fulfilled (or at least won't be part of the fulfillment). Leaders need to consult and share with each other in their planning and goal-setting. We all need to agree with Mike Steele of Dawn Ministries who exhorts, "We need to have a holy desperation in seeking God in order to determine His strategic viewpoint and plan for the city."

Vision Fulfilling Goal

What will the earth, or a nation, or a city look like when the vision expressed via Habakkuk 2:14 is fulfilled? The answer should necessarily include the condition in the city, and also the desired dynamic state of the Body of Christ.

Discovering Your City

What goal can the Body of Christ (the Church) pursue that when reached will fulfill the vision? The fundamental goals more and more nations and cities around the world are adopting for guiding and assessing their efforts, which fulfills the above vision and the mandate to "make disciples of all nations," are essentially as follows:

➢ See Jesus Christ incarnate in His Body, the true Church, in every segment of humanity in the form of healthy, outreaching gatherings of believers;

➢ See these gatherings distributed so there is one within practical (can get to) and cultural (would go to) distance of every person in every class and kind of society;

➢ See a wide spectrum of the Body of Christ working together toward penetrating every neighborhood with the transforming love, care, truth, joy and power of Jesus Christ, resulting in a measurable transformation of lives and society aligned with the righteousness of God—on an ongoing basis;

To summarize, the above goals...

- are "closure" oriented. That is, the conditions they describe fulfills the vision and encompasses the "make disciples" mission and imperative of Matthew 28 and Mark 16;
- encompass all the tactical ministries and methods involved in reaching the city;
- are measurable;
- require specific qualitative and quantitative Harvest Field and Harvest Force information to effectively "do the ministry" and to provide status and evaluation of effectiveness;
- are applicable to, and can be owned by, every Christian and ministry.

The above goals require specific up-to-date Harvest Force and Harvest Field information to facilitate reaching them, and for determining the status of the various factors involved in reaching them. For instance:

* "in every segment of humanity"-requires identifying, describing and determining the status of the various segments of the society - the Harvest Field.
* "healthy, outreaching gatherings of believers" - requires qualitative and quantitative evaluation of the gatherings of believers - the Harvest Force.
* "see these gatherings distributed" - requires identifying the geographic and ethnographic location/distribution of gatherings, and identifying and highlighting where they are not.
* "working toward penetrating every neighborhood" - requires both information relating to identity and location of neighborhoods, and also to the plans, goals and activity of the churches/gatherings/ministries.

> "A goal without a strategy or a strategy without tactics is a concept without a prayer."
> George Barna[2]

* "with the transforming love, care, truth, joy and power of Jesus Christ" - requires insightful analysis into the calibre of Christian life, as well as comprehension of successful methods relating to a variety of ministries and mandates, e.g. social, cultural, evangelistic and ethnic.
* "measurable transformation of lives and society aligned with the righteousness of God" - requires detecting and analyzing the qualitative changes in lives and society. Determining if these changes are aligning individuals and society more along the line of biblical principles and life.
* "wide representative spectrum of the Body of Christ collaborating" - requires identifying, describing and statusing those involved in the citywide initiative, and the type and level of collaboration.

These are very powerful goals pregnant with implications for all the ministries of the Body, as well as the quality of life of the individual believer. They are SCP (saturation church planting) goals. They are indicative of the transition in paradigm the Church is making from "growth" to "completion." (Obviously, growth is essential for completion.) It is the City Church perspective.

When these goals are attained, the immune system of the city and its neighborhoods are changed. The many elements of society have been impacted for righteousness.

However, accurate understanding is needed. In one area of Portland, Oregon, there is one African-American church for every 177 African-Americans. By saturation church planting standards, that area is saturated. That same area, however, has the highest crime rate in the city, and murders have been committed on church steps. Seemingly the Gospel has penetrated the area. However, overall transformation has been minimal, the warfare hard and difficult. Further understanding of the cause and effect dynamics of that area and society is required. Who committed the crimes? Were the criminals even from that part of the city? What creative ways are needed to reach the elements of society responsible for the high crime rates, whoever and wherever they are?

> *"Obedience is the one qualification for further vision."*
> G. Campbell Morgan

Mobilization-The Fundamental City-Reaching Strategy

A successful citywide strategy initiative will have a whole Church - whole city - whole Gospel focus. The fundamental strategy, then, is mobilizing the whole Church to reach the whole city with the whole Gospel. However, if those involved are not Spirit-filled and led, it will be a foundation with no re-bar and sure to crack and crumble over time. Achieving the aforementioned goals (p.4 & 5) will require a broad spectrum of the Harvest Force be involved in bringing into cooperative action the wide range of gifts, talents, skills, resources and tactics needed to reach every segment of society. It will require specific, accurate, up-to-date information regarding the Harvest Field and Harvest Force to evaluate how, when, and where these gifts, skills and resources can be used most wisely.

Imagine if the Body of Christ could unite around common information so that all are making decisions from the same set of facts! Each component has the same picture of the details, description and distribution of the peoples and problems of the city. All having the same picture of the Body of Christ, its description, distribution, size and status. All seeing what is collectively being done, and what collectively needs to be done. Each one determining the part they will play in reaching the whole.

> *"We serve a logical, orderly God, One who does not call us to compete with each other, but who prepares us for effective and cooperative ministry."*
> George Barna[2]

If and when this occurs, the Church in the city has the light (insight) and determination it will need to effectively carry forth the task of discipling the city. Even then, it will depend upon the spiritual life of the people and whom they are relying upon. Everything coming from goals, plans and themselves, or everything coming from God? (2 Corinthians 3:5)

Strategy versus Tactics

When we are talking about a citywide strategy, we also realize there may be many other ministry plans and efforts in the city that could, in themselves, be considered strategies also. Many of them may have whole-city ministry and vision. A united prayer effort would be an example. In the context of this book, and especially this chapter, we need to differentiate between the overall city-reaching plan and process which we call "strategy," and the myriad other plans and processes functioning in the city which in this context we refer to as "tactics."

In Jack Dennison's new book, *City Reaching: On The Road To Community Transformation*[1], he speaks more comprehensively to this issue of strategy versus tactics in the context of the whole mobilization process.

We can also find a helpful metaphor in diversified farming. The farmer's overall strategy is to effectively gather, preserve and market (or otherwise dispose of) all of the harvest. This will take myriad tactics ranging from understanding the soils, crops, seasons, equipment, finances, manpower, markets, etc. - to preparing the land, planting the seed, fertilizing the crops, cultivating and pruning, harvesting, etc., - to preserving and marketing the harvest - to caring for his family, and in making preparations for the future.

Likewise, in the city there are many individual and cooperative efforts involved in evangelism, church planting, community development, rehabilitation, etc., which should all be part of an overall city-reaching strategy. Some ask, "How do we get started in a citywide initiative?" In one perspective, if there are already a number of tactical ministries in motion, this could be considered as part of the citywide initiative, *if* and *when* the leaders of these tactical ministries all unite around the same overarching vision and measurable goals, and have the realization that it will take all of them cooperating and partnering together.

> *"City-reaching is the most significant innovation of the Church in this decade (in America) and will become the predominant paradigm in the next decade."*
>
> Jim Herrington
> Mission Houston

The reality is, there are many efforts taking place we would consider tactical (of course, they are rightly considered strategies in themselves) in an overall citywide initiative. Yet there may not be an overall citywide initative in process. However, much of this book is being written as if there were, and also, hopefully, help catalyze and mobilize these sorely-needed initiatives.

Such citywide strategies call for some structure that embodies the overall initiative for the completion of the Great Commission in the city. This doesn't overlook the fact there may be current citywide organizational structures and tactical efforts. There needs to be a team of servant leaders, including many of the ministry leaders, who will coordinate the citywide initiative in its broadest scope.

Don't Undersell Current Progress

In a meeting of leaders from 20 US cities Bob attended in Houston in February of 1999, many were asking the question, "What do we need to do to get started?" It turned out there were many tactical ministries already underway in several of the cities. Leaders were beginning to come together for prayer and planning. These were good and essential things.

However, the reply to the test question, "If you keep doing what you are doing, will the whole Body of Christ in the area be working most effectively and synergistically toward reaching the whole area with the whole Gospel resulting in significant transformation of the city?" was summarily, "No, not really. " Typically, there were many key people and ministries not yet working cooperatively toward the same overarching vision and goals.

Although at that time most of the cities represented had not performed initial assessment research, nor were there commonly-held measurable long-range goals, there was an eagerness to do whatever it took to effect positive change in their cities.

Just a few months later, several of those cities had made remarkable progress. Cities like Houston, Hampton Roads, Spokane and Seattle Washington, Portland and Corvallis, Oregon and Miami are well along in the process of forming envisioning leadership teams, as well as beginning the initial research.

These cities, for the most part, did not stop what they were doing. They were already involved in fruit-producing ministries. They needed progress in three fundamental areas: a) formation of core envisioning leadership team; b) articulation and ownership of a clearly-stated vision statement and overall measurable goals; c) obtain an accurate and up-to-date initial status assessment of the city and of the Church.

Prerequisites and Process
We can, then, consider the foregoing as prerequisites for mobilization of the Church in the city for reaching the city. These essential prerequisites are:

> 1. United, sustained prayer (pastoral and intercessory)
> 2. Visionary, perservering, mutually-supportive leadership

    3. Commonly-held God-given vision
    4. Commonly-held diagnostic information
    5. Commonly-owned measurable goals
    6. Extensive networking and partnering
    7. Effective communication of vision, goals and status

Proceed without any of the seven, and you may do many good things, but you will never reach your potential in mobilizing the Church for reaching the city. We will be expanding upon describing and contextualizing "commonly-held strategic information" in subsequent chapters.

A citywide initiative is a principle-driven /core-values driven process. All of the principles are operative at every level, but are experienced in somewhat of a sequential order. Again, you can find all seven of these playing a vital role in the Nehemiah story.

> *Nehemiah was committed before he went before the Lord, and had the inspired vision, goals, and the basic plan by the time he went before the king. This resulted from his persistent prayer of confession and repentance and his intercession for the city and people of the Lord.*
>
> *He became informed from those who reported to him, by carrying forth his own assessment, and by revelation. He was able to communicate the need and challenge on repeated occasions, and was able to form a network of those he mobilized such that every need was met including that of protection. He involved the people through vision and information to set the goal of building and completing the wall and restoring the nation to their Lord. The people declared, "Let us arise and build."*

When the whole Church holds in common overall vision-fulfilling measurable goals, coupled with an accurate picture of what is collectively being done and what still needs to be done, every congregation and church coalition can determine for themselves how they can best contribute to the city-reaching task both individually and collectively.

Synergy emanating from unity in diversity is the key.

This unleashes the entire Church, not just those who have chosen to participate in the agenda and limited goals of the more tactically oriented ministries and approach. The strategic effort attempts to bring alignment to the whole Church rather than attempting to coordinate the Church's activity around a few select needs and events.

Initiative Elements Expanded

Let's take a closer look at the elements in the process. The following outlines the salient components of each category.

Prayer and Intercession:
- Widespread, ongoing individual and united intercessory and warfare prayer.
- Active components of prayer, such as prayerwalking and "Lighthouses of Prayer," pastoral prayer, etc.
- Strategic prayer warriors and intercessors identified.
- Praying "on-site with insight" through spiritual mapping.[3]

Leadership:
- Identification of visionaries and the formation of a core envisioning leadership facilitating team or teams.
- Having strong mutual commitments built on relationships.
- Having a corporately owned, God-given vision (valid core values).
- Having vision-fulfilling measurable goals.

Common Vision
- Aligning with God's revealed will.
- Widespread ownership by leadership, pastors and laymen.
- When fulfilled, completes the Great Commission for the city.

Information and Evaluation:
- Initial assessment of the Harvest Force and Harvest Field including spiritual mapping.
- Determining current status, what is now being done, and what yet needs to be done, to complete the city-reaching task.
- Getting this initial information into the right form and right hands.
- Ongoing research and analysis (permanent lighting/illumination).

Corporate goal-setting:
- Leaders periodically gathered around up-to-date Harvest Field and Harvest Force information; making projections and setting goals for new churches/gatherings and believers.
- Annual or semi-annual congresses for establishing, reviewing and revising goals.

Networking and Partnering:
- Extensive collaboration and networking among denominations, churches, parachurch groups and key laymen/women.
- Networking structures in place, directories published, and clearinghouse established.
- Forged partnerships bringing complementary and mutually beneficial ministries into synergistic union.

Communication:
- Periodic conferences, workshops, seminars and congresses for: sharing information, evaluation, sharing case studies, feedback, corporate decision-making, initiating and nurturing cooperation, collaboration, partnerships and instruction and training.
- Publication(s) to keep the Church informed of various aspects of the city-reaching initiative. (A wide variety of media should be employed.)

Priming the Pump

During the initial phases of developing a Body-wide, city-wide initiative, identifying those key people, chosen and set apart by God, who potentially will make up the servant leadership team is of the first order. The initial visionary or "John Knoxer,"[4] must be identified. His or her vision-sharing role is something like passing a magnet under a piece of paper holding iron filings and other material. The magnet will move the filings, but not the other material. In like manner the "John Knoxer" passes the vision magnet by pastors and others in the Church to see who is magnetized by the vision - who can be drawn out for initiating the task at hand.

When he or she is vision-casting, it will be much more effective in the long run if this person, and those who initially respond, have the same picture of the city depicting both the current situation and also the task yet to be done. This requires some preliminary assessment and analysis consisting mainly of showing: zones or districts where churches are and are not, the ethnic distribution and percent Christian, and, economic levels, crime rates and other basic data that can be easily compiled.

Having this picture in hand accomplishes at least three things:
first, each person involved/contacted has the same meaningful picture of the city giving them the same frame of reference (which they might be gaining for the first time);
second, they can see the need and value of the information, and are likely to support obtaining further needed data; and
third, they will have information in their hands (well done color over-heads or computer slide-shows are excellent here) they can use with their friends, constituents, and perspective teammates and/or initiative participants.

This picture we call "prime the pump." It is used to catalyze and help launch the mobilization effort. Unless all are looking at the same picture and talking from the same set of facts, there is a risk of not reaching the potential of having the needed unity in diversity. And the potential for effective cooperative efforts will be lessened because of the lack of common understanding of the task to be done.

Once the leadership team has jelled somewhat, then a more detailed assessment and analysis will be in order. By that time there should be enough understanding and agreement regarding the goal and process of the initiative that the necessary resources will be forthcoming.

New Strategies, Structures and Movements

These are indeed exciting days! There is so much positive going on in this country and the world over. There is also a polarization taking place between the forces of evil and good. This is good, for if it wasn't occuring it would be because the Church was letting the world "squeeze it into its own mold" (as J.B. Phillips would translate Romans 12:2).

Over the past few decades we've witnessed several promising signs in the way of national and citywide strategy initiatives, international and interdenominational structures and movements. Organizations like AD2000 and strategies like DAWN have impacted nearly every corner of the globe, as has the Unreached Peoples initiative, and the emergence of what is being called the New Apostolic Reformation[5], and many others. The Global Prayer Movement has blossomed to where there are intercessors covering virtually every people and society on earth.

Newer movements and disciplines such as spiritual mapping, prayer evangelism, and the "new apostolic churches"[6] are proving to be vitally strategic in providing needed perspective, understanding, guidance and results. The potential spiritual mapping alone has for effecting transformation of societies, cities and nations is tremendous.

One newly arrived structure that is impacting world evangelization and has been quickly spreading around the globe is the Internet and WorldWide Web. We are still in the formative stages of the Information Revolution. Repeated quantum leaps are being made in communication and information management technology annually, and sometimes more often. Computerized mapping has come to the point where for many nations you can request information on an address or city, and a beautiful map can be printed off almost immediately with helpful levels of detail.

There has been a most encouraging trend toward interdenominational, inter-organizational, inter-church and international cooperation. There is still a long way to go, but today there is increased cooperation, partnershipping and mutual acceptance. When we have a realistic view of the task ahead, we will take the biblical mandate of unity more seriously.

At the end of the day...the bottom line is redeemed souls in the kingdom. It is the assembling and maturing of the Bride of our Bridegroom, Jesus Christ. Unless all of our structures, strategies and technology are resulting in making disciples of, and effecting transformation within, all segments of society and "filling the earth with the knowledge of the glory of the Lord," then they need to be challenged and reformed.

Salt can penetrate, but only works in touch. The Light must shine pure and bright. Our fundamental strategy needs to be one that penetrates every level of society with the shoe-leather theology of love. Each person on earth should be able to say, "Jesus loves me this I know, for the Bible tells me so." Experiencing the care, truth and love of Christ through some member of the Bride of Christ can make it so.

Then they will be able to say as I did some twenty odd years ago:

> O God, I cannot fathom eternity with you...
> Yet I know it's true.
> Blessed is my destiny!
>
> To look beyond the far beyond
> Past present faith and mind,
> And see the untold mysteries
> Held safe for those who find
> That such a reality exists.
>
> Who will know?
> Who can see this life past life
> And see the living God face to face?
> How can it be that any would see
> Thy Perfect Glory and Majesty
> That dwells in eternity?
> And yet I know this is for me...
>
> Before time began
> You set Your joy
> So it would grow as both
> Your love and fulness dwelled
> In those who in time beheld
> Your Son.

From the poem *Blessed Is My Destiny*
by Bob Waymire, 1978 (copyright)

Endnotes:

1. Dennison, Jack. *City-Reaching: On The Road To Community Transformation.* Pasadena, CA: William Carey Library, 1999.
2. Barna, George. *Turning Vision into Action.* Ventura, CA: Regal Books, 1996.
3. Spiritual mapping is defined in chapter three. Chapters four and five, and appendix "O" contain spiritual mapping related data descriptions.
4. John Knox was the Scotsman reformer who declared, *"Give me Scotland lest I die."* A "John Knoxer" is one who is highly committed to God and has the vision and burden to mobilize the whole Church. He or she is willing to make significant life changes in order to see their community or nation transformed.
5. C. Peter Wagner, *The New Apostolic Churches.* Ventura, CA:Regal Books, 1998.
6. Ibid

Chapter 2: The Strategic Nature of Information

Information plays a key role in every aspect of life. This is especially true in city-reaching. A primary task in the transformation of the city is the gathering, processing and communicating of vital data - *specific* information about the city (the Harvest Field): its societies and structures; its needs, visions and plans; and about the Church (the Harvest Force); its description, distribution, status, visions, goals and plans.

In Chapter 1 we observed the vital role information has in mobilizing the whole Body of Christ in the city to reach the city. You should keep this in mind as you read this chapter. Mobilization of the whole Body of Christ in the city to reach the whole city is the fundamental strategy. The overall purpose is to see the city's societies and structures transformed to align with the purposes and righteousness of God so that the city will be *"filled with the knowledge of the glory of God as the waters cover the sea."* (Habakkuk 2:14)

What is Information?

Information is data that has been processed to some level of order and understanding by the human mind. Some fifty years ago a scientist named Claude Shannon at Bell Labs published the first modern definition of information: *a message that reduces uncertainty*. Shannon even developed a method for calculating the amount of information, quantifying it by the amount it reduced uncertainty. For our purposes here, we will combine Shannon's definition with John Browning's and Spencer Reiss' definition[1], that is, information is *messages that change our worldview, however trivial*.

Our goal relating to information is to provide a message that *reduces uncertainty* within the Church, while also *changing its worldview-*

but in significant ways, not just trivial. It is also to get the message into the right hands.

> *Nehemiah and the messengers that came to him all had the same information, but only Nehemiah had, or at least was the only one that acted upon God's worldview. The report led Nehemiah to weep and pray, and this gave him wisdom and power to act. His heart's desire was to obey God, and his response was appropriate actions.*

Ultimately, the data and information that will be gathered and analyzed regarding the city needs to be acted upon. You want your research and information to be applied, and this by a wide spectrum of the Church. You want to see, from the embodiment of truth, whole sections of the city and whole segments of society transformed.

Two Truths that Set Men Free

If you want to get someone's attention, tell them, *"There are two truths that set men free."* If they are Bible-believing Christians, they may think you are some kind of a heretic, but they're usually inquisitive enough to hear you out. In the reality of the Great Commission to "make disciples" there are two "truths"...at least two realms of facts and realities...needed to "set men free." One is relativley helpless without the other.

> *"Truth is like a bird. It cannot fly on one wing"*
> A.W.Tozer

On the one hand, we have in the Word of God, absolute reality...truth. Yes, this *is* the Truth that can set men free. However, unless this Truth is effectively communicated to the audience so it can be acted upon, what is its relative worth to the individual, to groups, or to society?

Unless we have an informed, realistic understanding of our intended audiences, and of ourselves, we will never be able to reach our potential in seeing the power of God operative in people's lives.

Stated another way, *unless the Body of Christ has an accurate, up-*

to-date, meaningful understanding of its target audience, the Harvest Field, and also of itself, the Harvest Force, it will not be able to fulfill the evangelistic and socio-cultural mandates set forth in scripture.

The distance between the current Church's culture and that of the emerging generations is a case in point. The Church has preserved and protected many of its religious, social and cultural distinctives to the point it is no longer considered relevant by a majority of the unchurched. This socio-cultural evolution in society has gone undetected and/or uncorrected by the majority of the Church for the past four decades. The Church is so unfamiliar with the felt needs of the unchurched it hardly knows what to do.

> *"The social context within which the message is heard affects how it is understood."*
>
> Donald K. Smith,
> *Creating Understanding*

It's time to get in touch with the realities of our target audience:

- We must understand the mosaic of unchurched societies in the city, their needs and distinctives, their desires and aspirations.

- We must gain understanding into the spiritual history of the city. Spiritual mapping is needed to help in understanding the underlying causative factors of today's spiritual dynamics and conditions, especially those deleterious in nature.

- We need to determine what change-detecting sensors are needed.

- Why and how has the *salt* lost its savor in so many places and churches? (How are the churches doing in the shoe-leather theology and love area?)

- We must gain insights into the worldview and mindset of the current and recent generations regarding religion, Christians, Christianity and the Church. How can we understand their hopes and aspirations?

⊙ We need to understand why some churches and groups are growing, and others are not. Which churches are most effective and why?

⊙ We need to identify which segments of society the growing churches are reaching? How? Why? By whom?

⊙ We need to know who are *not* in the churches and why.

These factors and others make up the body of knowledge we need to have to effectively penetrate and effect change in the various segments of society with salt and light. Salt only works in touch. Even when the Church is doing a pretty good job in the *light* area, it often suffers in the *salt* area, and vice versa. Some churches are strong in social action and service, but weak in biblical teaching and discipleship. Some have good biblical expository teaching, yet hardly impact anyone outside their four walls. The most effective and healthy churches are those who are strong in both salt and light - internally and externally.

> *"Research can bridge the gap between our thinking and planning and the real world of our practice. Research can be the way we learn, not just the way we plan."*
> Bryant Myers[2]
> MARC

In the city-reaching initiative, you are ministering to an ever-changing target, and you must constantly update your contextual information to ensure that those who are lost and in bondage can be set free. You can't stop at a *snapshot* picture and draw your conclusions from that. You must be constantly monitoring and receiving feedback regarding your progress and effectiveness.

Sensors Needed

Too often the Church operates without the "sensors" needed to monitor its performance and progress. Some say, "We just let the Spirit lead." You do want to be under the guidance of the Holy Spirit, but you don't want only subjective evaluation. You need to be objective in determining how you are doing in response to the mandates from the Lord. He has given you your mandates, and revealed enough of His redemptive plan, that prayer-guided obedient action is called for. The information-gathering and analysis processes are constant, ongoing processes that enable you to detect whether or not disciples are being made, and if effective city-reaching is being accomplished.

Bringing the Task into the Light

Yes, you must have light for the task. Too often we labor under false suppositions and vain imaginations, ignorance and error. We're plagued by misconceptions and misinterpretations, outdated, superfluous and irrelevant information.

When we are plagued in these ways, the Kingdom of Darkness has a distinct advantage. We are engaged in Kingdom warfare: the Kingdom of Darkness vs. the Kingdom of Light. LIGHT can dispel the darkness, and expose the Prince of Darkness and his schemes and devious ways. Darkness cannot extinguish light, but always inhabits its absence.

You need permanent lighting, not just a peek with a flashlight from time to time. It has been well said, "Yesterday's truths are today's fictions." Each city needs an ongoing research and analysis function for generating the continuous illumination needed for the task.

Many pastors are in the position where they feel they have more tasks than time. They don't feel a need for more information, but for more resources of time, manpower and finances. Unless the "light" can convince them they are either placing their emphasis in the wrong place, or are not being as effective as they could be, then more light will probably have little effect. In fact, it can have a negative, hardening affect. On the other hand, many pastors will welcome information that will help them be more effective and efficient in their ministries, and in the stewardship of resources.

One of Satan 's schemes is aimed at keeping the Body of Christ ignorant and deceived. He does not want the Harvest Force to know the facts - reality. He wants us to continue to imagine we know the situation, and to believe what is published without question. He surely smiles when he hears, "We don't need all that research. We just need to follow the Spirit."

He would have the Church believe research is unspiritual and not realize that the process in itself is neither spiritual nor non-spiritual. Spirituality depends upon the motives, the applications, the attitudes...the "why" in the heart of those involved.

> *"Research is not something unspiritual or irrelevant to the business of ministry. It is rather the essential foundation for strategic effective ministry."*
>
> John Robb
> *Focus: The Power of People Group Thinking*

> *Nehemiah again provides us with a good biblical lesson on God-guided research. He was continually in touch with, and relying upon God, the all-knowing Master Information Manager. His motives were to see God's people restored to their Lord, and separated from the world (hence the wall). His process was prayer-guided and obedience-facilitated. The information obtained was utilized to motivate, equip and mobilize God's people ultimately to obedience, restoration, praise, worship and celebration of their God.*

Prayer and Information

Bob Beckett, a pastor in Hemet, California, realized the importance of prayer and information in the transformation process in his city. At one time, he relates, the prayer warriors of his church prayed for five days a week for transformation in the city. After several months of this, the prayer groups faded away, as they saw little happening. Beckett later observed, "We were striking out at the enemy but because of our lack of strategic information, we were incapable of isolating or discerning a specific target, aiming at it, and hitting it."

Ed Silvoso, in his excellent book, *That None Should Perish,*[3] strongly suggests, when city intercessors approach city leaders and ask for prayer requests, they should ask for specific things for which to pray. He says many are finding this strategic method of *prayer evangelism* very effective. He, along with other resource people, holds seminars spelling out *prayer evangelism* strategy in detail. In his book he says, "Intercessory prayer on behalf of the felt needs of the lost is the best way to open their eyes to the light of the Gospel."

Serious intercessors have a tremendous appetite for information. The more information they have, the better they are able to see the larger picture of what God is doing. To quote George Otis, Jr, "they want accurate targeting coordinates for their prayer, and they need information to do this. Since the prayer intercessors are the front line for the change in the city, information that you can get for them can be very strategic in changing the city and can strengthen the faith of those praying."[3]

After the Oklahoma City bombing, a company with demolition expertise was brought in to bring the rest of the building down. The top man, a Christian, told an interviewer an interesting statement. "The amount of explosive we use is not the most important issue," he said. "The most important issue is where to place the explosives."

> *"Effective citywide evangelism is based first on effective prayer and partnership. I would also suggest that good information is needed to pray effectively and to develop strong cooperative efforts. Let me ask you, How well do you know your city?"*
>
> Bill Bright
> Campus Crusade for Christ

The same is true in spiritual warfare praying. The issue is not so much how much prayer, but how strategic we can make the prayer. We need to pray in light of the facts of the situation and of the revealed will of God. More knowledge, either by research or revelation, enables more focused and effective prayer. Steve Hawthorne says strategic prayer is "praying on-site, with insight."

The Prophetic Message

We need to understand what the Spirit of God is saying to His Church about carrying out His mandates, and showing forth His compassion and redemptive power in the city. This "prophetic message" is the product and goal of our research and analysis. The Lord of the Harvest wants to lead us into understanding what must be done and how to do it, but we need to equip ourselves with an accurate picture of the Harvest Field and Harvest Force. In chapter 8 we further develop the Prophetic Message.

We can expect that message to become clearer as we dispel the darkness, and get in touch with the reality of conditions as they really exist, and not just how we might imagine them to be.

Men and women who seriously seek God's heart and mind are often astonished regarding the vision and conviction He gives them. Perhaps when you have become familiar with a certain situation, you experienced a strong conviction, in the light of God's expressed desires, that something should and could be done, and visualized what that could be.

Jim Montgomery, in wrapping up the chapter, "The Power of Information", in his landmark book, *DAWN 2000: 7 Million Churches To Go*, makes a highly significant observation when he states,

> *"One final word. In my mind, this type of church growth research can be boiled down to the simple need to know and understand how the wind of the Spirit is blowing over both the society and the Church in order to enhance our effectiveness in regard to our evangelistic mandate. From this understanding we can then get a more accurate picture of what the Spirit would want to accomplish through His Church in the succeeding months and years. This is what we refer to as the "prophetic message"[4] that emerges from the gathering and analysis of data."*

People with hearts and minds close to the Lord can evaluate a situation from His point of view and issue forth the prophetic word as to what is to be done.

Nehemiah was just such a person. Here was a man whose relationship with God is an example for all of us. As he waited upon God in extended compassionate and repentive prayer, he received not only the vision, but many parts of the plan that ultimately resulted in re-establishing the walls and restoring the people of Israel to God. And God moved on the heart of the king (Prov. 21:1) to supply protection and resources. Nehemiah faithfully transacted business along the line of the vision God had given him, even in the face of threats and pressures from within and without. His faith and action were the result of his constant communication with, and reliance upon, God.

This illustration of receiving and facilitating the "prophetic message" can serve as a model for every city-reaching endeavor. As Moody stated, *"God's work, done in God's way, will never lack God's supply."*

Information's Four Rights

Let's consider four "rights" that impact the value of nearly all of the information you will be using in either a citywide or local initiative. Basically, you need to get the right information, in the right form, into the right hands, at the right time. This is prerequisite to effectively mobilizing the Body of Christ for reaching the city.

You will probably detect the importance of the interrelationship of these "four rights." Violating any one of them can jeopardize your efforts. They are listed in their logical order.

1. The **right information.** Each step in the city-reaching process will have its information needs and requirements. The right information is pertinent, accurate, and up-to-date. Right information also means having the right amount of data...not too much or too little. For example, if you are collecting information on church attendance, how is the attendance defined (kids included?), what is the date of the information (all information collected during the same time period for the city), and how

accurate is the attendance statistic? At the same time, the budget information for the church is hardly relevant for the purposes discussed here, so why collect it - particularly if it would cause suspicion?

2. The **right form**. Having the right information in the right form is necessary for effective management, analysis, and communication. This is a very important element in the overall research and information picture. The right form means the information can have its maximum impact and effect. Don't undersell graphics and maps in your reports and presentations. A picture is still "worth a thousand words." A map showing the location of existing hispanic churches and hispanic population, for example, may dramatically higlight the location of a needed church plant.

3. The **right hands.** The right information in the right hands can work wonders. The right hands are those who can make the best use of it for achieving the goals. In the wrong hands, the same information can be counter-productive, harmful, and even defeating. Sooner or later the success of most efforts depends upon the *right people* being involved in the right way.

4. The **right time.** In most ventures time plays a crucial role. The right information made available too soon or too late could be worse than no information at all. The right time is determined by the need and development of your plan. There is a right time to gather, a right time to share, and a right time to apply the information.

Yes, when the *right information* in the *right form* in the *right hands* at the *right time* is coupled with the *right leadership, right vision, right goals,* and *right strategy,* then the potential of success is high. Portland, Oregon, is a city in which there has been considerable Harvest Field and Harvest Force information gathered and furnished to proactive leaders whose vision encompasses a citywide vision and strategy, and where there are measurable goals for saturation church planting. The process is also underway in several other cities, e.g. Houston, Seattle, Corvallis and Jacksonville. On the international level there are many countries where this process is well along, with neighboring Canada being an excellent example, together with several Latin American and Asian countries, including the Philippines and North India. Several countries in Africa have functional national initiatives.

Classifications and Definitions

We have found that the following terms and classifications of data and information are helpful in understanding the various roles information plays. We use them extensively. We've broken it down into two general classifications and four sub-classifications. They will be treated further in later chapters.

Harvest Force

Basically and technically the Harvest Force is made up of those who have surrendered their lives to Christ. This coincides with the saying, "You are either a missionary or a mission field."[4] Harvest Force information is that which identifies, locates, describes and statuses the Body of Christ in its various expressions, ranging from individual believers to local churches to denominations, parachurch organizations and institutions. All cults, Christian and otherwise, are part of the Harvest Field. Although there may be many nominals in some denominations, churches, and other places that are not much of a force for the harvest, nevertheless, for purposes of analyzing the city, all denominations and independent churches need to be included.

Harvest Field

Categorically, the Harvest Field includes every individual and every organization that is not part of the Body of Christ, the Harvest Force. Included are all religions including nominal Christians (although this will be difficult to determine in many situations) and cults. The Harvest Field is the context in which the Harvest Force finds itself (or herself). Harvest Field data includes information that identifies, locates, describes and statuses such things as: culture, ethnicity, language, politics, economics and commerce, religions (including nominal Christianity), society's mind-molders such as secular: education, media, arts and entertainment, etc.

Spiritual Mapping

Spiritual mapping is a fairly new research discipline, at least under this title. George Otis, Jr., of Sentinel Group uses this term to describe the processes of "determining why spiritual darkness seems to linger where it does," and "determining the reasons current conditions exist in the Church and the city."

Spiritual mapping seeks to determine the cause and effect relationship behind the social, cultural, physical and spiritual dynamics we find in the mosaic of societies of every city and nation. Otis reminds us there are deceptive strongholds in the community, and concerted intercessory and warfare prayers are needed to enlighten and guide the spiritual mapping to achieve discovery, understanding and remedies.

This will require an x-ray look below the surface. Satan has been at work in every city since its inception, and in some cities he has erected strongholds that are significantly inhibiting the growth and health and progress of the Church. It is possible through Spirit-led understanding and research to detect his schemes and effect corrective action.

According to Otis, spiritual mapping, simply stated, tries to answer three questions:
1. What is wrong with my community?
2. Where did the problem come from?
3. What can be done to change things?

Anyone serious about understanding in-depth spiritual mapping of their city needs to obtain the book *Informed Intercession*[5] by George Otis, Jr.

Identity, Location, Description and Status

The information we need falls into one or more categories. These categories apply to both Harvest Field and Harvest Force data/information. You can find expanded descriptions and illustrations in Chapters 5 & 6.

   Identity - includes the name and the type of entity. "Type" or "kind" of entity facilitates classification and grouping. For example, the type may be "church" and the name "First Baptist." Or "denomination" and "Nazarene." Or "ethnic group" and "Native American." This would be basic directory information.

Location - a vital indicator. It is important we have a picture of the distribution of both the Harvest Field and Harvest Force, and their relationship to one another. This is the actual geographic location of the entity, its latitude and longitude or specific address. It is NOT only a post office box number. This is also basic directory information.

Description - includes any information that tells of the form and function of the group, organization, ministry, etc. An example would be *an inner city church ministering to the homeless through provision of food and shelter, with a strong emphasis on personal evangelism and nurture home Bible studies. It holds services every night each week. It also has a job placement ministry.*

Status - information which tells the current condition or measurement. We may provide the status of a program by describing how it is currently doing, or by a percent of completion. This is a measurable value. For example, a denomination in the city may have 2000 members, 75 churches, and have an annual growth rate of 6.7%. It may be ministering mainly to upper class Anglos, and have two Bible schools with a total student population of 265.

The Need for a Closure Vision

When considering the issue of "completing the task," we can call on two biblical metaphors for insights. One has to do with warfare and the battlefield, and the other the diversified farmer and his harvest. The battle commander and the farmer have one vital point in common. They both are after "closure" - for completing the task. Although both must pursue many tactics, each one's overall strategy is to reach completion. The information they need to support their entire efforts is far more than if they were engaged in one skirmish or battle, or had only one crop to grow.

Our over-arching supreme goal should be to fulfill the mandate of "making disciples" and seeing significant redemption in and of society. This implies reaching a dynamic status of discipling, such that all newborn generations will be able to experience the love, care, truth, joy and redemptive grace of our Lord on a continuing basis.

Conclusion

We said in the beginning of this chapter , "Our goal relating to information is to provide a message that *reduces uncertainty* within the Church, while also *changing its worldview--but in significant ways, not just trivial.*"

From the beginning of time man has searched to understand how the world was created, how it works, and then predict how the world will work in the future. This knowledge is too deep for man, and the more we discover, the deeper the mystery. The discovery of this knowledge has the potential for making a positive impact on the city, moving it to become aligned with God's righteousness and the fulfilling of the prophecy, *"the (city) will be filled with the knowledge of the glory of the Lord as the waters cover the sea."*

Endnotes:
1. Browning, John and Reiss. Spencer. *Encyclopedia of the New Economy*, Wired Publishing, April, 1998
2. Myers, Bryant. *Reflections.* Monrovia, MARC Newsletter, September 1997.
3. Silvoso, Ed. *That None Should Perish.* Ventura, Regal Books, 1994
4. Jim Montgomery. *DAWN 2000: 7 Millions Churches To Go.* Pasadena, CA: William Carey Library, 1989
5. Otis, George Jr. *Informed Intercession.* Ventura: Renew Books, 1999

Chapter 3: Spying Out The Land
Part 1 - The Preparation

In Chapter 1 we looked at mobilizing the Church in the city towards becoming a City Church that is a vital force in transforming the city, its societies and individuals. We considered the role information plays in that process.

In Chapter 2 we looked at the strategic nature of information, its attributes and applications.

In this chapter we prepare the way for the process involved in gathering the information needed to underwrite the overall city-reaching process. We will look at the various *phases, categories, levels* and *layers* pertinent to the research process. The next chapter leads us through the steps in the process itself. Then the subsequent two chapters (and Appendices F & G) look at the specific Harvest Force and Harvest Field information you need.

Early on we want to emphasize, *spying out the land* is a specialized process and not just anyone can or should do it. This will become more evident as you work your way through the chapter. Another reality is, *information in itself doesn't guarantee success - although you can't get there without it.*

Not Information Alone

When the nation of Israel was camped in the desert near the Promised Land, God told Moses, "Send some men to explore the land of Canaan, *which I am giving to the Israelites.*" (Numbers 13:2) This was their promised time, or *kairos*[1] moment. At this *kairos* moment, Moses then selected one man from each tribe of Israel. He commissioned the twelve to go into Canaan to "*spy out the land*" with some specific instructions regarding what to look for. (Numbers 13:1-20). They had a survey outline given to them by God.

The mission lasted forty days, but most of the spies didn't share an optimistic report on the return. The land was indeed rich and fertile, but the cities were extremely well fortified, large, and the people who lived there were like giants. Of the twelve spies, only Joshua and Caleb brought back an optimistic report urging the Israelites to go in at once and take the land. The other ten focused on the giants and missed the purpose: the trip wasn't to determine *whether or not* to take the land, but to see and report on what they had inherited, and to help learn what would be involved in taking the land. Only the two believed God when He said, "I have given you the land."

> *"Research must be directed by, and answer the questions of, leadership or mission strategists. This is the key to research making a difference"*[2].
> Bryant Myers, MARC

The ten focused on the giants, and the two focused on the promise. The two also saw the giants but knew they were no match for their God. All of them had the same information, but only Joshua and Caleb had God's worldview. As a result, all of the Israelites, except Joshua and Caleb, plus those born after this event, spent the rest of their lives wandering in the desert. No, information alone doesn't guarantee success.

God Is Behind It All

This is a lesson for us today. Those involved in obtaining and painting the picture of the Promised Land, which in our case is the city, should never lose sight of the fact that God has said the knowledge of His glory will fill the earth (Habakkuk 2:14). Cities are a highly significant part of the earth. We also know it is not His will that any would perish but that all would come to repentance (2 Peter 2:9). And we have many other promises to latch onto assuring us God will be with us in our city-reaching efforts. Ours is to be faithful and obedient.

Another point regarding that spy trip; initially only the twelve were accountable and had the information. Once the *congress* was held and the information distributed to the larger body, the entire nation held the

information and was accountable. The same is true in the city.
At the start, those commissioned for the research return with the information and share this first with the leaders that commissioned them, and then with the broader Body in the initial congress. Once the Church in the city holds the information, God holds the entire Church accountable. Until then, the Church is only accountable for the spy trip.

And another thing, don't make too hasty an analysis. Stay open and objective. Give the data you gather a fair opportunity to speak for itself. Don't draw final conclusions from initial analysis, and don't try to prove your own presuppositions. If the ten had withheld their judgment until they all got together, and stirred in more of the ingredients of God's promise and plan, the whole outcome may have been different, and millions could have experienced the promise, instead of a few. When God is with us, the minority becomes the majority.

10 **minus** faith in God = defeat and wandering
2 **plus** faith in God = victory and possession

It does take both realities to set men free. One of these was the *rhema* of God (His Word) promising the land was theirs. The other was the contextual knowledge the spies brought back. Always check to see both are included in your final conclusions. Keep making the main thing the main thing.

And, by the way, that was Nehemiah's trick too. He mixed vision with faith. Works every time, if the vision is from God. And if it is, Oswald Chambers exhorts us to *"Transact business along the line of the heavenly vision, no matter what the cost."* People might talk you out of goals, but they can't talk you out of vision. So we need to be off to spying out the land...in preparation for occupying it for and with the Kingdom.

This chapter (3) and the next (4) are given to understanding:

- Classifications and terminolgy of research
- Phases and levels of research and analysis

- Survey and information management team
- What information is needed
- The survey process
- Costs and timelines

Classifications of Research

In research discipline there are terms and perspectives that help in understanding the process and the product. Before we get into the process you will want to familiarize yourself with some of them.

Quantitative and Qualitative Research

All of your research and analysis efforts will come under one of these categories, or a combination of the two.

Quantitative methods have mainly to do with statistics and quantifiable measurements. Qualitative methods are more subjective, and the information is normally gathered more by interview and observation. For example, the former tells us how many churches there are, and whether or not they are growing. The latter tells us why they are growing or not growing, and what is taking place from a spiritual perspective. Comprehensive analysis necessarily includes both. Standing alone, neither completes the picture. Wrong conclusions or suppositions can be drawn from quantitative research alone.

Qualitative, on the other hand, can vary depending upon who is doing the interviewing or observing. Understanding, insights, and checks are needed. When gathering Harvest Force data especially, validity and reliability can be issues. Often data such as membership varies in definition and practices in counting. Much is estimated, and some of the estimations can be far afield of reality.

Special care must be taken in who does the interviews and how they are carried forth, for the interviewer can significantly impact the response from the interviewee. (Interviews are treated in some detail later in this chapter and in Appendix-E.) When compiling case studies you will employ both quantitative and qualitative research and analysis.

Our friend, Steve (Sang Chul) Moon of Korea's Research Institute for Missions-KRIM, writing for the WEF training publication, provides us with the following diagram (3.1).

Quantitative Research	Qualitative Research
Etic[2] View	Emic[2] View
Statistical generalization	Logical generalization
Questionnaire Survey	Interview and observation
Appropriate for a broad view	Better for in-depth analysis
Evaluating segments of a phenomenon	Holistic understanding of a phenomenon

Figure 3.1

Some feel you cannot quantify qualitative information such as the effectiveness of prayer, where reconciliation is taking place, and how victorious Christians are. Although this is sometimes true, some objective quality of measurement can be fairly accurately ascertained and qualified by using "cause and effect" relationships, and assigning numerical values to particular responses or effects.

Library and Field Research

Library research involves information already published and available for acquisition (yet often open to interpretation). This may be printed, on electronic media, or readily available via the Internet. The sources are varied, but it is termed "library" for it is the kind of information you could find in a public or perhaps university library. Or it may be readily available from a public, church, parachurch, etc. office.

In any event, library information is published information that is available without need of interviews, observations or field surveys. Usually there is a good amount of *library research* that can be performed by untrained or minimally trained personnel.

Field research involves gathering information not currently published, or if it is published, some field research may be necessary to validate the data. *Field research* usually involves one or more of the following: interviews (face-to-face, phone, etc.), observation, trained survey personnel, and survey forms.

There are situations where *field research* may also involve some amount of intensive investigative *library research*, such as situations where building a case study history involves digging through historical records in libraries and other available documents.

Phases and Levels

In the context of this book, research for the city-reaching process is set forth in three levels or phases:

Phase of Citywide Initiative	Level of Data
1. "Prime the Pump" or "Catalytic"	1. Initial
2. "Pre-Congress"	2. Primary
3. "Continuation" or "Ongoing"	3. Extended

These levels and phases correlate, in a general way, with the sequential process steps of a citywide strategy initiative focusing on mobilizing the whole Body of Christ for reaching the whole city. Completing this task involves penetrating and saturating the whole city with the whole Gospel and life-giving gatherings of believers: to see the people and societies in the city transformed to align with the righteousness of God. Ongoing monitoring is carried forth for the purpose of evaluating this task.

Having said all that, please note, there is such a close relationship between levels of data and the phases to which they generally apply, we could almost use them interchangeably. However, we will refer more to phases than levels in an attempt to coincide closely with the overall initiative sequence steps.

Phase-One - Mobilizing the Key Leadership

The purpose of this phase is to get enough data to mobilize the key leadership for the city initiative. This research consists of gathering the *initial level* assessment data needed for the "prime the pump" (catalytic) phase of the initiative (Nehemiah 1:3).   This first-level basic data can usually be obtained in minimal time and with minimal effort, often requiring only "library" research.   Its purpose is to bring to the attention of a core group of pastors and other leaders the fundamental status of the city.   The data will be automatically updated in the other phases.

Phase-one information identifies:
* *Where you are now* (where the Church is and isn't in relation to the various segments of society), and compares it to:
* *Where you need to be* (in order to reach the overall measurable goal for the city), which provides initial insights into:
* *What is yet to be done* (in general terms).

> This is to say, *"We're here. But we need to be there. This is what needs to be done."*

It provides a *benchmark*, a reference point for measuring future progress and effectiveness. With the picture of *what yet needs to be done*, you begin forming the prophetic message which guides and launches you into the "mobilization and penetration" phase. Again, you must keep in mind this can apply to both the city and the Church, or any of their parts.

> *There is a corollary here with Nehemiah. In response to the initial information regarding Jerusalem and God's people, he wrestled with and thoroughly caught God's vision. While Nehemiah was in compassionate and repentive prayer God began to reveal His restoration plan for the city and nation. Nehemiah used this initial information to recruit the initial resources needed.*

Phase-Two - Mobilizing the Church

This (primary/pre-congress) research involves additional library plus field research in order to paint a more detailed picture of the Church growth history over the past ten years, and to provide information regarding the makeup and status of the societies in the city. This includes which churches are growing and not growing, where, among whom, and to some minimal extent, why.

An important role of Phase-Two *primary* level data is to continue to develop the "prophetic message" God wants to use to challenge and encourage the Church. This will provide the foundation for making projections and setting corporate goals for new churches and believers. This data also identifies specific areas in the city and the Church where revolution and transformation is needed. In citywide initiative, or DAWN strategy parlance, this is "pre-congress" data. (This is a congress vs. conference because of the process in a congress of formulating and enacting corporate goals.)

> *The corollary with Nehemiah continues. Upon his arrival in Jerusalem, he carried forth his own on-site research (2:12-15). He presented this in the context of all that God had done and was doing in regards to his being in Jerusalem. He challenged the people who responded with, "Let us arise and build" (2:17,18). Subsequently, he set forth the detailed plan for each family based upon his research and plan, and the restoration of city and people followed (Phase 3).*

Phase-two (primary level) data will need to be updated as a minimum in preparation for each congress. Some data could and should be updated annually, such as church-related statistics. One reason for this is you will be able to provide some churches and organizations with up-to-date data. A periodic publication is one way to do this. Another reason is you will be able to detect significant growth pattern changes early (good or bad). This will alert you to successful methodologies, and help to detect problem areas early. Others can benefit from this information and analysis. You can also begin building case studies to share at the next congress or workshop, or in a publication.

Phase-Three - Occupation and Transformation Phase
This research involves more *extensive* level research and analysis and correlates with the ongoing operational phase of the citywide initiative. This phase, for example, involves understanding the worldview

and mindset of the unchurched. It identifies why conditions in the city are the way they are. It supplies insights into the cause and effect relationship regarding current ills within the Church. It sheds light on why some segments of society seem more resistant than others, and suggests the best methods for effective evangelism and initiating new gatherings of believers within them.

It involves continually gaining deeper insights into what it will take to increase holistic Church growth. It will identify the why and wherefore of spiritual strongholds, and suggest corrective action. It will help put the finger on what kind of revolution is needed within the Church to make a continuing positive impact on the various segments of society in the city. It will help the mayor, chief of police, and others understand how the Church is, and/or will be, working together to increase the quality of living and morality in the city.

During this phase, there is nearly continuous monitoring of the Harvest Field and Harvest Force. One purpose of this ongoing extensive monitoring and analysis is to help ensure the enemy can no longer go undetected and unchallenged in the efforts he uses to dominate and control various elements within the city and within the Church.

> *During the restoration process of Jerusalem, of that nation Israel back to their God, Nehemiah was in constant contact with his context in four areas: the work on the wall, the society of the Israelites, the taunts and attacks of the enemy, and his God .*

Some cities may already have the structure, facilities, equipment and personnel needed. What determines the starting of Phase 3, however, is where the initiative is in its overall city-reaching strategy and process. The milestone for the transition is usually the first congress where corporate goals for new churches and believers are set by a wide representation of the Body in the city.

These three phases/levels are not cast in concrete, and will from time-to-time, city-to-city, and place-to-place have some fuzzy edges. There will be some variations in what data is needed when. Transformation in the Church and in society is a continuing process and can only maintain a positive trend if insightful measurement and evaluation takes place on an ongoing basis. Timely, pertinent, understandable and accurate feedback is essential.

A Summarizing Scenario

You have a burden for seeing your city impacted by the Gospel, resulting in significant revival, restoration and transformation. Each phase of the citywide initiative requires appropriate level information from each category or layer to achieve this.

A picture is obtained showing the location of all churches by size, ethnic group, district and neighborhood. You can also see the population per church ratio and easily detect which areas and people groups need more churches, and which segments of society are most needy. Articulating the vision and sharing the information with key leaders helps identify those having a similar vision and burden for seeing a transformation take place in both the Church and the city.

Once this core group of leaders is on board, you take the next step, which is to obtain primary information relating to the dynamics taking place in the city and the Church. This information and analysis reveals where the Church is growing and not growing and why, and has implications for what and how things should be done to make a positive impact in discipling the city. Areas where significant change is needed within the Church are identified, and case studies are prepared.

This picture is shared with the broader Church Body at a congress in order to motivate and mobilize them towards action. At the congress, the Body sets new corporate goals for new churches and believers. (Congresses should be repeated every 2-3 years.) Ongoing research and analysis continues the task of gathering extended data leading to understanding the "causes and cures" needed for successful, God-centered, transformation of the societies within the city.

Categories and Layers

In Chapter 2 we described two basic data categories, i.e. Harvest Field and Harvest Force. In one sense, these two categories are all-encompassing. That is, all data relating to the spread of the Gospel will fall into one or both. Chapter 2 also mentioned an additional category: spiritual mapping.

We find it helpful to group the information needed for analyzing and discipling nations, cities and people groups into these three categories or "layers."

1. Harvest Field data describes the context in which the Church finds herself.
2. Harvest Force data describes the institution of the Church, the true Body of Christ.
3. Spiritual mapping data is x-ray data identifying reasons *behind the scenes* for why things are the way they are.

We like the concept of *layer* because the data in each category can be overlaid much the same as you would overlay overhead transparencies, or combine a select variety of layers in a computerized mapping system. There you have different types of data on different map "layers." For example, individual layers may contain: various geopolitical boundaries, ethnic group locations, streets, lakes, highways, rivers, parks, buildings, churches, adult bookstores, etc. Using that same concept you can overlay any combination of Harvest Field, Harvest Force and spiritual mapping data which will often result in eye-opening discoveries.

Preparation for the Survey

When embarking on a survey you need to spend adequate time in planning and preparation. Don't take a shotgun approach. You want to minimize the *"I wish I had thought of that,"* and *"I should have been better prepared"* statements when you get into your survey and/or information management. Take time to plan. Don't epitomize the sign that reads, "Planning is what we do when we don't have anything else to do." And be only interested in *applied* research. Only do the amount of research necessary to support a sound and relevant strategy.

In addition to providing the roadmap for your survey and analysis, a well laid out plan is a good recruiting tool for:

- Recruiting personnel
- Recruiting finances
- Mobilizing workers, finances and initiative ownership
- Cooperation, networking and partnershipping

Your initial planning should include:

- **Clear identification and understanding** of the *target area* and/or *target people(s)* to be covered/included
- **Schedule/major milestones/timeline** (start date, data gathered date, analysis complete date, initial/final report due dates)
- **Information requirements** (what data will be needed when? Identifying some basic data sources for *library* and *field* data)
- **Personnel requirements** (correlated with schedule/timeline)
- **Budget and budget authorization** (also where the funds are coming from and when)
- **Strategy for obtaining cooperation** and understanding on the part of those needing the data, and those who potentially will be furnishing the data (e.g. vision-casting, endorsements, announcements, data feedback to providers, etc.)
- **Survey form preparation** (requires use of experience of others, see Appendix-D for some sample basic forms.)
- **Information management preparation** (implications for, and lists of hardware and software and operators, data entry and management plan, decisions/selections re: database, spreadsheet, graphics & mapping, etc.)
- **Survey training** (library and field—including interviews)
- **Analysis training**--if required

The Survey and Information Management Team

We need to consider the team that will gather and manage the data. Seldom will all the aspects of a citywide survey be carried forth by one person, especially if you include the information management task.

Although a "prime the pump" survey (initial overview picture, or "pre-research") and preliminary picture can be achieved by one person in a relatively short period of time, when you get into the operational phase of a citywide initiative, the team will necessarily include additional persons, especially if the leaders are to have the accurate, up-to-date data and pictures they need in a timely and communicable fashion.

You need to consider the various functions to be carried forth, and then match these functions with qualified people, and adequate resources, and authority.

For instance, over time you will need:

A. **Intercessors** - Researchers are discovering that in cities experiencing transformation, it is generally started by intercessors, often no more than one or two. Early Harvest Force research should identify where these intercessors are in the city. As the work proceeds, it is the intercessors who will pray for the protection of the researchers and leaders, and for the provision of spiritual discernment concerning the analysis.

B. **Supervisor or manager** - who is responsible for determining, with other leadership, what is needed, why it is needed, when it is needed, and what form it needs to be in. This person could well have investigative and information management skills, and if he or she has skills in preparing surveys and designing survey forms, that is a plus. This person might also participate in the surveys and analysis in some way, depending upon the person and situation.

C. **Research assistant** (one or more) - this (these) person(s) will be involved in library and field research, and perhaps some data management. They will need appropriate training in data gathering. Some will need training in how to conduct interviews. (This is covered later in this chapter.) If trained, they could also be involved in analysis. Assistants take on tasks that are based on their gifts; i.e., a people-oriented person is more comfortable in interviewing and the more introverted type normally enjoys a day in the library.

C. **Information manager** - although you may have several people that are computer competent, can do data entry, manage the data, and do some graphical and/or mapping analysis, you still need one person that has the basic responsibility for the overall management, storage and stewardship of the data. This person needs to interface (in a good relational way) with the supervisor/manager, and also with the leadership that will be using and presenting the data.

Note: You can get by with part-time help for a while, but this is not optimum. Be careful to assure your information and analysis is not compromised, for then the overall initiative will be compromised. When the light dims, darkness moves in. Don't look for just warm bodies. It would be like a general sending soldiers out with no training. They won't be equipped for the situation, and can put the effort in jeopardy.

In the next chapter we will look at the survey process.

Endnotes:
1. "Kairos," *(says Theodore Bovet,)* "is an opportunity imposed on us by God. We can grasp it, but also fail. It is not our own time that we choose for ourselves, but a commanded opportunity and a definite step in God's previously conceived plan of salvation for mankind." Bovet, Theodore. *Have Time and Be Free. Richmond:* John Knox Press, 1964 p.26
2. Myers, Bryant. *Introduction-MARC Newsletter.* Monrovia, CA: MARC Publishing, September 1997
3. *Etic* and *emic. Etic* denotes objective observation where the measurement and/or results are independent of the observer. Quantitative measurements are usually *etic*. In *emic* research there is a subjective element wherein the results are impacted by the observer's judgement or presence. Qualitative research is generally *emic*.

Chapter 4: Spying Out The Land
Part II - The Process

We now turn our attention to the processes involved in gathering and managing information you will need to support the various plans, strategies and ministries involved in reaching the whole city and all of its parts and peoples. This applies to both Harvest Force and Harvest Field data.

You must keep in mind you are embarking on a spiritual enterprise that will require "putting on the whole armor of God," and standing firm. You are going to be bringing light into darkness. The Kingdom of Darkness has had its way with much of the city for a long time and will not voluntarily give it up.

You will need spiritual discernment and guidance for your task, and a protective covering of intercessory warfare prayer. It is very important that you assemble a group of faithful warriors to pray for you and others who will be involved in dispelling the darkness. You should continually give them feedback when their prayers are answered and also regarding the details and concerns of the battle.

It would be difficult to overemphasize the importance of the information that needs to be gathered, and how it is gathered, in the overall assessment and analysis of the city. We have considered the strategic nature of the information. Now we need to look at the process of obtaining the right information in the right way.

For example, you will have to employ several different methods for obtaining the information needed. In some cases, who gathers the information, and how it is gathered will determine its quality and validity.

Many of the persons doing the research will find themselves in privileged roles and positions. They will often be in situations where they can "sow seeds" in the questions they ask, or observations they make.

The information you will be gathering has incredible potential. It may be used by a wide variety of people for a wide variety of purposes. It will be needed for setting goals, identifying and correcting ingrained problems, determining effective methods, mobilizing resources, evaluating needs and effectiveness, and several other strategic applications. It can and hopefully will play a crucial role in mobilizing the

> *"Research is not something unspiritual or irrelevant to the business of ministry. It is rather the essential foundation for strategic effective ministry."[1]*
>
> John Robb, MARC

whole Body of Christ in the city to reach the city with the transforming love, care, truth, joy, peace and power of our Lord Jesus Christ. The information must also be secure, for in the wrong hands it can do much damage. Much of the Church and denominational information will need to be treated as proprietary.

Diligence Required

You will need to pay attention to detail. This is the place for diligence and dependability. Satan has had a heyday in the past. He is quick to take advantage of and exploit false suppositions, vain imaginations, and just plain old error. Also, you will be entering new waters. You will be investigating many of the causative factors that have rendered many of the segments of the society of the city to various levels of degradation morally, physically and spiritually.

Likewise, you will be investigating many of the causative factors relating to the fact the Church has had problems reaching certain segments of the population and generations.

When you reach the goal of getting the right information (accurate, up-to-date, pertinent data) into the right form, in the right hands, at the right time, then great strides can be made for the Kingdom of Light.

The Body can move ahead in touch with reality, and decision-making will be based upon commonly held facts. You will begin to witness "redemption and lift," and a variety of significant transformations.

When this information synergy occurs, you will be assisting the Body in gaining credibility...an absolute necessity for the transformation of the city. When anyone in the city-reaching process and pipeline loses credibility, the entire city-reaching initiative can suffer. Satan will always be looking for a way to undermine you, so be diligent. This applies especially to those who are gathering the facts.

The following guidelines can apply to every person on the team. Appendix-L contains some "common pitfalls of research," plus additional survey guidelines and helps.

Do's and Don'ts
Do:

- **Pray** – Focused, strategic and sustained prayer is necessary for obtaining and maintaining the vision and research.
- **Use Data to Interpret Data** - Don't draw conclusions too quickly. Look at the data in the context of the other data.
- **Develop Accountability** – Be sure you are working under the covering of supportive fellowship, prayer warriors and mentors.
- **Be Accurate** – Satan deceives by hiding facts, but also by twisting facts you obtain. Use multiple sources. Examine the source, and verify the information you receive. Respect the mentors that challenge your findings.
- **Be Disciplined** – Be sure your goals are clear and you are moving toward them. Don't go on wild goose chases or fun trips. Keep the main thing the main thing.
- **Avoid the "Snapshot" Approach** – Assume God is moving dynamically in the area and you are researching a moving target. What's true today is not necessarily true tomorrow. You are watching a motion picture, not slides. Beware of sampling.
- **Keep the Task and Vision Before You** – Use visuals to keep the picture of where you are going in mind – large maps, photographs of the city, etc.

- **Be Sure Your Motivation is Correct** – Avoid making decisions simply to profit, control, or to increase your own prestige. Maintain a spirit of humility.
- **Protect the Unity** – The end doesn't justify the means. As you work, put priority on the unity of your ministry team. Cooperate so synergy can result. This will be reflected in the outcome.
- **Be Compassionate** – Remember people are human, and not just a number. The end purpose is the transformation of souls and the city.
- **Secure the Data** – Your information is strategic. Be sure it's protected from inadvertent access, and that you protect your own use of it with regular backups.

Don't:
- **Underestimate the Enemy** – You are working on the front line!
- **Let Pride Control You** – Information is a powerful force in the world today, particularly strategic information. Avoid taking pride in the information you are getting and using it to control others, or for selfish ends.
- **Misinterpret Data** – It's easy to use data to support your own assumptions rather than seeing new revelations. Be open to new insights.
- **Make Decisions with Incomplete Data** – Don't jump the gun in drawing conclusions. This can put you in the position of trying to explain a wrong conclusion when all the data has been analyzed. Joshua made a covenant with the Gibeonites without consulting God or getting the true facts. Later, they had to honor this covenant and it cost the Israelites dearly.

Obtaining the Information

We will look at *what to gather* and *where to get it* in later chapters. In this section, we want to look at the *methods for gathering*, or *how to gather* the information.

The variety of informational needs require a variety of methods and skills be employed in obtaining the needed data. We will look at sev-

eral methods, keeping in mind that each type will have its requirements regarding the skill level of those involved in the process. For
example, you may want to involve different people in doing some of
the library and field research, from those carrying on person-to-person
or phone interviews, where good interpersonal and social skills are
very important.

How to Use Survey Forms (See Appendix-D for some sample forms.)

Preparing good survey forms is both an art and a science. Poorly designed and utilized forms consume your resources without providing
usable and reliable data. In fact, they may cause more damage than
help, for you may be misled by the response without realizing it. There
are some rules of thumb that are wise to follow:

1. Don't use complex and lengthy forms unless you have a very
    specialized audience that is committed to cooperating. Get
    only the information you need, and during initial phases, you
    may wish to start with even shorter forms. Surveys using long
    forms are often counter-productive.
2. Have someone experienced with surveys and/or analysis re-
    view your forms.
3. Run a limited pilot survey to help evaluate the forms. Select a
    representative area and/or segment of society and perform your
    survey. Experience teaches that you will modify your forms
    and/or methods.
4. Keep to one subject. The survey (external in the neighborhood
    or internal to a church) should have a single purpose. Keep
    multipurpose surveys separate even though some may be filled
    in by the same person. Changes will be simpler. Record keep-
    ing, data trails, data entry, source, date, etc. will all be safer
    and more straightforward.
5. Be as objective as possible. Furnish multiple-choice answer
    selections whenever feasible rather than asking a question in-
    viting or requiring them to write narrative answers (with the
    exception of obtaining some general observations or com-

ments). They may not interpret the question as you intended, and some handwriting and meaning are hard to decipher. For example, rather than ask, "What ministries are being carried on by your church?" list the possibilities with a place to check those that apply (box or line). Then make a place for "other" to be written in. This simplifies data entry and prevents lengthy responses which may be difficult to interpret.

6. For statistics, provide blanks both for that statistic, and also for the data date to which it applies. Assure you can accurately determine the data source, especially if the data is second hand.

7. There are two *unpardonable sins* in research and analysis. One is to not date the data, and the other is to not identify the source. A lot of data is not useful because it is not known to what year it applies, or where it came from. Was it empirical data (real "hard" data), an estimate, a wild guess, a calculation, or what? Every data record should have fields for *data date* and *source*.

8. Keep an audit trail. During the data entry, a sign-on screen should ask for the user's initials and password. These initials and the edit date should be stored in a transaction file with the entry data. This transaction file is then printed and processed to update a database.

Personal experience relates that Patrick Johnstone (Operation World), Ron Rowland of Wycliffe/SIL (Peoples Database), David Barrett (World Christian Encyclopedia), and other top-level researchers/publishers agree. Their credibility depends upon the validity and verifiability of the data they publish. Yours may also.

How to Do Phone Surveys (Many guidelines from "Interviews" apply. See Appendix-E.)

Without some prior notification of the respondent/interviewee, phone surveys are notoriously risky. The response is usually minimal, and you have a hard time talking to the right person and/or obtaining exactly the information you are after. If you are calling a church for instance, you will have to penetrate the secretarial defense line.

To make phone surveys most effective consider the following:

- Best results can be achieved when those being called are expecting the call, and have already made a commitment to provide the information because of their familiarity and support of what you are doing. Tell the secretary that person is expecting your call.
- Make your appointment for the interview ahead of time. Let them know what you will be asking so they will be prepared.
- Be able to give a good reference known to the person being called. Assure them the referenced person(s) supports the survey and/or the overall effort.
- Send out a letter of explanation ahead of time, written or signed by someone the person knows, or on a familiar letterhead. Say you will be calling to set up an appointment to obtain the information via phone, or in person if they so desire.
- In situations where many or most of those to be contacted meet periodically, such as at a pastors prayer breakfast or conference, an announcement regarding the upcoming survey, and an explanation of why the data is needed and how it will be used can significantly increase the rate of return and enhance the accuracy.
- Assure the person(s) called that the information is being treated appropriately. Exercise special care with proprietary information. Tell them how the information will be used. Mentioning they will receive a copy of the survey results also helps.

How to Do Interviews (See Appendix-E for additional interview guidelines.)

Interviews are excellent tools when carried forth skillfully. Usually this requires some training. Both the interview process and the questions need careful consideration. It takes a special skill and discipline to perform an objective interview.

During the interview process, good and frequent note-keeping is crucial. Time must be allotted *after each* interview to record that part of the interview that you could not do during it, because of lack of time. You will gain insights as you go on interviewing that will escape if you do not document them immediately. Therefore, avoid back-to-back interviews where possible.

During the interviews, you will gain insights not otherwise possible. However you should realize that how you are perceived by the interviewee will determine to a significant extent the caliber of information you receive.

It is important when making the contact for setting up the interview appointment that you are ready to make clear the purpose, how the information will be used, who will have access to it, how it will benefit them or their cause, etc. You can gain credibility if you can give as a reference someone or some cause known to them.

In each case, you need to be prepared to explain verbally, or in written material, the purpose, the sponsor, who will benefit, and how the data will be handled, managed and utilized.

Where is the Data?

Data sources for Harvest Force and Harvest Field information is covered in some detail in their respective chapters (Chapters 5 & 6). Much of the data you will need to paint the overview picture of the city and the Church is readily available. Much can be obtained from libraries, the Internet, denominational headquarters, government office, law enforcement, and several other sources.

If you are in the formation stages of an initiative, and there is no readily available, accurate picture of the city, you initially will probably want to obtain more of an overview status of the city and the Church before you do an in-depth survey. This "prime-the-pump" data will get you into the process and familiarize you with some of the challenges and opportunities, as well as with some data sources. This will also provide up-to-date information which can be used quite strategically in launching or furthering the citywide initiative.

What data sources can you identify that are likely to have and provide information pertinent to the following?
- Identity, distribution, description and status of the various seg-

ments of society, e.g. ethnic, religious, economic, cultural, social, political, elderly, youth, arts and entertainment, etc.

- Identity, distribution, description and status of denominations, churches, gatherings, small groups, parachurch groups, and Christian service ministries.
- Identify and describe areas in the city, or segments of society where significant transformation has been, or is taking place.
- Demographics and vital statistics
- Distribution of churches by geopolitical areas and ethno-cultural groups. Identify areas (zones, tracts, districts, neighborhoods) with no churches. Determine who are in the churches, and who are not (re: ethnic, cultural, religious, social, economic roots and affiliations).
- Describe the religious and political history of the city. Identify enemy strongholds.
- Determine the impact and influence, or lack of impact and influence, the Church is having on the various elements of society.

How Long Will It Take?
How Much Will It Cost?

These are commonly asked questions. Especially when you are planning a citywide strategy initiative for the first time. Some see the need and importance of getting an accurate, up-to-date picture of the city, and propose a survey and analysis project. And some may automatically think it is an overwhelming task requiring a lot of finances, personnel and time. However, this isn't necessarily so. You want to be interested in doing *applied* research. And as previously mentioned, only do the amount of research necessary to support a sound and relevant strategy.

Several considerations come into play. Maybe an illustration will help. When I (Bob) was with Overseas Crusades, in 1979 he carried out a nationwide survey in the Philippines. The entire effort took about two *months* of intensive library research, about three *weeks* total traveling around the country doing field research, a couple *months* of analysis, and one return trip for a *week* to check out holes and get some questions answered. It took about another month to complete the report. The entire effort cost approximately $2,000, not counting salary or travel to the Philippines, but including considerable travel within the country. (That being 20 years ago, this would probably be doubled or possibly tripled by now.)

This information (analysis report and data) has had, conservatively, dozens of applications and uses, including setting the basis for the projections by the national churches at a DAWN congress. (Dr. Donald McGavran and Jim Montgomery used the report as the basis for the book, *The Discipling of a Nation,*[2] which was distributed at the congress.)

In some cities, the initial effort and budget has involved setting up an ongoing "information resource office," including sophisticated computer and mapping hardware and software. Some have paid hundreds, even thousands of dollars, for databases for their city. So when you ask someone involved in this latter situation, they may say surveying your city will be expensive. It really depends upon how you set up and execute your plans.

You talk to others who have performed surveys using volunteer personnel and sophisticated hardware and software, and you can get a different story. Someone who is computer-literate regarding databases can team with one or more involved in gathering the information, and produce some very useful information in a relatively short period of time, and for very small financial investment. This is especially true when doing a Phase-1 survey involving mostly Library Research.

An ideal situation is where there are several leaders and churches who see the need for the research and will make a commitment of dollars, people, time, and possibly equipment to make it happen. There will be a need for a good plan, budget and timeline (see Figure 4-1). There needs to be a serious degree of realism as to what is involved. Not just any warm bodies will be appropriate. There needs to be clear lines of responsibility so corrective action can be taken if the research begins to falter. The best approach is for a knowledgeable person or persons to draft a timeline and budget. Get it approved by the leaders. Each church and/or organization then make a commitment and contribute the needed finances and possibly other needed resources.

There are several variables to consider. Those wanting to obtain a baseline picture of the city, including basic demographics, distribution of ethnic minorities, vital statistics and church locations, can produce a basic data picture, including maps, for a minimum investment in time and dollars. The pace at which process will move through the timeline will depend upon the quality and quantity of leadership.

Timeline

Normally, when planning a citywide or nationwide initiative, a rough time frame of 2-4 months is allocated for the Phase-1 initial assessment research and analysis (Figure 4-1). This culminates in a report and presentation depicting an overview picture of the status of the city, and of the Church, and in general terms, *the task yet to be done*.

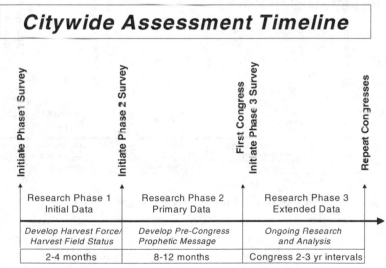

Figure 4 -1 Citywide Assessment Timeline

This survey and report becomes the first step of a process of gaining common goal ownership. It will aid in corporate goal-setting at a large citywide gathering or "congress" to which all the pastors, Church/parachurch leaders, and key laymen/laywomen are invited.

Once the leadership commissions further assessment, the Phase 2 survey is launched (Figure 4-2). This involves obtaining the growth status of the Church in its relationship to society. This process usually takes between 8 and 12 months. The results of this analysis are presented at the congress. Using the growth history and projection, the challenge is made for the Body to set new corporate goals for new churches and believers for the next 2 to 5 years.

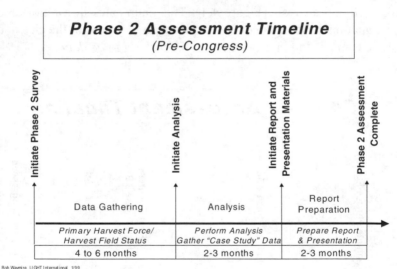

Bob Waymire, LIGHT International 1/99

Figure 4-2 Phase 2 Assessment Timeline

The congress is usually repeated at intervals of 2-3 years, where the up-to-date status and analysis is again presented and goals updated. The data presented also has many implications for needed action by the Church. Jack Dennison of CitiReach addresses this aspect of the city-reaching strategy and process in his book, *"City Reaching: On The Road To Community Transformation."*[3]

Getting Started

Prior to the formal Phase-1 survey, some "pre-research" can be accomplished. Some already available Harvest Field, Harvest Force, and spiritual mapping data can be assembled. This picture would paint a very general view of the city, e.g. population and pop density, major ethnic and economic distributions, and perhaps some minimally reached areas and people groups. This preliminary picture is usually assembled from readily available census data, city planning reports, real estate materials, and the yellow pages (to give a general idea of the number and location of churches).

This picture provides an excellent tool for "priming the pump." In providing a preliminary Harvest Field and Harvest Force description and status, this initial picture is highly valuable in the hands of the vision-casters and leaders for getting others on board in the embryo stages of a citywide, region-wide, or neighborhood initiative. It is also helpful in showing the value and power of the information, and getting commitments and cooperation for doing a more in-depth benchmark survey.

Depicting the information in tables, maps and graphs provides for maximum communication. In some cities, maps are available that depict much of the status of the city, and some even show church locations. We found this in Knoxville, Tennessee, where a local mapping company had produced a huge wall map containing the locations of churches, and various geopolitical boundaries. Although the data was not totally complete (little is) or for the current year, it certainly provided, with only minimal qualifications, an excellent preliminary picture and a good starting place.

Computerized maps are nice, quick and easy, but others can be as effective. Most good computerized mapping systems, such as Atlas GIS or ArcView, are integrated with a database and are powerful analysis tools. These systems are very reasonably priced for the power they offer, and you can obtain good city street and address files with them.

A set of color overheads in the hands of the right person(s), depicting a graphic picture and status of the city, can be a very powerful motivation, recruiting, and mobilization tool. Special binders are available that hold the transparencies in such a way they become a flip chart very handy for small meetings, or, the transparencies can be easily removed for projection.

Time and Cost Summary

The time and cost of surveys and analysis vary greatly according to: the quantity and kind of information needed, when it is needed, what form it needs to be in, and how it will be used.

The "rule of thumb" time frame for the Phase 1 survey is two to four months (cf. Figure 3-2). This presupposes certain data and applications. The Phase 2 survey, analysis, and report should take between eight and twelve months and in some cases more (cf. Figure 3-3).

The cost factor can range from a few hundred dollars, including materials, postage and transportation, to many thousands when there are investments for data libraries, hardware, software, hired computerized mapping, hired survey personnel, hired data management, and/or sophisticated publications and presentations.

The next two chapters discuss what Harvest Force and Harvest Field data are needed, and where to find it.

Endnotes:
1. Robb, John. *Focus! The Power of People Group Thinking.* Monrovia, CA: MARC Publishing, 1989 p.32
2. McGavran, Donald and Montgomery, Jim. *The Discipling of a Nation.* Pasadena, CA: Global Church Growth Bulletin, 1980
3. Dennison, Jack.*City Reaching: On the Road to Community Transformation,* Pasadena, CA: William Carey Library, 1999

Chapter 5: Gathering The Harvest Force Facts

It is said there are three prerequisites for a general to lead his forces to victory in a war. These are to know:

1. The enemy's strength, location, strategy, preparedness.
2. His own forces - their strength, location, tactics, preparedness.
3. The context of the land, the battlefield, its description and conditions.

In a spiritual war the same thing is true. Ephesians 6 makes it plain that we are already at war. To win the war, we need information about the enemy, our own forces, and the land in which the battle takes place. The battle is for the souls of men and women, the real "land" to be occupied.

We should never consider the unchurched the enemy. The one exercising fundamental control of them is the enemy. However, when we want to pin down the source of many of our problems, we can learn from that great philosopher, Pogo who declared in one tough skirmish, "We've met the enemy and he is us!" In one sense, this describes the Church today. We're often our own worst enemy. If and when the Body of Christ begins functioning near its potential, with spiritual and knowledge-based insight, we will find the

> *"Research of the right kind can help us know where we are, and what our trajectory is. If we can locate ourselves, we can orient ourselves so we are pointing toward our vision once again."*
> Bryan Myers[1]
> *Perspectives*

world to be a much better place, and millions more will be released from the enemy's snare. *We all need to become "worshippers" before we become "workers," lest our efforts result in wood, hay and stubble.*

In this chapter we will primarily be looking at data about the Harvest Force, or in the above terminology, Battle Force. In church growth parlance this is often referred to as "institutional" data, that is, God's institution on earth, the Church.

There are dynamic forces (spiritual, economic, social, cultural, political, ethnic, religious) already working in the city, and the Church is in the midst of them. The Church's task is to "make disciples;" to effectively communicate and demonstrate the love, care, joy, truth and power of Jesus Christ; to be penetrating salt and revealing light. Although the Church can be seen, its basic reality is unseen. We have a purpose statement defined in Luke 4:

> *"The Spirit of the Lord is on (us), because he has anointed (us) to preach good news to the poor. He has sent (us) to proclaim freedom for the prisoners and recovery of sight for the blind, to release the oppressed, to proclaim the year of the Lord's favor." (Luke 4:18,19)*

The Church, Christians, and Christianity already have a reputation in your city...with the city government officials, with the unchurched, and among the churches themselves. Many factors impact the Church's reputation. The churches and para-church groups are carrying forth many ministries that could and should impact the life and lives of the city for righteousness. Some are, some are not.

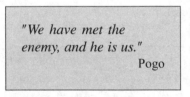

"We have met the enemy, and he is us."
Pogo

The effectiveness of these ministries is determined against criteria that may differ from group-to-group, from city segment to city segment, and even person-to-person.

On the negative side...

There are identifiable and noticeable elements of society missing from the Church, or only minimally represented. Some of these elements can be classified by age, some by occupation, some by race and ethnicity, some by religious background and heritage, some by economic level or status, and some by social distinctives and status. There are a variety of reasons for the lack of representation, some are external to the Church, some are internal. One of the reasons may be that over the past few years the Church has not been furnished and/or challenged with the right information in the right form at the right time in order for it to be aware of these missing segments. Another probable reason is the Church did not have in place a detection system for self or societal analysis. There are other reasons yet to be uncovered.

And on the positive side...

On the other hand, there are also some areas in some cities that have experienced, or are experiencing, a very positive transformation. This impact is related directly to one or more churches, and usually to one or more visionary and proactive leaders in the Church. In a few cities, transformation is occuring in areas where high crime

> *"Evangelism is not complete without the gathering of new disciples into the dynamic fellowship of a local church. The missionary task is not merely to organize a church on foreign soil, but to initiate a Christ-ward movement which will propagate the gospel throughout the entire culture — and eventually other cultures as well."*
>
> Steve Hawthorne, Ralph Winter, *Perspectives on the World Christian Movement*

rates, gangs, poverty and pornography previously have been rampant, but today are minimal. Where high school dropout rates were very high, and are now the lowest in a decade or more. The morality quotient has also raised noticeably.

The Heights, a section of about one hundred thousand population, in the center of Houston, is one such area. The mayor and other city officials have recognized the basic causes for the positive change were the local churches and parachurch groups in that area, and their demonstrated love and care for all ages. Over the years, Urban Outreach Inc. and other groups, have implemented care-giving programs for every age group, but mainly via the youth.

One of many such programs is the Youth Club begun in 1993. This grew out of meetings between Urban Outreach and the principal of

Hoge Middle school. It focused on after school programs and activities. Behind the scenes, Urban Outreach speerheaded Harvest Field, including spiritual mapping, research of the area. The theory was, the more they knew about the history of the area, how the diverse cultures had been interacting, the type and cause of the crimes, the spiritual history, who were jobless and why, the number of single-parent families, the expressed physical and other felt needs of the families and youth, etc., the better they could design and implement programs and activities that would be effective over the long haul.

Now in the area there are fifty-two churches cooperating, many area businesses are involved, and the city has made the parks, swimming pools and other facilities available. Urban Outreach has helped organize volunteers for mentoring and tutoring the kids to help them in their studies, and for taking state tests (on one standard state test the Heights' percentage of improved scores is the best in the city). They teach leadership skills, help the youth find jobs, and maintain a "job bank." They have a wide range of activities, e.g. sports, drama, camping, etc. for involving the youth.

Urban Outreach says because many kids never get any attention, they feel abandoned and have no one they can trust. This usually manifests itself in any one of a variety of negative ways. One way they help build esteem is in mentoring and tutoring. They have two volunteers work with one student. The youth learn someone really cares. They take small groups of kids on special camping trips designed to provide a fun and and a loving, caring environment.

Urban Outreach has demonstrated community transformation can be more than a good idea, a vision, or a goal. In the Heights in Houston it is a reality. This is one of the best "shoe-leather love and theology" demonstrations we have seen or know of in the nation.

A wide variety...
Some churches are healthy, growing and reaching out to a broad spectrum of the city and various segments of society. There is a wide variety in the leadership styles of the churches, and the gifting of the leaders. There are many different churchly structures. Some churches

meet only in one structure. Some meet in a variety of structures at various times, and have a variety of service types and styles. Some are "cell churches," and some are churches with cells.

Some churches have strong evangelistic outreach programs, others are mostly nurture centers or hospitals. Some multiply churches, and some multiply members. Some are led by apostles, some by prophets, some by evangelists, and some are led by pastor-teachers. Some are large, some are small. Some are authentically Christian, some nominally so.

George Barna indicates from his research that *only 10-15% of churches are effective change agents today.*[3] However, this can be an effective catalyst for city-reaching.

The Opposition

There is another matter we must consider that contributes significantly to the challenge of city-reaching. That is, we have an enemy that definitely does not want it to be accomplished.

Nehemiah wasn't long into his city and nation restoring enterprise before he came face to face with the enemy. The people in Jerusalem had no more than just declared, "Let us arise and build!"

and started to work, when a trio of ridiculers from the surrounding area began to mock and accuse them of rebelling against the king. (2:17-20) Repeatedly from then on, Sanballat, Tobiah and Gershem tried to thwart the work of the Lord.

> *"We cannot simply save individuals in the city and expect that the city will get saved. If the Church does not deal with the systems and structures of evil in the city, then it will not effectively transform the lives of that city's individuals."*
> Robert Linthicum

Nehemiah was also beset by opposition from within. His own people confronted him with some weighty challenges (Chapter 5). The enemy's attack was both internal and external. In both situations, Nehemiah solved the problems in consort with the Lord by accurately identifying the source of the problems, and by standing firm with God for righteousness.

Like Nehemiah, there must be the constant awareness that "the battle is the Lord's." City-reaching is not easy. The Kingdom of Darkness is alive and well, and reclaiming the land will be a constant challenge...but the victory is promised. (2 Corinthians 2:14 *"Thanks be to God who **always** leads us in His triumph through Jesus Christ..."*) The heart of the battle must be fought in the heavenlies, for "our struggle is not against flesh and blood" but against the rulers in the spiritual realm.

Our challenge is to be able to respond with a valid, "Yes!" with proof when anyone in the city asks, "Does anyone care about me?"

What is the Picture of the City Church?

A strategic element in carrying forth the initiative to thoroughly reach the city is to gain insights into the health, growth, dynamics, scope and effectiveness of the Church as a whole, and of the individual churches and parachurch groups. This information will be used to motivate, equip, catalyze and mobilize the Body of Christ for taking the whole Gospel to the whole city, and to be a more effective transformation agent. Enlightened research reveals where the Church is in relation to where and what

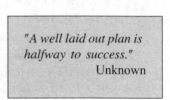

"A well laid out plan is halfway to success."
Unknown

Christ desires it to be, and provides the basis for future planning.

As previously mentioned, an initial picture will also, in a "prime the pump" fashion, provide the visionary leaders and catalyzers with a basic picture to use in helping to launch the initiative. This could and should ultimately and verifiably impact for righteousness every element of the Body, and every segment of the city's heterogeneous mosaic.

Painting the picture of the Church in the city will involve both *library* and *field* research. An initial picture can be fabricated relying mainly on *library* research. This picture can be painted with fairly limited resources of personnel, time and finances. The information needed for providing insights into why conditions are the way they are, and for guiding and underwriting effective methodologies and transformation will require various kinds of *field* research, and--will be ongoing.

Crucial Questions Needing Answers

Before we look at an outline of the various data categories let's consider six categories of questions relating to the Harvest Force to keep in mind when doing the data gathering, processing and analyzing. It is not intended to be complete, but a representative listing. These categories were selected for highlighting because it is in these areas that many of the commonly known ills are impacting the Church today. Use it as a check list to see how you are doing in the process.

You will be embarking on extremely serious and important business. The end result of your research and analysis can be pivotal in your city's current and future history. Few cities or nations have been in a position to witness what the Lord can and will do when His Body is functioning symbiotically and proactively around commonly held vision, goals and information.

When you are gathering, processing and analyzing the data, obtain answers to the following Harvest Force related questions:

1. Prayer Evaluation
* Is there a united prayer effort organized in the city?
* Do the leaders pray together on a consistent basis?
* Is there consistent and strategic prayer walking?
* Is there consistent and persistent intercession for the city, its peoples, and government?
* Has contact been established with city officials (mayor, Chief of Police, etc.) for the purpose of prayer?
* Have prayer lighthouses (or neighborhood houses of prayer) been established? If they have, what is the city coverage?
* Have pastors attended prayer summits? What percent?

2. Vision and Goals
* Have the leaders cast a clear and concise vision? What is the

vision?

* Is the vision an overarching vision encompassing the whole Church and the whole city?
* Are there measurable goals owned by a large spectrum of the Church, that when achieved will attain to the vision?
* Where vision exists, is it a closure vision? Or is it limited to an activity or growth vision?
* Is there a citywide initiative in place already? Who is involved? What is its known purpose? What is the current status?

3. Equipping the Saints

* Is there adequate understanding and administration of the 5-fold ministries (Ephesians 4:11) in equipping the saints? For old and new churches? What percentage of the churches?
* Is the leadership pushing balanced equipping (pastors, elders)?
* Is there instruction on spiritual gifts? How widespread?
* Is there involvement in training (doing it) in evangelism, small group leadership (nurture and evangelism), etc.
* To what extent is missions being emphasized?
* Identify some of the key apostles, prophets, evangelists, pastors and teachers in the city.

4. Body Life

* To what extent is there inter-church, inter-denominational, inter-organizational cooperation and fellowship?
* Is there a presence of a functioning *overall citywide strategy initiative with commonly held vision and goals*? (Don't confuse this with processes and tactical ministries such as crusades, Promise Keepers, etc. and their goals and strategies.)
* Where is reconciliation taking place within the Body?
* Where is reconciliation needed?

5. Relevancy of Gospel Communication

* What generations are the Church effectively reaching? By what measurement? What are the salient factors?
* Are there widespread ministries for reaching singles of various ages and backgrounds? Can you give illustrations?
* Is the Church ministering effectively to single moms? Business

people? Senior citizens? Minorities? Politicians?
* Which ethnic/ethnolinguistic target groups are being reached? Not being reached? How? Why?

6. Outreach Ministry
* Are holistic "mission outposts" established throughout the city? Where can more be located? What should be their primary ministries focus?
* Which churches have benevolent outreach ministries beyond their internal family? Are these doing effective evangelization through meeting physical, emotional and social needs?
* What is the ratio of evangelistic (outreach) cells per church for the Church in the city? For the fastest growing churches? For the reproducing churches?
* Are social, economic, moral, psychological and political transformations taking place? Where? What are some examples? What factors are involved?

Note: You have probably thought of other crucial questions relating to the description and status of the Church. List these and keep them handy along with those above.

Needed Harvest Force Data

Let us now look at the data categories applicable to denominations, local churches and parachurch groups. *Not every one of the following data items applies to all three categories, however.* The categories below can be confusing, as it looks like (and there is) duplication between the sections. Your basic task is to identify the Harvest Force and the dynamics of this Harvest Force. The Church in the city, as the Body of Christ, is your primary target of analysis.

Most of this information can (and should) be made available to all the churches, which helps in overall Body understanding and acceptance, and also may end up getting some errors corrected.

It may be difficult to get some of the information. Some individual churches and denominations are often quite protective of their internal status, ways and means. Yet you need to find ways of obtaining the data, since only by doing this can you get the true picture of the Church in the city. You may want to use linked tables to keep public information and proprietary information separate, yet in the same database. This provides you with flexibility in data management and selection, and will build up trust with the donors.

"Read Me!!"

The **Expanded Harvest Force Data Descriptions** are located in **Appendices-F & F-1** which are corollary with this chapter and section. These appendices cover all the detailed data listings for the following categories. **F-1** provides a "phased" listing. Also, **Appendix-H** provides further treatment of the data.

Data Category Outline

 I. Basic Administration and Ministry Descriptions
   A. Basic identity
   B. Goals and programs
   C. Ministries description
    1) Evangelism
    2) Missions
    3) Benevolence
    4) Community development
    5) Media
    6) Education and training
   D. Target peoples
   E. Target areas
   F. Stance on socio-cultural issues

 II. Churches and Related Statistical Data
   A. Churches (English speaking)
   B. Churches (non-English speaking)

    C. Small Groups (by age and purpose)
    D. Average weekly attendance (worship or main service(s))
    E. Active baptized members
    F. Baptisms - "believer's" and infant
    G. Pastors and/or staff
    H. Intercessory prayer cells

III. Other Harvest Force Data
    A. Local churches - information not included above - unique to local churches.
        1. Predominant ethnic orientation
        2. Seating capacity
        3. Number and types of services
        4. Weekly meetings/services
    B. Parachurch groups
        1. Organizational affiliations
        2. Index of non-profits
    C. Other corporate Church data
        1. Identification of special efforts and groups
        2. Identification of key Christians in special posts

Data Sources

Usually there is not very much local church, or Christian organization data available via public sources, at least not up-to-date data. However, there are some good exceptions. It very well may be that your city already has a directory of churches, ministries, denominations, and/or parachurch organizations. (Remember, everyone who is genuinely "born again" is part of the Harvest Force. However, all Protestant churches should be included as a minimum in your directory without trying to make judgments as to their biblical stance. A directory that includes all churches and worship centers for every religion (even cults) can be a valuable asset.)

1. Denominational Headquarters Data

    Perhaps there is a denominational or church association office in your city or area. They usually maintain annual reports on all of the churches under their jurisdiction. They may also have some graphical analysis, or even maps showing the distribution of their churches and ministries.

In any event, contact the denominational office (which in some situations may be combined with a local church) for each denomination, and explain why the data is needed and how it will be used. In cities where there are too few churches of one denomination to have a separate office, often one of the church's pastors is the local "superintendent."

Many denominations also have state or regional associations that maintain records for all of their affiliated churches, and these should be contacted if the information is not available locally.

Some groups of churches, or affiliations, claim they are not a denomination, but have centrally kept records.

In addition to statistical data, obtain information (reports, articles, etc.) relating to the various ministries and programs the denomination is currently involved in, or sponsors. If there are some success stories that have been published, it will be wise to accumulate a sampling of these which may help in the analysis, and provide case studies.

2. **Local Church Data.**
   The local church data is normally obtained through a local church survey of the city, or region of the city. However, some information may already be compiled (such as a listing of churches) by any one of several different groups in the city, whether Christian or other. With the current level of information technology, many information banks are finding their way to the Internet and various Web sites. Some churches have their own Web sites.
   In Chapter 3 we discussed several different survey methods and techniques. Additionally, some local church-related sample survey forms have been included in Appendix-D which you

may find helpful in surveying local churches.

As previously mentioned, sooner or later a good *church directory* will need to be compiled. This information changes often, including pastors and phone numbers, and not quite so often, locations. If you are just starting the process, you will probably find the Yellow Pages helpful. However, these will not be complete, nor necessarily up-to-date. Although this may suffice for some "initial assessment" picture, and could be used in the "prime-the-pump" situation for motivation or recruiting involvement in a citywide initiative, it will not support needed church growth analysis.

Check with local associations of evangelicals, ecumenical councils, and youth organizations. Also remember that every non-profit organization registers with the state. The state corporation office (or library, using electronic access) may be able to furnish you with a church list. You may be able to get this in electronic form, then edit out those you wish to omit.

Often, some parachurch group has already compiled a directory of churches. Check with the local ecumenical council, Youth for Christ, evangelical and/or pastors' associations, etc.. Check the Internet and the Web. Today there are more and more databases becoming available that track annually the telephone numbers and addresses of all businesses and churches. Contact Mapping Center for Evangelism[4] or Strategic Resources Ministry[5] for more information and leads on these databases.

Contact the city offices, including the planning office, and see if they keep a record of churches and other Christian organizations. Some cities do.

3. Parachurch Organizations Data

Most parachurch groups present in the city will have an office. Since there can be a wide variety of Christian organizations that come under the parachurch label, it may well be there is not a comprehensive directory available. A helpful directory would include Christian schools, seminaries, Bible schools, clinics, benevolence, campus ministries, sending agencies, literature, evangelism, Christian media [radio, television, films, recordings], arts and entertainment, consulting firms, research groups, etc..

Check with the local evangelical or ministerial association to see if a recent directory already exists. Over time contact will probably need to be made with representatives of every parachurch group to determine the extent of overall ministry the Church has in the city.

In addition, there may be some sending agencies in your city. Also contact the Rescue Missions. Some parachurch groups are involved in coordinating or catalyzing citywide ministries of evangelism, training, etc..

Notes:

1. Keep in mind the object of the research, which is to determine the identity, location, description and status of the Harvest Force in the city/area. Also keep in mind, you don't need to gather everything you could gather. That is, you need to surmise what data is needed and not needed and when. Therefore, you must keep in mind the goals and what you plan on doing with the data and analysis.

2. Just remember to ask yourself "Why do we need this?" It takes time, effort, space and finanaces to obtain, maintain, analyze and publish information. Know what you need and how it will be used. Also remember you want to generate a clear picture of what yet needs to be done, and be able to communicate this information to the leaders and the Body.

Help the Future

When you are spying out the land, you will find there is quite a disparity among organizations and churches with regards to what information is gathered and maintained. One of your challenges will be to help rectify this through demonstrating how and why the data is needed. It is an education process. The best way to do this is to tell stories of how the data you already have is being used to reach the city. Don't get discouraged at the start. As the research process evolves, you will gain more stories. Tell people they will be able to see the aggregate of all the data and analysis at some point in time (such as a conference, publication, congress, etc.) This assures them there is a definite Church-wide purpose in what you are doing. Only at that time will they really begin to accurately understand why and how the data is valuable...even powerful.

The involvement of leadership is essential in both the maintenance and collection of the data. One of their roles is to convince denominations and churches of the need to maintain needed data (e.g. *attendance, small groups, prayer cells ,etc.)*. And another is to explain why the data is needed, and to encourage them to cooperate in furnishing it promptly when it is needed. Unless the Church has the information needed for insightful evaluation of Body life, effectiveness in ministry, and overall progress, the Church can drift undetected from its purposes and goals.

In your investigation and survey, always pursue the information you know will give you the best understanding of the situation. Reflect this on your forms and in your reports, whether or not the data is available. You are involved in a process that includes education, enlightenment and seed-sowing.

The Next Chapter

In the next chapter we'll look at gathering the Harvest Field facts needed for providing an accurate, up-to-date picture of status and dynamics of the city. When you couple the picture of the Harvest Field with that described in this chapter for the Harvest Force, you will have the foundational data needed for objectively analyzing what God has been doing, and what He wants to do in the not-too-distant future in the city. This *prophetic message* could and should lead the Church in the city into new and fruitful efforts for "discipling" and transforming the city.

Endnotes:
1. Myers, Bryant. *Perspectives*. Monrovia, CA: MARC Newsletter, September 1997
2. *Urban Outreach Inc.* is headquarted in the Heights section of Houston, TX. It was founded in 1993 by Duncan Ragsdale, who still serves as Director. Their programs are designed for the purpose of "bringing together clergy, laity, school children and their parents." You can reach them at: 205 E. Ninth Street, or P.O. Box 70129, Houston, TX 77270-0129, Ph: 713-869-4281. Ministries of Urban Outreach include: Love Your Neighborhood, Heights Youth Rescue, Heights Outreach, Heights Youth Club, HYC Drama, HYC Fine Arts Academy, HYC Leadership Sports, HYC Camps and Clinics, Donna's Kid-Mentoring, Heights Outreach Pastors Fellowship, Heights Leadership Institute, Heights Town Planning, and Lighthouses for Houston Neighbors.
3. Barna, George *What Effective Churches Have Discovered: Insights on Ministry in the Late Nineties*. A Christian Growth Seminar by George Barna, Copyright, 1997 George Barna, Barna Research Group, 2487 Ivory Way, Oxnard, CA 993030
4. *Mapping Center for Evangelism: www.map4jesus.org*
5. Strategic Resources Ministry: www.lia-pdx.org/res/srmhome.htm.

Chapter 6: Gathering The Harvest Field Facts

C ities are composed of two heterogeneous societies who challenge accurate and thorough description and assessment. They are both a complex mosaic of races, religions, cultures, economic diversity, politics and social stratas. They are both a challenge to those who desire to understand the inner workings to bring about broad sweeping positive changes.

One of these societies is the Church, the Harvest Force, whose description and status we looked at in the last chapter. The other is the context in which the Church finds herself, the Harvest Field, and we will look at portraying its description and status in this chapter.

In your (or any) city a person could rightly declare, "Well, it might be like that in the part of the city you live and work in, but that doesn't describe my situation. Where I live and work it is quite different." Only a person who lives, walks and breathes the city can really begin to know its ins and outs, the whos and the whys, the unique worldview of its citizens. Even then they must have their "senses trained to discern between good and evil."

It will be necessary for the data gatherer and analyst to "walk the city," visiting a wide variety of areas and neighborhoods, from downtown - to the industrial parks - to the residential districts - to "skid row(s)." Later in the Spiritual Mapping section of this chapter, there are a couple anecdotes that illustrate this point. They are actual cases.

You want to see the diversity of the city through geographic and ethnographic lenses as well as through God's eyes. You also want to understand the felt needs of the city. This is not the needs as you see them, but rather the needs as they see them. It is through discerning and ministering to the felt needs that the real need is met, that of a new life in Christ. That, of course, is the ultimate goal.

> *When Nehemiah learned of the need in Jerusalem (1:3), his God-given goal was to see Jerusalem and the people of Israel redeemed and restored to their God. Everything he did from that point on worked toward that end. The Apostle Paul in entering Athens (Acts 17:16), saw the great need there, and moved immediately toward meeting that need.*

Remember the old story of the blind men and the elephant? One person felt the tail, and described the elephant much as the tail. Another felt a leg, and described the elephant from this perception. Another felt the trunk, and again *saw* a different animal. Only by sharing and working together could they get a reasonable perception.

In the same way, we tend to view the city through our own perceptions and needs. We have to move beyond this to get a true perspective.

The remainder of this chapter is given to assist in the redemption of your city and all of its societies through obtaining an insightful understanding of its character and dynamics. The Harvest Field data points (set forth in **Appendix-G**) have been considered carefully in the context of a citywide and Body-wide Church mobilization strategy initiative. When this data is gathered and properly analyzed, the Body of Christ in your city will have one of the most valuable tools it can possibly have. When effectively communicated, the Body will have light that can significantly dispel and overcome the darkness.

The Assessment of the Harvest Field

Performing an in-depth survey of the Harvest Field is a large and continuing task in view of the dynamics of change taking place in the city. If you are performing an "initial assessment," then you will want to collect all of the information outlined, for there is a vital need for establishing a baseline data reference for the city. Subsequent updates may vary in their frequency and depth. However, it is vitally important that as thorough an understanding as is possible and practicable of the city be achieved to develop foundational strategies and plans, and to implement appropriate methodologies.

Crucial Questions Needing Answers

Similar to the Harvest Force there are a myriad of questions begging for answers regarding the city and the populace. Many of the questions are alluded to in the various data category listings outlined in this chapter and **Appendix-G**. However, the following list of questions and their answers are basic to determining the past and current impact the Church is making in the city, as well as helping to obtain insights into some of the more subtle dynamics of the city. You will probably think of many more, plus additional categories, and it would be a good idea to add them to the list. Keep these in mind as you are embarking on your data gathering. Review them again as you begin your analysis.

Remember, what you are doing is vitally important to the Church and to the future of the city. There are many people, including those outside the Church, that will be keenly interested in the results of your research and analysis. Take the time and effort to make it thorough.

Seek to find the not-so-obvious answers to the following:

1. The Unreached and the Unchurched

There are two huge stumbling blocks in the path of the unchurched. One is the completely distorted and/or lack of understanding the Church has of the unchurched, their worldviews, needs, hopes, opinions and aspirations. The other is the distorted view and understanding of authentic Christianity, Christians, the Church, and churches, held by the unchurched.

Why do these huge stumbling blocks exist? What understanding does the Church need, and what appropriate actions should it take to remove these hindrances to the True Life awaiting those who will put their faith and trust in the Lord Jesus Christ?

The following questions need answers in your city. You will think of others. Make some effort to find the answers through study, surveys and interviews. Some analysis results may already be available. Each of the following 10 questions relate to the unchurched. (Works like George Barna's can give you further insights into determining the mindset of the unchurched.[1])

1. What percentage of unchurched people have rejected God, or think He is irrelevant to their lives?
2. What percentage have just rejected the Church, or think it is irrelevant to their lives?
3. What percentage of the people truly understand the basic tenets of Christianity? How many of these same people can describe the reasons or basis for what they do believe?
4. What percentage have more than a passing interest in spiritual matters? What percentage are involved in New Age, Spiritism, the occult?
5. What is most important to people? Being helped? Having friendships? Getting good employment? Having a good marriage? Making money?
6. What are causes people feel they can connect with?
7. What percentage of the non-regular churchgoers want their children to get good moral training?
8. What percentage of the unchurched have any interest at all in the Bible?
9. What percentage say they are tolerant of different faiths? Of these, what percentage think Christians are narrow-minded? What percentage have a favorable impression of Christianity? Of churches?
10. How many feel they would like to try to go to church, but are afraid they will have a bad experience?

Additional questions relating to the unchurched and/or unbelievers:
* What are the main reasons given by the unchurched for their not attending a Christian church? For not becoming a Christian?
* Who are the least-churched people groups in the city? How would you describe them geographically, socio-culturally, eth-

nically, and economically?

* Who are the least churched age groups in the city? How would you describe them ethnically, socio-culturally, economically, occupationally, and educationally?

* Which social events (music, sports, drama, etc.) would be most likely to attract the teenage and young single adults? Young marrieds? Middle aged? Seniors?

2. Needs-Social, Moral, Physical, and Spiritual

* Which segments of society have the greatest need in each of the areas? How would you describe their needs? Where are these people located? What is (are) the predominant age group(s)?

* Which groups, organizations or individuals in the city are being highly successful in meeting needs in these areas? What *do* *they* attribute success to?

* What are the biggest problems as reported by the schools? Elementary? Middle? High? College? What efforts are currently underway to solve them?

* Which areas of the city experience the highest crime rates? Violent crimes? Nonviolent? Which stratas of society? Ethnic? Economic? National heritage?

3. City History

* When was the city founded? By whom? For what purpose?

* What have been some of the major milestones in the city's history? Policy-wise? Industry and commerce? Religious? Moral?

* What have been major times of crises in the city? What was the cause? What was the result? Is there any impact still being felt today?

* What took place in the city's history that can be directly attributable to its current spiritual and moral condition? Do these conditions still exist?

4. City Leadership

* Who are the key leaders in the city? What are their positions and responsibilities? What are their religious beliefs? What is

their reputation regarding morality? Honesty? Servanthood?
* Who are considered the biggest problems regarding city leadership? Why? What are their areas of responsibility? What is their circle of influence?

5. City Growth and Expansion
* What have been the newest residential expansion areas? Are new churches planned for these areas? By whom? What type of services?
* What expansion projects are on the drawing boards? Residential? Commercial? Heavy industry?

6. Transformation and Revival
* Which areas of society are most needy in terms of transformation? What kind of change is needed?
* Which areas have experienced significant transformation in the past 5 years? What were the factors involved?
* What efforts should have resulted in transformation but failed? Factors involved?
* When was there significant revival taking place in the city? Who was involved both from the Church aspect and the populace? What was revival attributed to? How long did it last?
* Are there any current signs pointing to revival? What are the signs? Who's involved?

You may want to increase this "checklist" based upon your own, or someone else's, experience. Obtaining answers to these questions will go a long way toward equipping the Church for significant progress, as well as bring a new level of awareness and accountability.

Defining Basic Guidelines
There are several guidelines that should be followed when gathering and storing data for the categories that will follow.

1. Identify each data record as to primary data source and data year. Do not assume data gathered in the current year is for the current year. Double check the assumption.
2. Where available, gather data for:

- The entire MSA (Metropolitan Statistical Area)
- Main geopolitical divisions (e.g. zones, districts, counties)
- Census tracts
- Zip codes

3. Don't forget the Yellow Pages, or the Internet/Web. Often these can be good sources. Don't make them your sole source for any category, as any one source probably won't have complete data. The purpose for which those listings were generated is probably different from yours.

4. Use multiple sources for the same data when possible. This acts as a double check. However, be aware that multiple sources may really be propagating the same data, and that data may not be accurate. Some quote each other and you have a "chicken and egg" situation.

5. Play the devil's advocate with all data. Ask yourself why you should consider it valid.

A Note Regarding Geopolitical Entities Definitions

1. Get or generate a list of entities, such as school districts, zones, counties (in the MSA), neighborhoods, zip codes, census districts, etc..

2. Get maps of entities (see the city planning commission, local governments, or mapping companies)

3. If you are doing computerized mapping, you will need the "boundary file" layers for these entities. If the city is doing mapping, these layers may be available from the city at little or no cost.

Outlining the Data Categories

The following outline describes the categories of data needed to be gathered to paint a comprehensive picture of the city, its past and current history, its societies, and its dynamics. Described after this, and near the end of the chapter, are locations where much of the data can be obtained.

Data Categories (Ref: Appendix-G)
1. Demographics
    A. Population
    B. Vital statistics
    C. Households
2. Ethnic/ethnolinguistic groups
3. Socio-cultural groups
4. Social concerns and needs
5. Cultural traditions and events
6. Arts and entertainment
7. Media
8. Economics
9. Industry and commerce
10. Religions
11. Government and politics

IMPORTANT NOTE
The Expanded Harvest Field Data Description (Dictionary) and Data Table are located in **Appendix-G** which is corollary with this chapter and section. This appendix covers all the detailed data listings for the above categories.

Spiritual Mapping and City History

The strategic importance of the research discipline termed spiritual mapping has rightfully been coming to the forefront of the Christian mission. This has largely been born out of George Otis, Jr.'s experiences and observations over the past 15 years or more.

Otis's extensive travels which have taken him to every continent and to hundreds of thought-capturing sites have led him into a keen understanding of the cause and effect relationship behind the social, cultural and spiritual dynamics we find in the mosaic of societies of every city and nation. He has recently published *Informed Intercession*[2], which promises to be the landmark work for spiritual mapping.

No city can experience significant widespread lasting transformation unless the principles of spiritual mapping have been, and are being applied. The city today is the result of its total social, cultural, physical and spiritual history.

Without understanding why things are the way they are in the communities of your city, achieving proper remedies and lasting transformation will be impossible. Melting the tip of the iceberg does not remove the dangers just because it is not visible from the surface. Informed insights into the socio-cultural and spiritual history are needed, and can be achieved when the orderly investigative process of spiritual mapping is followed.

> *"Spiritual Mapping is the process of superimposing our under- standing of forces and events in the spiritual domain onto places and circumstances in the material world."*
>
> George Otis

Otis observes,

"Before you can establish an effective evangelistic and/or intercessory plan, you must first try to understand why things are the way they are. How has your community come to be what it is today? What do you know about the origin of contemporary hindrances to the gospel?

"To answer these questions it is necessary to examine the historical and spiritual roots of your area. Who were the original peoples? What factors or motives led them to found a permanent community?

"You will also want to investigate significant confluent events like natural disasters, military invasions, and the influx of new religions. How did these occurrences alter the life and identity of the community? Did the inhabitants of that time attempt to resolve the traumatic circumstances by entering into pacts with the spirit world? Did their actions compound or modify earlier arrangement?"

He goes on to state,

> "History is not a collection of accidents that pop out of a social vacuum. Just as there is a sense and cadence to the universe, so is there a rhyme and reason to our communities. To discern this rhythm, however, we must listen to the entire concerto of our history, not merely the latest stanza."[3]

And then, according to Otis, we must "heed the warning lights on the dashboard of life. We must go beyond dialogue. We must do the things that welcome the Lord into our society. We must determine why spiritual darkness lingers where it does."

Your city has people and events in its current and past history that are significantly influencing or impacting the city today. We've included in **Appendix-O** a sizeable sample of spiritual mapping related data items. These can get you started on your own spiritual mapping of your community. So much has occurred in this area over the past few years the case studies are multiplying rapidly of where spiritual mapping and simultaneous and subsequent intercessory and warfare prayer are resulting in strategic spiritual breakthroughs and victories. Be sure to obtain Otis' book, *Informed Intercession,* and the videos Sentinel Group produced depicting case studies of transformed cities around the world.

For example, in one city an inner-city church requested some mapping of their neighborhood, which was essentially their mission field. Unlike a census tract or zip code, the neighborhood had a name and a history. By understanding this history, the church could begin strategic prayer and ministry.

There is a real need to think strategically in getting the information you need, and to know what you need. In one city the researchers tried to eliminate getting church attendance because it was so hard to obtain. The issue isn't how difficult the data is to obtain, but how crucial the data is for supporting the strategy. Church attendance data is high priority data.

Data Sources

The following data sources assume an assessment survey for the Metropolitan Statistical Area (MSA), or significant segment (target area) of the city. You will find there are other good data sources.

A. Demographic and other Harvest Field Data.

Much of the data you will need is library data that is already published and may be compiled into usable reports. These days, much data is available on electronic media (disk, CD, Internet/Web, etc.). The following should provide you with a good start. Don't be too gullible regarding published data. Just because it's available doesn't mean you need it. Just because it is in print doesn't make it accurate. Find out how and when the information was compiled, by whom, and for what reason. Some information is assembled for promotional purposes and is biased. Try to validate the data, and in your database enter the source and data date for each piece of information. (Not doing so is a researcher's unpardonable sin.)

1. City, County, State, and National Government Offices.
It will pay in the short and long run for two or three people to spend some time in the city offices getting familiar with the Planning Office, and other offices that have data regarding the population (for example, ethnic minority offices, social services, etc.)

Maps. Obtain a good large map of the city you can use for your general use. Also obtain as many thematic maps as you can showing such things as: population distribution, population growth rates, identity and distribution of religions and worship centers, ethnic distribution and media, crime, economic stratas/distribution, etc.. If you haven't used maps much, you will find they are powerful tools as you begin to get a progressive revelation and picture of your city or area. Many individuals involved in national and citywide initiatives use maps very effectively, and are part of their basic toolkit.

One pastor's wife who was starting some research in their new pastorate in a small town found a city map (complete with houses and churches) on the wall of the mayor's office. She asked for a copy, only to be told it was their only copy and they could not lend it out. She asked if she could borrow it during the lunch hour and she would get them a few copies. They let her take it. Think strategically!

Note: Computerized mapping is quite popular these days. Most cities either have their own systems, or are furnished maps by a service agency in the city government. Find out what they are doing, and try to learn what mapping software/packages they are using. There are several groups in the U.S. who provide mapping systems and/or mapping services for the Christian community, such as Global Mapping International, Mapping Center for Evangelism, Strategic Resources Ministry, Percept, and several others. The list is rapidly growing.

Statistical (e.g. census, etc.) reports. Often city-generated reports will contain considerable data you are interested in. For instance they may have data on the location and size of mosques, churches, temples, porno points, etc.. Get as much data on disk or CD as you can, but assure it is in a usable format. Try to obtain actual geographic data points as well as aggregate data. For example, getting actual locations of where murders, car thefts, and burglaries occur shows cluster patterns and spacial and other relationships. These are visible if you are mapping aggregate data, say, like the number of burglaries per neighborhood or zip code. To do this, it is often necessary for the researcher to build trust with city officials. This usually takes time.

Note: It is really a plus if you can find a Christian or other sympathetic person in the city government who can help with locating, accessing and furnishing the data needed. Many city government personnel have the "civil servant" spirit, and are willing to help. City government offices often have maps that will be very useful.

2. Libraries (city, county, and university) and universities.
Library. We suggest two or more people be involved in the Li-

brary Research, especially in the library. A variety of aptitudes and perspectives will prove beneficial here. In major universities you will often find a "government document section," and/or separate research library and map library. These are good depositories for all types of local, state, national and international data. Many times they include annual statistical updates and projections. Many cities have neighborhood associations that maintain information at the neighborhood level.

University. At the university, check with the various departments and determine where you can find copies of Masters and Doctoral theses (perhaps they have a "Commons" area, or a special section in the library where copies are filed). You very possibly will find professors, especially sociologists and cultural anthropologists, who are very glad to partner in some ministry orientation for the city. This may take the form of them involving their students in performing research on a particular Target Area or Target People of special interest to you.

Seminaries. If your city has a seminary, you may find they will also be willing to cooperate. Consider their students potential resource people for helping in the city, and you will often find they are eager for the experience, seeing how it could benefit them in future ministry. Every discipline of study should be a candidate for your obtaining help in analyzing the city. Talk with the professors. Tell them your purpose and need for gaining insights and data that can help lead to a transformation of the elements of society.

Sundry. You should be on the lookout for papers on such things as: ethnic diversity and needs, population analysis, crime analysis, community development and needs analysis, health and welfare, media, religion-related, human behavior, worldview, social issues, etc.. These are data (data is singular or plural) helpful in determining how best to penetrate and reach society with the Gospel, and in assisting to mobilize and allocate resources effectively. That is to say, you may find some good help for both the disciple-making and the management processes. The newspaper section of the library can be a good resource for contemporary data.

3. Independent Research and/or Analysis Organizations.
Today there are many organizations doing research and analysis. There may be some in your city, even if it is a smaller one. They do work for marketing, development, real estate, banking, and other groups who are trying to determine what the current and future potential is for sales, employment, expansion, building, industry, etc.. Some even do human interest research, including worldview and mindset/opinion, in order to tailor advertisements.

4. Other sources
There are many other sources of data other than the three mentioned above. Some of them are:

* Real estate offices. Some offices use sophisticated computer programs that can do address matching, and locate and draw maps for nearly any desired real estate entity. The larger offices also routinely do a variety of population, economic, property and market analyses.

* Chamber of Commerce. Most chambers maintain listings of business and business opportunities, churches, social service groups, sports organizations and schedules, arts and entertainment entities and schedules, etc..

What's' Next?

The next step in your discovering your city is to learn what the data has to tell you. The next three chapters speak to the area of analysis and to developing the "prophetic message" that needs to be communicated to the Church in the city. The final chapter considers ways to effectively communicate that message.

Endnotes:
1. Some books by George Barna are: *Generation Next, Evangelism That Works: How to Reach Changing Generations With the Unchanging Gospel; User Friendly Churches; Virtual America*;...all by Regal Books. Also you can contact Barna Research Group in Oxnard, California for further help.
2. Otis, George Jr. *Informed Intercession*, Ventura: Renew Books, 1999
3. Ibid, chapter 7, p.5

Chapter 7: Analysis - Introduction to the Process

You have now come to the point in *discovering your city* that you hold a massive amount of information and now you want to make this information work for the Church in transforming the city. You are ready to take a careful, objective and methodical look at what the assembled information has to tell you. You want the data to reveal its many secrets.

You've been able to make some observations along the way, but now you need to refine the ore to obtain the hi-grade. Other people may hold much of the same information you are holding, but haven't seen it in the same light in which you will see it. The Holy Spirit will reveal to you insights and lead you into the truth as you are prayerfully involved in the analysis.

A Word of Caution

At this point, you are moving to the front line in spiritual warfare. You can be sure the enemy does not want you to see things the way they really are. He has maintained various strongholds for a long time, and holds many captive. Once you have the analysis results you will be upsetting the status quo... disturbing the balance of previous things, both in society and the Church.

> *"Unless the fellowship in the Christian assembly is far superior to that which can be found anywhere else in society, the Christian can talk about the transforming love and power of Christ until they are hoarse, but people are not going to listen very hard."*
>
> Canon Michael Green

You can be assured there will be some eyebrow-raising revelations. You will also be gaining insights into the reasons things are the way they are, and see many implications for what needs to be done. Prayer is essential here, both for obtaining enlightenment and insights into what has previously been hidden or distorted, and for mental, spiritual and physical protection for yourself and for others involved in the analysis.

Review the Vision and Goals

This would be a good time to review the overall strategic goal stated in Chapter 1. It may be in your city you have worded the goal differently, or perhaps you are still working on the level of several tactical goals and the wider Body has not yet become involved in an over-arching, city-reaching strategy. The forthcoming analysis will provide insightful status with regard to the goals, and will (or should, in any event) lead to determined courses of action toward achieving them.

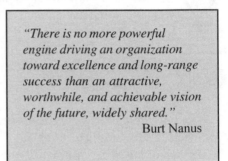

"There is no more powerful engine driving an organization toward excellence and long-range success than an attractive, worthwhile, and achievable vision of the future, widely shared."

Burt Nanus

The previously stated, over-arching goals (see Chapter 1) are:

Ø *To see Jesus Christ incarnate in His Body, the true Church, in every segment of humanity in the form of healthy, out-reaching gatherings of believers;*

Ø *To see these gatherings distributed so there is one within practical (can get to) and cultural (would go to) distance of every person in every class and kind of society;*

Ø *To see gatherings that are dynamic, and working toward penetrating every neighborhood with the redeeming and transforming love, care, truth, joy and power of Jesus Christ, resulting in a measurable transformation of lives and society aligned with the righteousness of God - reaching every generation on an ongoing basis.*

Ø *To see a broad and representative spectrum of the Body of Christ in the city collaborating in the overall city-reaching process of taking the whole Gospel to the whole city.*

What You Are Looking For

When you have completed your analysis there will be:

* an accurate, up-to-date status of the overall city-reaching goals;
* revealing pictures painted of the Harvest Force and Harvest Field;
* insights into why things are the way they are in the Church and in the city, including the impact history has had on current situations;
* specific conclusions drawn;
* concrete recommendations regarding specific actions the Church in the City should take;
* a clear *prophetic message* to the Church taking into account the current condition of the city, and how the Church needs to proceed.

You will have looked at all the evidence (the data) and drawn many conclusions. This revelatory information made up of the data and the analysis report containing the Prophetic Message will be of utmost

> *"Why do churches and denominations die? The answer is simple. Because they change the wrong things, and hang on to the wrong things."*
> Elmer Town

interest to the denominational leaders, to pastors and churches, to parachurch groups, and to those coordinating the overall citywide strategy initiative.

The accuracy and adequacy of analysis will have a direct impact on how effective the Church in the city will be in reaching the goals of seeing lives and the city transformed by the love, truth and power of Jesus Christ.

The Analysis Process

In previous chapters we've been establishing the foundation of information needed to determine: what has been done, what is being done, and what is yet to be done - towards reaching the goals of seeing the city saturated with gatherings of believers showing forth the redeeming and transforming love, care, truth, joy and power of our Lord Jesus Christ.

We now want to look at an overview of the analysis process which will portray a clear picture of inner-workings of the Church and the city. There are five aspects:

*	The tools of the process	(Chapter 7)
*	The steps of the process	(Chapter 7)
*	Performing the analysis	(Chapter 8)
*	Developing the "prophetic message"	(Chapter 8, 9)
*	Communicating the results	(Chapter 10)

In this chapter we consider the first two.

Tools and Types of Analysis

The analysis process itself is a powerful tool in unlocking the hidden secrets of information. There are, classically, four types of analysis tools for converting the raw data into a more revealing and useful format. Most likely you have already formatted some of your data into one or more of them.

1. Statistical/mathematical
2. Graphical
3. Cartographical (maps)
4. Factorial

Utilizing these methods, you will be able to have the data reveal to you its hidden secrets. Don't do your analysis a disservice by omitting some of these tools.

Note: **Appendix-H** contains the details of the process for formatting the data for each of the following types of analysis. **Appendix-H** is companion to Chapters 7, 8 and 9.

1. Statistical/Mathematical Analysis

Statistical analysis is as important in the process of understanding Church growth and non-growth as the measurement of a patient's vital signs are to the doctor or nurse. Without the needed details, it is impossible to make an accurate and insightful assessment of actual conditions, causes and effects.

A trained eye can look at a table of data containing denominational statistics for churches and active members (or attendees) and immediately make several revelatory observations. A statistical table covering church and active member numbers for the past 5 to 10 years is of special worth. Appendix I contains some sample tables.

Three particularly useful mathematical calculations are: growth rates, population per church ratio, and average church size.

Observation can detect good growth, poor growth, anomalies in growth, presence of certain diseases, and compare the relationship between the growth of churches vs. members. This provides insights regarding growth potential.

2. Graphical Analysis

Graphical analysis is a very vital and powerful tool. Graphs provide a dimension of understanding and intelligence not possible by any other means. This is especially true for comparison in size or rates. Often it is a graph that will lead you to investigate anomalies, or good or poor growth because of the comparative analysis they afford.

Graphs are a good way to communicate the results of a survey and analysis in order to help make the greatest impact. This is especially true for making projections and setting new growth goals. New projections for growth based upon several different growth rates can easily be seen and compared on a line graph.

The three most common graphs are: line, bar (or columnar) and pie. See Appendices H & J for examples.

3. Cartographical Analysis (Maps)

Cartographical analysis is a very powerful tool that often is not used to its potential. Maps provide a spatial relationship and comprehension not afforded in any other way. They should be a part of every citywide or local area survey and analysis. They also provide an excellent "execution" tool for ministry implementation.

Maps can be used for depicting various status measurements and conditions. Any kind of data having a spacial element can be depicted on maps, including compound information on one map. An illustration would be a map depicting the distribution of Asians and their percent Christian, or "population per church ratio" by census district. Or depicting high crime rate areas in reference to porno points. The themes that can be depicted on maps is nearly limitless, as is the combination of overlays.

Unlike graphic images, maps are a composition of layers, with the components of each layer constructed using combinations of latitude and longitude coordinates, which can be arranged to form lines, points and polygons. (Polygons are many sided, enclosed figures for which area can be measured.) For example, one layer may be a collection of polygons representing zip codes. Another layer of points, such as church locations, has each point defined by the latitude and longitude location of each church. Highways and rivers are constructed of lines.

See Appendix-K for sample maps, and Appendix-L for more information relating to mapping software and city data files.

4. Factorial Analysis

Factorial analysis in the context of this publication pertains primarily to ascertaining the factors of growth and non-growth of the Church in a city or people, and the factors impacting social, cultural, religious and political conditions. Statistical, graphical and cartographical analyses all play their parts in facilitating factorial analysis.

The factors of growth or effectiveness can be: national and/or local, contextual (Harvest Field) and/or institutional (Harvest Force), external and/or internal to the denomination or Church. (Nehemiah had both internal and external factors he had to contend with in building the wall and restoring the people of Israel to their God.) Because all these have potential influence on Church growth, certain basic data needs to be gathered to understand the context and the basic Church description and status. Once the factorial analysis gets under way, then further investigation will probably be needed as additional questions arise and holes need to be filled.

Steps in Performing Analysis

The following nine steps (with their sub-steps) give an idea of what the analysis process involves. This list is not exhaustive, but gives an idea of some of the methods used to gain an informed understanding of the Church and the city. In the gathering and managing of the data, you may have already converted some of the data into the following formats. Each table, map and graph will provide you with more illumination and understanding.

1. Prepare Basic Data Tables
   * Prepare tables for Harvest Force and Harvest Field (including spiritual diagnostics), and combinations of both.

2. Perform Statistical Calculations and Analysis
   * Calculate: growth rates, population per church ratio, church size, attendance as percent of population, etc.
   * Make interpolations/extrapolations for missing data.
   * Identify trends.
   * Identify current and historical status (demographics, vital statistics, economics, etc.).
   * Calculate projections for new congregations and believers.

3. Perform Graphical Analysis
   * Prepare line, bar, and pie graphs.
   * Plot Church growth history.
   * Plot current Church distribution.
   * Plot Harvest Field distributions.
   * Plot growth projections for new churches and believers.

4. Perform Cartographical (mapping) Analysis
   * Prepare a variety of maps (entire metro area, plus selected

districts, zones, etc.).
* Basic geography and ethnography (e.g. distribution of ethnic groups by geopolitical entity).
* Harvest Force themes (e.g. distribution of churches).
* Harvest Field themes (e.g. crime rates vs. economic levels).
* Combined or compound themes (e.g. population per church ratio by geo unit).

5. Perform Historical Analysis
* Identify significant spiritual, religious and political events that have occurred since the founding of the city.
* Determine which historical events or conditions are impacting the city today, both positively and negatively.
* Relate significance of early monuments and sites to location of current moral and political conditions, both good and bad.
* Identify and try to explain contradictions in the historical record.
* Determine what and how conflicts in the Church's history are impacting the Church today.

6. Perform Factorial Analysis
* Determine causes and factors of good growth and poor growth.
* Determine type of growth (e.g. conversion, transfer, biological, etc.).
* Determine extent of corporate Body life, (e.g inter-organizational cooperation, partnerships, united prayer efforts, etc.)
* Compare current status against goals. Highlight the "task yet to be done," and the implications for seeing the city transformed to align with God's righteousness.

7. Identify and Obtain Additional Data Needed
* Identify data needed for verification and/or clarification.
* Identify data needed for filling gaps.
* Identify case studies that would be valuable.
* Obtain needed/missing data and/or case studies.

8. Prepare Summary Report (Chapter 9)
* Summarize observations.

* Set forth conclusions.
* Outline report.
* Create report.
* Make recommendations.

9. Communicate the Results (Chapter 10)
* Identify communication strategy (methods and means).
* Prepare presentation materials.
* Prepare overhead transparencies depicting results.
* Prepare special articles.

Some Guidelines and Observations
As you begin or continue the analysis, there are a few guidelines you would do well to review and keep in mind.

1. Don't draw conclusions too fast. Learn to have a discrete, critical eye. Often data interprets data.
2. Look at research and analysis done by others.
3. Don't be afraid to say you "don't know," or that "the data is incomplete." Doing otherwise jeopardizes credibility and the validity of your data and conclusions.
4. Do make projections and draw your own conclusions. You are probably the most familiar with the situation as the result of your research and/or analysis.
5. Conscientiously try to not let your own doctrinal opinions influence the conclusions. Keep the results as objective as possible.
6. Identify sources and dates, and other pertinent data, on all tables, charts and maps.
7. Treat your data as secure information. Don't share it with those that have no need to see it in the context of the mission.
8. Approach the data with a dependency upon the Lord to provide guidance and insights.

Remember, relying heavily upon estimates and derivation will get you into trouble sooner or later. Go the extra mile in effort and perseverance to obtain hard facts and perform tedious analysis. The reward will be worth the effort. Do not yield to the temptation to manipulate the data to make it align with your presuppositions. *Careful treatment is required, but the fruits are rewarding.*

In countries, such as Ghana, when the first factual survey of the nation was completed, Ross Campbell, who coordinated the effort, exclaimed, *"When we completed the survey and analysis, nothing was the way we imagined it. We have had to change our whole strategy for 'churching' this nation."* The analysis will change your worldview of both the Harvest Force and Harvest Field in your city.

In San Jose, California, when a very preliminary picture and analysis of the city was presented to the leaders, they were overwhelmed by what they saw. They could see from this initial report various areas of the city with no churches, or where there were no churches relevant to the particular context (as in the case of the Native Americans).

Normally, however, healthy churches grow both qualitatively and quantitatively. In some situations, in order to reach various segments of society, churches start new gatherings. This form of growth is needed more and more as our research tells us the new wine isn't attracted, nor does it have its needs met, by and in the old skins.

Stay objective. Let the analysis tell you what the situation really is, and what is needed. Don't use the analysis to prove your, or disprove other's, opinions and points. Strongly opinionated and/or judgmental observations by the analyst are taboo and very risky. Such actions will frequently cause loss of credibility because of suspicion that the results reflect his or her bias.

Staying Objective

Often some organizations may be experiencing good growth while others may find growth slow or "impossible." Compile case studies of good growth, where the factors/causes are pinpointed, well documented, and described. The case-studies should be kept as objective as possible, letting the facts speak for themselves.

Takes Time

We should point out the accumulation of data, the knowledge base, and the insights derived all take time. There is no quick and easy way to understand your city. First, you see the situations that exist, then your understanding into why things are the way they are begin to evolve. You will go through the analysis process making discoveries that will help others be more effective and focused. Each time you go through the process your knowledge base will grow, and you will become a more valuable asset to your city and the Church.

You need to be gaining keener insights and better understanding of why the church is ineffective or effective than did your predecessors. There must be better and more thorough measurements of the seemingly subtle areas that help detect drift and trends that have rendered the Church dangerously separated from the existing, and especially the emerging, cultures.

Although many insights and conclusions can be drawn during this formatting process of arranging the data in tables, graphs and maps, do not make them your final conclusions. Resist the temptation to go public before you have completed the factorial analysis process and final report. If you are pressured to draw preliminary conclusions, make it very clear people understand they are preliminary and inconclusive. Tell them the analysis is incomplete, and to exercise caution in how they use it.

What's Coming Up?

The next step in analysis is the actual formatting of the data, and performing the four types of analysis outlined in this chapter. Chapter 8, and corollary Appendix-H, speak to this. Appendix-H leads through the step-by-step process of the various types of analysis. Chapter 8 contains a check list for determing the factors of growth. Preparing your final report is outlined in Chapter 9.

Chapter 8: Analysis - Painting the Picture

I n this chapter we will work through the process of learning and developing the message God has for the Church about itself and the city. This "prophetic message" will need to be communicated to the leaders, and the rest of the Church over time. The next two chapters will speak to the packaging and communication of this message.

The analysis will illuminate and change the Church's perception regarding the Harvest Force, Harvest Field, and spiritual condition in the city. You need to be prepared to ponder the implications of what you will be discovering; double check your conclusions; make sure you get the information into the right hands in the right form, and in a timely manner.

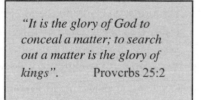

"It is the glory of God to conceal a matter; to search out a matter is the glory of kings".　　Proverbs 25:2

As you are involved in the analysis process, remember there are modern tools and information resources at your disposal. This Information Age is a boon for the analyst. You can sit in your own office or home and access an astonishing amount of data and information management and communication tools.

Madison Avenue takes full advantage of these tools to sell their products, exploiting the human nature's desire for *position, passion and possession.* Should not the Church take advantage of these same powerful tools to capture hearts and minds for the Kingdom of God? Since our culture is being more and more conditioned to hearing and learning things via the media of the Internet and Worldwide Web, would it not be wise for the Church to also take advantage of this media to facilitate the transformation of our churches and society?

When Global Mapping International started developing mapping tools in 1983, computerized maps of cities existed, but were rare, expensive to generate, and certainly not in the public domain. Now, less than two decades later, you can buy CD's containing maps of any city in the US or go onto the Internet and obtain, or even create, a map of your city from any one of several Internet sites.

This is all to say that as you are analyzing and painting the picture of the city and the Church, keep in mind there are an increasing number of modern tools, techniques and technology to assist you.

Working Through The Process

You have processed a lot of ore. Now you want to refine the precious metal and mold it into usable forms. You now are ready to implement the analysis steps outlined in the last chapter by performing the steps outlined below.

1. **Format the data as outlined in Appendix-H**. Refer to Appendices-I thru M for sample tables, maps, graphs and growth rate calculations. You may have already put much of the data in these formats. It is essential you follow the process as outlined as closely as possible to support the conclusions, factors and final analysis report. Data reveals many hidden secrets when in these formats.

   Note: You may want to refer once again to **appendices F-1 & G-1** for determining which data is most appropriate for the particular phase of city-reaching you are involved in.

2. **Perform statistical/mathematical calculations specified**. Calculate growth rates, population per church ratio, average church size, percentages of populations for various entities, etc..

3. **Review the tables, graphs and maps** that were prepared per instructions in **Appendix-H**. Make observations. These will provide you with many of the answers to the questions listed later in the chapter. They may provide other answers you are looking for. It is more than likely they will also raise questions. Keep a record of the questions.

4. **Perform historical analysis and basic spiritual mapping**. Refer to pertinent section in Chapter 6 and also **Appendix-O**.

5. **Perform factorial analysis.** Review the "Fundamental Determinations," and "Factors To Consider" outlined in this chapter. Make as many determinations as you can from the data. Answer as many of the questions as can be supported by the data. You may want to make copies of these two check lists to have them handy.

6. **Keep a record of missing or additionally needed data.** Arrange for obtaining the data, and/or for assuring the data is maintained in the future by the churches and denominations.

7. **Write down all observations, conclusions and recommendations.** Go to the next chapter (Chapter 9) which outlines the preparation of the formal analysis report where you will formally document all your results. Various *ways and means* of communicating these results are outlined in Chapter 10.

Factorial Analysis

Factorial analysis focuses upon determining the contribution various factors have upon the results at hand. It is through this type of investigative analysis you find out why things are the way they are. For instance, when you see a church that is growing faster than all others in an area, why is this? What are the contributing factors? When you find a generational group minimally reached, what are the reasons?

It is exactly in this area where we are often fooled. Without careful diagnosis we take a chance on drawing wrong, false or incomplete conclusions regarding why something is the way it is. Often things are not the way we imagine them to be. As mentioned before, often *yesterday's truths are today's fictions.* Some things cannot be extrapolated linearly. Some logical interpolations are in error. It is the job of the analyst to penetrate through all the smoke and fog to the clear facts. This will frequently require you to obtain further clarifying data. You may need to mine a lot of ore to get to the higrade. Don't short-circuit the process.

Where to Begin

Your investigation into why things are the way they are needs to begin with the review of the data you have in the various formats. You need to surround yourself with the tables, graphs, maps, and any interview or other pertinent records and notes that have been accumulated. Previously, we suggested you may want to make copies of some checklists to have them handy.

Review the vision and goals and make a list of those things you need to know in order to gain an accurate, up-to-date status of the vision and goals (such as those outlined in earlier chapters). You may need to status additional goals. Study the materials and note those things that help provide the answers. Also note any: *apparent* or *suspicious* anomalies (abrupt changes or questionable variations in numbers, curves and trends; missing data; etc.), fast growth, poor growth, unchurched areas, etc..

If something seems out of place or doesn't align with the other data, don't automatically assume it is in error. You might miss something important.

> **Suggestion**: *After you have made your initial analysis, do not publish it immediately. Show it to someone whose judgment you trust to see what questions or observations they might have. And you also may want to let some of your conclusions and recommendations sit a day or two or more, then revisit them for further study and evaluation. Often first impressions are not what they seem, and time can bring new perspective. Be a careful and thorough analyst. You want to build, not jeopardize, credibility. This is Kingdom business. Be as objective as you can. Draw attention to the facts, and for the most part let them speak for themselves.*

Fundamental Determinations

During the analysis process, you will want to make the following determinations. Generally these pertain to:

a) *what has been done* - including what worked and what didn't? Why are we where we are today?
b) *what is being done* - who's doing what, where and how? What are the results?
c) *what is yet to be done* - qualitatively and quantitatively for the Church in the city to reach the goals and fulfill the vision?

For example:

* You want to *see the city from a historical perspective*. What are the events that have the most influence in making the city what it is today? Who were some of the key figures? What things of the past are still influencing the life of the city for good? For bad?

* You want to *build the summary picture of the current distribution and status of the population*: the vital statistics, trends, immigrations, ethnic groups, density (by districts or zones), crime rates, poverty levels, religious adherants, income levels, etc.

* You want to *identify the distribution and status of the churches* in the city. What growth and ministry methods have been most successful in the past? What are they now? Which churches are growing and where? Who are they reaching and *not reaching* and why? What are their plans and goals? Who and where are they targeting? What new wineskins are needed?

* You want to *describe the dynamics of the city*, its peoples, its hurts and needs, its strengths and weaknesses, its aspirations, its ethnic, social, cultural, economic, and religious makeup. How would you describe the relationship between the city government and the churches and Church leaders? Good? Strained? Non-existent?

* You want to *describe the peoples and segments of society* in the city. What are their distinctives (linguistic, cultural, religious, economic, social)? To what extent are they being evangelized? Are they being exposed to the whole Gospel? Who

are their leaders? What are their felt needs as a people? In which groups are the churches growing? Multiplying? How do the unchurched perceive the relevance of the Church to their own lives?

*   You want to describe in both geographic and ethnographic terms *where there is no continual witness for Jesus Christ.* Where are new gatherings of believers needed? What type will be best? Who should be involved? What ministries are being effective?

*   You want to get *an insightful picture into what the Church* (that is a majority of the churches and parachurch groups combined) *is doing collectively.* What is the type and level of cooperation? To what extent is there common goal ownership? United prayer? United planning? Who are the servant leaders? The city elders? The apostles?

*   You want to *learn how effective Salt and Light has been in the city.* Where is the Light the strongest? Where is Salt penetrating and flavoring society? Where is it arresting corruption?

Factors To Be Considered

The following listings are provided to help you during your factorial analysis in determining which factors are contributing to the conditions being described or statused by the data. These listings are samples, and not exhaustive.

1.   *What are the factors (internal and/or external) of growth for those churches that are growing? What is the best or most effective "growing edge?" Why? What is the type and quality of growth? Why?*

    Some possible factors:
    a. Good biblical preaching and teaching
    b. Outreach orientation of leaders and of teaching
    c. Proliferation and distribution of small groups - nurture, evange-

listic (share, care, bear and prayer groups) or both;
d. Good involvement in fervent intercessory prayer
e. Contemporary, culturally relevant services
f. Effective equipping of the saints
g. Proactive servant leaders
h. Clear vision and challenging goals
i. Meeting of felt needs (physical and emotional) in the community
j. Periodic evaluation against goals and objectives
k. Large percentage of lay involvement
l. Up-to-date societal analysis and understanding
m. Culturally relevant methods of evangelism
n. Consistent pattern of realistic self-analysis for evaluating strengths and weaknesses
o. Sensitivity and program design for each age group
p. Adequate facilities
q. Strong missions program
r. Strong benevolence program
s. Wide variety of youth activities
t. Responsive populace
u. Etc.

2. *What are the factors (internal and/or external) contributing to the non growth of some churches, in addition to being weak in areas described above where growing churches were strong?*

Some possible factors:
a. "Social strangulation" (not relevant to the surrounding society and culture)
b. Lack of owned vision and goals
c. Entertainment syndrome vs. equipping and sending
d. Services not relevant or appealing to new generations and other unchurched
e. "Pedestal syndrome," e.g. pastors or clergy supposed to do all the work, or too position conscious
f. "Church development syndrome" i.e. imbalance between nurture and evangelism whereby the church focuses overly on nurture and internal development at the expense of outreach

    g. Growth vs. completion focus; lack of self evaluation
    h. Etc.

3. *What are the reasons why some areas and peoples in the city do not have an appropriate number or type of gatherings or churches?*

    Some possible factors:
    a. Lack of goals and purpose
    b. Lack of awareness or concern
    c. Lack of information - people not informed of condition
    d. Lack of appropriate research and evaluation
    e. Lack of cooperative plan for saturating the whole city with gatherings of believers
    f. Absence of citywide strategy initiative
    g. Lack of properly trained people for starting new culturally relevant gatherings in the various types of people
    h. Hostile environment
    i. Plans not followed through
    j. Etc.

4. *Why is the Church not making a bigger impact upon society as regards: arresting corruption, moral degradation, substance (drug and alcohol) abuse, crime rates, hungry and homeless?*

    Some possible factors:
    a. Lack of alternatives and activities for youth (e.g. sports, entertainment, counseling, job training, camping, etc.)
    b. Lack of social services by the Church in areas of: medical help, financial aid, job training, job placement, family counseling, drug rehabilitation, etc.;
    c. Lack of definitive data regarding actual conditions
    d. Non-contextualized methods of evangelism
    e. Lack of spiritual diagnosis (detecting causitive factors)
    f. No goals or plans to do so on the part of the Church or churches
    g. Lack of united intercessory or warfare prayer
    h. Need for more sensitive or pertinent law enforcement;
    i. Lack of Christians in government

  j. Lack of presence and penetration in needy areas
  k. Lack of unified vision and compassion for the city
  l. Etc.

5. *Why has the Church (churches, parachurch groups, etc.) been ineffective in winning and maintaining members of the last three generations (i.e. Boomers, Busters, Generation X)?*

  Some possible factors:
  a. Churches too traditionalized
  b. Right statusing information not available or adequately communicated
  c. Lack of knowledge of the different worldviews
  d. Insensitive or ignorant of felt needs or aspirations
  e. Lack of right type of leadership
  f. Lack of culturally relevant services and activities
  g. Inadequate contextualized evangelism
  h. Etc.

6. *What are the main contributing factors to the progressive development of citywide cooperative efforts (such as prayer, evangelism, benevolence, church planting, etc.) that are being carried forth?*

  Some possible factors.
  a. Visionary leadership ("John Knoxers" - "Give me the city lest I die.")
  b. Proactive, relational leadership team
  c. Existing united prayer effort
  d. Widespread ownership of biblical vision
  e. Good Body-wide communications
  f. Widespread common goal ownership
  g. Widely held, up-to-date status picture of the city
  h. Ongoing research and analysis
  i. Effective spiritual mapping
  j. Accurate assessment of segments of society
  k. Comprehension and worldview of the unchurched
  l. Etc.

7. What are the main contributors to a *non-existent or weak development* of citywide cooperative efforts?

   Some possible factors:
   a. Lack of vision and "John Knoxer(s)"
   b. Lack of initiative by key people and leaders
   c. Absence of united fervent prayer movement in the city
   d. Confusion between "tactics" and "strategy;" resistance on part of churches
   e. Lack of clear vision
   f. Lack of commonly-held goals
   g. Lack of an up-to-date status picture of the city as a motivation and mobilization tool
   h. Leaders unfamiliar with the strategy concept
   i. Etc.

Determine What "Sensors" are in Place

Now that you have been through the lion's share of managing and analyzing your city and the Church, you are in a good position for helping to make the future better. You have seen which data was not available and why. Questions have arisen for which there are no answers because there was no monitoring of those areas.

One of the challenges that faces our citywide analysis is determining the factors that impinge on how effectively the Church is tracking and monitoring the dynamics of change taking place within society, and within the Church. This tracking and monitoring is dependent upon there being adequate and functioning measuring mechanisms.

Too often the Church is surprised at the great amount of change that has occurred undetected. Conditions have deteriorated to a sad state of affairs unbeknownst to those who could have done something about them if they had only known earlier. In some situations there is great growth and revival happening in a church or area and no one else is aware this is taking place, let alone know the cause and effects, or principles at work.

Two of the reasons are:

a) there is no periodic or ongoing monitoring, tracking or communication taking place to detect or inform, and this applies to local churches and denominations, as well as to contextual situations in the city;

b) there is not clearly and/or commonly accepted criteria for measurement. Attendance vs. membership is an example. Identifying transfer vs. conversion growth another.

Action: Note and describe (include in your final report) where there is an absence of criteria and methods for detecting:

A. When and where overall Church growth is far below potential, or drifting in that direction.

B. Which elements or segments of society are in need of churches, small group meetings, houses of prayer, or other forms of Christian presence.

C. When and where positive transformations are taking place in society resulting from the Church's ministry and/or presence.

D. The presence or lack of inter-organizational cooperative efforts for prayer, evangelism, benevolence, etc..

E. Which churches and groups are involved in effective evangelism and the starting of new gatherings and churches.

F. When the social and cultural gap is growing between that of church meetings and that of the unchurched in society - especially for the current generations.

G. The lack of contextualized strategies and structures —e.g. social events where unchurched are invited, outreach "outposts," small group Bible studies, taking the message to the market place in socially relevant clothing (e.g. music, drama, films, videos, etc.).

Summary and Conclusions

Now that you have performed the analysis, you should have discovered the following:

1. Which case-studies will be most appropriate for communicating to the leaders and wider Body.

2. There are holes in the data that need to be filled, and mea-

surement and monitoring processes that need to be instituted.

3. There are many (apparent) anomalies that need to be explained, requiring further explanation and investigation.

4. You have observed areas where what needs to be done is quite obvious, and you feel you have some viable observations and recommendations to offer.

5. There are some very culturally appropriate and effective ministries being carried forth which should be adopted and/or adapted by others.

6. You have a fairly solid reference for statusing the measurable goals and progress to date.

7. You now have established a baseline for referencing and measuring future progress.

This information and emerging picture will be of utmost importance to those leading the citywide initiative, or potentially so. Many others will be vitally interested in the information, once they know it exists.

You now have a very valuable package of information. Your next challenge will be to get all the information into a communicable format. In addition to the formal analysis report you should prepare, you will also want to format the data for communication in a variety of media, ranging from color overhead transparencies, to summary presentations on the Worldwide Web.

You and the leaders will need to think through the variety of audiences you will need to communicate to, and also who will do the communicating.

As we stated in the introductory paragraphs of this chapter on "painting the picture", current-day technology provides a wide spectrum of powerful and attractive media. Plan to take maximum advantage of it.

What's Next?

In Chapter 9 you will prepare the analysis report and set forth the "*prophetic word*" God is saying to the Church in the city. Then, in Chapter 10 you will find helps for a variety of ways the information can be communicated.

Chapter 9: Developing the Prophetic Message

I n *discovering your city* you are now entering the final phases of developing the Prophetic Message. In this final phase of the analysis process you will be learning what the Lord of the Harvest is saying to His Body, the Church.

There will be a growing anticipation and excitement as you begin to see the pattern of God's working in the city. This whole process has been much like the missionary in India watching a man weave a tapestry. With the man behind the tapestry, he saw nothing but the shuttles going back and forth. As the missionary moved in front of the rug, however, he could see the beautiful emerging picture and pattern in the tapestry.

Insightful analysis is analysis carried forth under the guidance of the Holy Spirit. With your physical eyes you have seen the physical elements of the city. But hopefully you penetrated beyond that. The true world of reality is unseen by our physical eyes, and seeing the true and full picture requires the quickening and anointing by the Holy Spirit of our spiritual eyes. The usefulness of

> *"The prophetic message essentially communicates the vision of how fast the Church ought to grow over the next five to ten years and what methodologies will be most productive in bringing about growth."*
>
> Jim Montgomery
> *DAWN 2000: 7 Million Churches To Go*

your analysis, and the power that will be released by the Prophetic Message for achieving positive eternal results will correlate with the extent you involve the Lord of the Harvest in the process.

It should also be pointed out again (this was mentioned in Chapter 6), that the accumulation of data, the knowledge base, and the insights derived all take time. There is no quick and easy way to understand your city. First, you see the situations that exist, then your understanding into why things are the way they are begins to evolve. You will go through the analysis process making discoveries that will help others be more effective and focused. Each time you go through the process, your knowledge base will grow and become a more valuable asset to your city and the Church.

You need to have keener insights than your predecessors or previous analysis as to why the church is ineffective or effective.There must be better and more thorough measurements of the seemingly subtle areas that help detect drift and trends that have rendered the Church dangerously separated from the emerging cultures.

The Prophetic Message

When we speak of the message, we are primarily talking about the "Prophetic Message" or *rhema,* that communicates where the Spirit of God is moving in the city, and what He wants to do in the not-too-distant future. (This Greek word implies power in the spoken or written message; that is, when it is spoken it intiates the change through its authority.) This word needs to ring a clear message like a bell in the early dawn which can be heard by all. Or perhaps more appropriately in our situation, as the Apostle Paul reminds us in 1 Corinthians 14:8:

> *"...if the trumpet does not sound a clear call, who will get ready for battle."*

It is hard to motivate from many voices. Until there is unity and the city leaders are working together, effecting change will be difficult, if not impossible. A clear, concise, relevant message is needed. This mainly comes from the analysis.

Jim Montgomery states,

> *"From an analysis of the data indicating what the Holy Spirit is doing in and through society and the Church comes the message of what this suggests for the future. This is perhaps the most sensitive and crucial aspect of the whole process, for the Church will be motivated to bold new action only to the degree*

that it believes that the challenge is truly from the Lord. Jesus said that his sheep hear his voice and they will not follow another...The Church cannot proceed effectively until it clearly perceives the direction the wind of the Spirit is blowing."[1]

Analysis Report

Preparation of the analysis report is of key importance. Here is where the final process of developing the Prophetic Message(s) occurs. We mention messages in the plural for in all reality there may (at least should) be two distinct but complementary messages forthcoming.

* One derived primarily from the data describing the status of the physical, or the "seen" elements.
* The spiritual or "unseen" elements derived from spiritual mapping. This latter provides insights into why things are the way they are, and provides specific material for informed intercession.

Your report will contain significant potential for impacting the Church and the city. In some cities, this report will be providing, for the first time, an accurate, up-to-date status of the city, its components, its history, and of the Church. In others, it will provide an up-to-date status of the progress being made in the already existing citywide initiative. In any and every case it is an important document warranting careful and skillful preparation. The factual content and analysis results are very important, and of equal or greater importance is how the facts are presented and communicated.

This report will be a "prophetic message" to the Church and give direction for the future. It will challenge the Church to take appropriate action for finishing the task of "making disciples" of the city.

You want to take special pains to assure the report is capable of effectively communicating the facts in an unbiased manner. Strive for balance in accentuating both the positive and negative situations. You may miss some subtle factors, but don't miss the obvious due to hurry or lack of checking. Have a few others review a draft of the report before making it available to a broader audience. Allow for this in your preparation schedule.

Even if there is no formal citywide initiative in progress, you would do well to provide the status of the Harvest Field and Harvest Force in relation to the over-arching goals stated in Chapter 1, and to do this for the whole city and its main geopolitical and ethnographic subdivisions.

Report Content Outline

The following is a sample outline of contents for the analysis report, followed by an expanded description of each section.

1. ***The General Summary and Conclusions.*** Here you want to capture the attention of the reader. It should be concise (3-5 pages). It should give a short statement of purpose, summarize the findings, and outline the main implications for action needed by the Church. If a busy leader picks up your document, he should be sufficiently challenged to read the entire document.

2. ***The Vision, Purpose, and Problem.*** This section outlines the conditions the Church was facing, why the survey and analysis were commissioned, and who commissioned it. The vision, core values, audience, needs (felt and real) and goals are identified here. (You may need different report versions for different audiences.)

3. ***The Methods.*** This section describes how the research and analysis were carried forth. You want to convince the reader the process was thorough and objective. Describe the methods, schedule, tools and techniques that were used.

4. ***The Data and Analysis Picture.*** Here is where you present the data tables, graphs, maps, any case studies, and the factorial analysis of both the Harvest Field and Harvest Force. Include sample projection tables and graphs for new churches and gatherings. You should draw attention to the data and factors that formed the basis for your conclusions.

5. ***Observations and Recommendations.*** Those who perform the survey and analysis are best positioned for making learned observations and recommendations. Give suggestions for goals and projections. Propose specific actions to be taken.

Notes:

1. One good strategy is to break the supporting data off to appendices (as we did in this book) and keep the text in story form. Describe the summary information and prophetic message in the chapters in as much story form as possible.

2. During this overall process you have included some "spiritual mapping" data. Now would be a good time to look at Otis's book, *Informed Intercession,*[2] and review his chapter on "Briefing the Troops."

Content Description

Note: Most of the following listed tables, maps and graphs may have already been prepared. You will now need to select and arrange them in order to communicate the most effective message.

1. ***General Summary*** **(3-5 pages)**
   a. Make a general statement regarding scope, coverage, and importance.
   b. Summarize crucial findings (e.g. population per church ratio, unchurched or least churched areas and peoples, areas of greatest physical and moral needs, rates and factors of growth of population and Church, segments of society least-churched, high crime areas, etc.).
   c. Give a graphic overview (tables, maps and graphs) of Harvest Field, Harvest Force, and combined.
   d. Describe general observations (general, re: each zone/district, re: major ethnic groups).
   e. Give general conclusions and recommendations including crucial factors and spiritual issues.

2. The Purpose and Problem
  a. Describe why the research was commissioned.
  b. Tell who commissioned and funded the survey.
  c. Describe the vision of those commissioning the survey, the core values, purpose, and a list of the goals.
  d. Describe the scope of the survey and analysis.
  f. Describe the intended audience for the information.
  g. Describe the prayer support structure for commissioning, defining the strategy, and interpreting the results (prayer summits, prayer walking, lighthouses of prayer, etc.).
  h. Tell who to contact for more information, or copies of the report.

3. The Methods
  a. Tell when the survey was begun and completed - list phases.
  b. Tell who supervised and who carried forth the work.
  c. Tell how long was spent in each aspect and phase of the survey and analysis.
  d. Describe the survey methods used, including library research, field research, phone surveys, interviews, etc..
  e. Describe forms used and who they went to. (Put sample forms in an appendix.)
  f. Describe the analysis process and methods, and the basis for the conclusions.

4. The Data and Analysis Picture
Harvest Field
  a. Give a general description of the city and its geo-political subdivisions, using narrative, tables and maps.
  b. Give a demographic description (including vital statistics) with breakdowns by geopolitical subdivisions - using tables, maps and graphs. Include various age breakdowns and gender.
  c. Give an ethnographic description and status showing distribution of all ethnic/language groups including demographics, primary religions, and economic status, using tables, maps, and graphs.
  d. Describe the distribution of religions and the nonreligious using tables, maps and graphs.

  e. Describe the economic distribution and status by census and/or zip codes, plus other commonly used subdivisions.

  f. Define the areas of projected growth in the city by subdivision, using tables and maps

  g. Highlight the areas of high crime, pornography, gangs, slums, and occult activity - using tables and maps. Identify any historical or current causative factors resulting from your spiritual mapping/diagnosis.

  h. Identify other locations and activities considered to be entrenched spiritual strongholds of the enemy of man's soul.

  i. Identify and give the status of the educational institutions (beyond high school), including the number of graduate and postgraduate students, and countries of origin of the students.

Harvest Force and Combined picture

  a. General listing, description and status of the Harvest Force, i.e. denominations and parachurch groups, regarding name, year of origin in city, staff size, total number of churches, total number of attendance, number of members, number of educational institutions, number of medical clinics, and other entities making up the Body of Christ in the city.

Note: You may want to compile or commission a separate directory of churches and Christian organizations, their ministries and/or focus.

  b. Provide a picture of the distribution of the Christian and evangelical population by geopolitical and ethnographic subdivisions. Use tables, maps and graphs.

  c. Provide a picture of the distribution of churches, indicating size, denominational affiliation, whether traditional or house church, and by ethnicity and language. Use tables, maps and graphs. Provide for map overlays over other themes, such as population density, ethnic distribution and economic levels.

  d. Provide the "population per church ratio" status using tables and maps - for geopolitical subdivisions and ethnic groups.

  e. Provide for each denomination a "growth rate" table and graphs for churches, attendance (where data is available) and for members, including the semi-log line graph--depicting rates over the past 5 or 10 years.

f. Provide tables and graphs depicting projections for new churches and believers based upon current and increased rates - for next 5, 10, and 20 years. (Ref. Ch. 7)

g. Provide a table and maps depicting the areas (down to census tract or zip code levels) having no churches, or a minimum number of churches. Repeat for ethnic/language groups.

h. Drawing from your spiritual diagnosis/mapping data, provide insights into why human misery continues, and why there is such a resistance to the Gospel and its messengers.

5. *Observations, Conclusions, and Recommendations*

Note: You will need to make observations to bring attention to important areas and items. There may be some qualifications needed for some data, descriptions or pictures, and these should be stated.

Make observations regarding:

a. The general spiritual condition and status of the city and the unchurched.

b. Areas and peoples of the city where there are causes for real concern.

c. The attitude of the city and area governments toward Christianity and the Church.

d. The history, current status, and distribution of the Church.

e. The areas of effectiveness (highlights) and the ineffectiveness ("lowlights") of the Church.

f. Areas of needed focus of, and action by, the Church.

g. The extent of unity or disunity and cooperation of the Church in the city.

h. The successful methods and not-so-successful methods carried forth by the Church.

i. The relevancy of the Church to the unchurched (as observed by church attendance, surveys, interviews and/or the Church's culture vs. the current generation's cultures).

Conclusions and Recommendations

a. State the conclusions that can be a "rallying cry" for the Church.
b. Give a conclusion regarding the overall relative worth of the survey and analysis, considering what has been discovered and documented, and how it can be used.
c. Give conclusion regarding the status of, or need for, a progressive, united, citywide strategy initiative for achieving the goals which this survey was statusing. (Ref. Ch.1)
d. Give conclusions and recommendations regarding where and how the Church in the city needs to work more symbiotically and cooperatively.
e. Give conclusions and recommendations regarding growth projections for the future, and what these should/could be.
f. Suggestions as to applications and uses of the information.

Conclusion

It would be hard to overstate the importance of your analysis report. All the time and effort spent is relatively useless if the information isn't put into the right form and put into the right hands, at the right time. Although the content may vary according to each situation, the importance does not.

> *"It is the hard, cold facts that time and again have motivated the Church in a nation to action."*
>
> Jim Montgomery
> *Then The End Will Come*[1]

It is a good idea to have one or more people review the report before you publish it, or put it into widespread distribution. Someone who is not closely familiar with the subject, but is representative of the wider audience would be good, as well as those who have a keen interest in the research and analysis. Ask them to be candid with you regarding their impressions and their recommendations.

When people receive this prophetic message God has for the city, hopefully it will help galvanize the Church to action. However, they will realize that seeing effectual, lasting transformation will not occur over night. It will be a huge, God-sized task. But now they will have a much clearer understanding of what it will take.

Jack Dennison reminds us, "There are no quick fixes, no overnight solutions. For the microwave chef who expects instant results, city reaching will not meet their need for immediate gratification."[3]

Your report, as good as it is, is basically a snapshot for a certain time. Although it contains much meaningful data that will be of good value for a long time, it also contains data that, by the time you publish, will be outdated. Someone needs to be considering when the next picture should be painted, and what changes you want to make next time.

Now ask the Holy Spirit to take this "light" and see that it is used in a very meaningful way to help illuminate the Church and the city in such a way the Spirit of God can effect meaningful transformation, and ultimately be able to say, *"the city has become filled with the knowledge of the glory of the Lord as the waters cover the sea."*

The next chapter will help you with ideas for communicating this information in a variety of formats to a variety of audiences.

Endnotes:
1. Montgomery, Jim. *Then The End Will Come.* Pasadena: William Carey Library, 1997
2. Otis, George Jr.. *Informed Intercession.* Ventura, CA: Renew Books, 1999
3. Dennison, Jack. *City Reaching: On the Road to Community Transformation.* Pasadena, CA: William Carey Library, 1999   p.228

Chapter 10: Communicating the Message

You now have a message the whole Church in the city needs and hopefully wants to hear, see and respond to. You have teamed with the Lord of the Harvest to formulate His Prophetic Message to the Church. Under His guidance you have been able to construct the picture of:

- ◆ *What God has been doing in the city.*
- ◆ *What God wants yet to do to fulfill His mandates.*
- ◆ *What the enemy has wrought in the city.*

You are able to see many of the implications for what must be done to *see the city filled with the knowledge of the glory of the Lord as the waters cover the sea.*

Earlier we said we must get:
- ◆ *The right information.*
- ◆ *In the right form.*
- ◆ *Into the right hands.*
- ◆ *At the right time.*

Up to this point we have focused on getting the *right information* into the *right form*. Now we turn our focus to getting this information into the *right hands* at the *right time*.

Sounding the Call for Action

Our earlier discussion of *"two truths that set men free"* has application here. You now have a body of factual and potentially powerful data, but this alone has little effect unless and until it is effectively communicated. Now it must get into the right hands (some Nehemiahs,

John Knoxers, key pastors, leaders, city elders, and others) who will take the information and couple it with God's revealed will and the faith that leads to obedient action. That is, those men and women true to God, who will act strategically upon the Message of Truth when they receive it.

There may be some situations where it is not known who these men and women are. Some of these future leaders will seem passive until your information reaches them. Then, much like iron filings sitting among the chaff, your information acts like a vision magnet that passes and draws the filings out.

On the other hand, if a citywide saturation church planting initiative has already been launched, then there will be those awaiting the information to use in various steps of the motivation, equipping, mobilization and transformation processes.

This will not be a "once for all" situation. The information you communicate will hopefully create change, even initiate a sorely needed revolution in the Church which then will need to be monitored, analyzed and fed back again...and the process goes on. The city is a community of communities. Each community needs to receive the message clothed in the most appropriate clothing.

Jim Montgomery points out:

> *"The prophetic message essentially communicates the vision of how fast the Church ought to be able to grow over the next five to ten years and what methodologies will be most productive in bringing about that growth. It is the message that provides the content for personal contacts, messages delivered in churches, seminars, congresses, articles, books and other communications."* [1]

And we could add it is the message that provides content for: informed intercession, united prayer meetings, pastors meetings, key leaders meetings, city council meetings, seminars, Love in Action meetings, etc. It provides the substance for the motivation, mobilization and transformation that is to be forthcoming. The goal and challenge is to get the information into the hands of those who will make the most effective use of it...in a timely manner.

The Audience

There are four specific audiences for your information and the *rhema* message that is sent. The content and method of communication varies with each of these:

+ *The city leadership and the gatekeepers.*
+ *The larger Church body of the city.*
+ *The larger Church body beyond the city.*
+ *Those in the city that have not had a personal experience with Christ.*

There are other select categories of audiences listed on the next page or two. With each group, you must remember to communicate the message in the context, vocabulary, media and needs of the audience you are trying to reach.

Reaching the Leadership

The first audience is a specific individual or groups of individuals involved (or potentially so) in some aspect of ministry within the city. We are talking about proactive leadership and movers and shakers ranging from the overall citywide initiative, to leaders of a variety of tactical ministries, to pastors and parachurch and denominational leaders, to key equippers and planners. *A specific strategy here is that you wish to pull this leadership together in unity.* Avoid taking any initiative that would harm this unity, even if this means lost time or difficulty in reaching a specific objective.

This audience would include (in addition to those above):
+ Prayer mobilizers and warriors.
+ Citywide strategy initiative mobilizers and leaders.
+ Tactical ministries mobilizers and leaders.
+ Denominations and leaders.
+ Parachurch organizations and leaders.

At the beginning, avoid overwhelming the people of this level with large amounts of information. These are all busy people, and at the start all they essentially need is the summary result and the supporting data. These are your Nehemiahs, and all Nehemiah needed at the beginning was the condition and needs of the people at the spiritual, emotional, and physical level.

At the later and deeper research, the detailed results are shared *only* at this level. For instance, the larger Body can assimilate general summary data, but there are details of factorial analysis and case studies that need to get into the skilled hands of those who know what best to do with them. Many of those involved in some aspect of leadership, training, or planning will find much of this information very meaningful. Growth rate tables and graphs excite some people, and put others to sleep.

Reaching The Body of Christ in the City

The second group you are trying to reach is the citywide Body of Christ. It will be strategic in the overall scheme of things if certain summary data are furnished to a wide spectrum of the Body. They need to be involved in the process at an early phase if you expect them to take ownership with the leaders on the larger vision. They make up the force that will carry forth the essential work at the grass roots. Without them, there will be no societal transformation or revolution. The task of leadership will be made much simpler and effective if all the Harvest Force has the same pertinent information. It is much easier to unite and mobilize people who have the same information as the leaders.

This audience would include all those in whom Christ dwells, e.g.:
♦ Local churches and pastors.
♦ Laymen (of all stripes).
♦ Students/Youth.
♦ Media (all types and varieties, Christian and secular).
♦ Prayer mobilizers and warriors.
♦ Citywide strategy initiative mobilizers and leaders.
♦ Tactical ministries mobilizers and leaders.
♦ Denominations and leaders.
♦ Parachurch organizations and leaders.

♦ Select city leaders and offices (Church and civil, government and industry).

♦ Arts and entertainment.

Beyond the City

Another audience you need to reach includes those people beyond the city that may want to learn what has taken place, or is taking place, in your city. They may be looking for case-study models to consider for their own plans and strategies. Transformed cities are already using books, videos, and the Internet to share what God is doing in their city to help other city initiatives.

Reaching the Lost

Finally and importantly, you need to consider the message to the lost of your city. Those that are lost and without hope need to hear the Good News of the Gospel, that God is working in the city, and that there is hope for the transformation of their own personal lives. This will take careful thought and good skill. In some situations you can put a certain kind and amount of data in the newspapers with good effect. For instance, where there are ministries to the needy, and/or special counseling available, etc. that have been discovered in the analysis.

The Media

The media to be utilized will largely be determined by who the target audience is for the particular data. For instance, you may have promised a copy of the report to the pastors and parachurch groups who participated in the surveys, and you would want to mail this to them when available. An ideal way for reaching many audiences is to make the presentations in person, such as in seminars or workshops, however this takes more time and administration on the part of both parties.

> *"...cultural appropriateness is a major factor in media effectiveness"*
> Donald K. Smith
> *Creating Understanding*

Below are listed several different media to be considered.

Publications - one time, occasional and periodic.
When you begin publishing a periodical, which is strongly recommended, take time to carefully consider what will be involved, regarding: the demands of time and scheduling, your audiences, the format, and the cost. A periodical is very effective and practical for reaching pastors and leaders, especially when you want to get a flow of information to them over time. See "Materials" in the section that follows for more information on the forms the publications could take. (*See Appendix-P for samples*)

Seminars, Consultations and Workshops

Gatherings of this sort provide an excellent vehicle and setting for communicating the message. These can be select people who have known responsibilities and/or interests in the information. The setting is one given to discussion and interaction.

Conferences and Congresses

Conferences are a good venue for communicating the message. You usually will have general interest groups and can tailor the message accordingly. Congresses are a very essential tool in the overall city-reaching process, as this is where a large percentage of leaders gather together to consider the current state of things, and to set goals for the future. (It is this "goal-setting" that distinguishes a congress from other gatherings, such as conferences.)

Some key aspects in planning the Congress:
- Invite a cross-spectrum of denominational and parachurch leaders.
- Hold the Congress on neutral ground.
- Present the Prophetic Message and the research results that support it.
- Challenge the leaders to set goals at the Congress.
- Ask each denomination and group to set its own goals (work in small groups).
- Add the individual goals together to get the larger corporate goal.

Meetings

In any city on any given day there are probably several key meetings taking place (committees and otherwise) involving people who can or could play vital roles in reaching the city with the living Gospel. In meetings like these, the information can be communicated effectively.

There is one city leader known to the authors that keeps overhead transparencies of maps and graphs depicting the status of the various zones in the city in a special binder that can be used as a flip chart. He uses this very effectively in small meetings, including in restaurants. He also has overheads of tables and graphs statusing a wide variety of pertinent information, and is always ready to share needs and what God is doing in the city.

Radio and Television

In many cities it will be possible to communicate the message over radio and/or television. This can reach a broad audience, however, who is being reached is often unknown, unless the station or program director has some audience survey results. On television, graphics can be utilized effectively.

Internet/WorldWide Web

The WorldWide Web is becoming more and more a household item, and there is a large amount of information and data that can effectively be displayed for access via the Internet. However, you are depending upon them to access the information, so don't make this your sole communication tool. However, don't underestimate the power

> *"One thing we do know is the telecommunications revolution will enlarge the role of the individual with more access to information, greater speed in execution, and greater ability to communicate to anyone or to great numbers anywhere, anytime. All trends are in the direction of making the smallest player in the global economy more and more powerful."*
> John Naisbitt, *Global Paradox*[2]

of information in this medium. You may also be able to find models and samples of research being carried forth by other cities. Other cities may find your data helpful as well.

In placing information on the Web you should consider:
- Purpose (why you want to communicate what).
- Audiences (who you want to have what data).
- Content (including procedure and authorization for posting).
- Format (including data format, maps and graphics).
- Provision for feedback (data updates, responses).
- Security (relating to sensitive and proprietory data).

Information Resource Center(s) (IRC's)
Hopefully, each city will have one or more Information Resource Centers (by whatever name) that obtains and maintains data and information pertinent to city-reaching. This can be a broad scope of data, but should be well managed such that the validity and source are readily known, and the data can be made available practically and efficiently.

This "center" should be linked strategically into the overall city-wide initiative. To best serve its public, it could have readily available quality materials (reports, maps, graphs, etc.) at a reasonable price. In some situations it is this "center" that is the hub and home for most of the information we have been talking about in this book. And in some situations, it may be the generator of surveys and analysis.

Bible Schools and Seminaries
Don't under-estimate the need to furnish data to Bible schools and seminaries in the city, or the state. You need to do what you can to bridge the gap between education and actuality by providing accurate, up-to-date, relevant information to Christian and other educational institutions. This will help increase the relevance of what students are learning to actual city conditions. There is especially an urgent need in the area of sociology and worldview to provide current data for understanding the mindset of the unchurched.

Arts and Entertainment (including sports - Christian and secular)

Some of the most effective communication to a broad audience takes place via the arts and entertainment media. Cold facts don't communicate too well by themselves at times and to some audiences. However, if you can get people involved in the arts and entertainment to comprehend the message that needs to be communicated, they can often do miracles in communication. Drama, music and art are especially powerful communication tools.

The Materials

Reports

In addition to your final analysis report (Prophetic Message), there may be other reports that have been generated. This is often the case following a formalized survey and analysis effort. In some situations this has taken the form of a book. The *Discipling of a Nation*[3] by Donald McGavran and Jim Montgomery is an example. This was based upon a nationwide survey and analysis of the Philippines performed in 1979, and was generated primarily from a formal analysis report by the researcher.

Periodical *(see Appendix-P for samples)*

As previously mentioned, a periodical can be a very powerful, strategic and persuasive tool and can greatly enhance any initiative's effectiveness. It helps all those involved to have the same timely information. It does not have to be fancy or voluminous (many start with 2 or 4 pages). It does need to be very informative and be of interest to pastors and parachurch leaders, as well as key lay persons. Because the publication should always carry some statusing picture relating to the Church, and to the city's Harvest Field, it will be of interest to these groups if it is well done and consistent.

You want to "count the cost" before starting a periodical. It requires time and discipline as well as finances, but it is well worth the investment when done properly.

It is important to design the publication well, and have something in every issue that will make the recipients want to pick it up and read it. Including case studies of various groups in the city help here. Also, having a schedule of events pertinent to city-reaching can be a plus.

A map or graphic can enhance the communicability. Pastors and leaders are usually interested in what others are doing, and how their own organization fits into the whole picture.

Overhead Transparencies (individual and slide presentations)
Overhead transparencies (OHT's) should be in your arsenal of materials. Although computer slide shows can be used in many settings, there are still a variety of situations where OHT's can be a most effective tool (see Meetings in the previous section). They can be used without projection in some settings. Keeping a set organized in a special binder makes them readily available for communicating in different situations, from small meetings without projection, to large conferences where the images can be projected.

Videos and Computer Slide Shows
In this day and age, videos and computer slide shows are commonplace. VCRs are commonplace. Computer projection equipment is becoming more common and affordable. This is true in the USA and fastly becoming true in Developing Nations. Often the same slides fabricated for a slide show can be used as OHT's, and vice versa. The authors do this consistantly. Videos incorporating the analysis results portrayed graphically are excellent tools and can be stand-alone (not requiring anyone to accompany them).

Computer Graphics (tables, maps, graphs, etc.)
Computer graphics have the potential to be powerful communication tools. In addition to the slide shows mentioned above, there are a variety of applications for computer graphics. The types and generation of the graphics have been treated elsewhere (e.g. Chapter 8 & appendices I, J, K). Computer generated maps can find a variety of formats ranging from being furnished/sold separately in hard copy, to being put on the Web. The same is true of tables and graphs. Graphics communicate in a realm and with an effectiveness that is impossible in any other way. Don't undersell the good use of graphics.

Additional Communication Guidelines
Here are a few thoughts and guidelines regarding presentation of church growth and other analysis from both positive and negative experiences:

a.   Don't assume your audiences have a good foundational under-
     standing of and for what you are presenting. Make your pre-
     sentation comprehensive enough that newcomers (whether
     leader or layman) will be able to get the impact of what you
     want to communicate.

b.   Present the positive growth data or picture, and the factors of
     growth first. Accentuate the positive, and leave most of the
     negative to self discovery.

     A good ploy is to identify another group that is growing well
     under the same circumstances as the slower growing and em-
     phasize the factors involved. In this way those not growing
     will hopefully make the discovery of some things to help cor-
     rect their slow growth. It's best to accentuate the positive, not
     the negative.

c.   Use graphics as much as possible. Not only are these good
     communication tools, but they can make more of an impact,
     and can be more easily remembered. Additionally, others can
     use them effectively to reproduce a portion of the presentation
     for use with their own group or audience.

d.   Stay objective. Refrain from offering opinions and guessing at
     reasons. Do not put yourself in a situation where you could
     possibly lose credibility because of subjective comments. Once
     you lose credibility in one area it overflows into others.

     Let the facts speak for themselves. Be ready to describe how
     the data was gathered, treated and analyzed, but be careful in
     going beyond the facts in guessing with "what ifs." Let others
     do this, but not those who have gathered and analyzed the data.
     If you stay objective and present the facts accurately and in
     good taste, you will gain or maintain your credibility, and you
     and your work will be of inestimable value in the future.

e.   It will be wise to prepare up to a dozen visuals (overheads,
     computer slide show, or color prints) or more that portray the

status picture. These can be used in a strategic manner in a variety of situations, ranging from one-on-one meetings, to making presentations to a large audience. Those involved in motivation and mobilization will find the materials to be of inestimable value in achieving unity in understanding the situation, which is key to a viable cooperative city-reaching effort. Make them available to other leaders so they can use them with their constituency.

Conclusion

All the arduous work involved in gathering and analyzing and fabricating the picture of your city will all be for nought if the data never gets out of the files and into the right hands. You have a message and picture that hundreds, even thousands need to see and hear.

Plan early what you want to communicate, whom you want to receive it, and how you want to communicate. Taking this into consideration as you go through the entire process will help you to determine what information should be packaged in what form. You will also need to have the media ready so the message won't get outdated and stale before you get it into the right hands.

Today's technology is a boon for you. There are so many creative and wonderful tools and vehicles for managing, packaging, displaying and communicating the message you will probably find yourself challenged with determining which is best, rather than being hampered by lack of means. Take advantage of the Internet.

Be creative and tenacious, and remember, fundamentally it is the Lord's message and ministry. Partner with Him every step of the way.

Endnotes:
1. Montgomery, Jim *DAWN 2000: 7 Million Churches To Go"* Pasadena, William Carey Library, 1989 p.184
2. Naisbitt, John. *Global Paradox*, Avon Books, 1994
3. McGavran, Donald and Montgomery, Jim, *The Discipling of a Nation*, Colorado Springs: Global Church Growth Bulletin, 1980

Appendices

Definitions and Descriptions of Church & a church

(This is excerpted from the article, *What is (a) Church*, by Bob Waymire,
December 1999. Article is available at: www. discoveryourcity.com)

Introduction: What is Church? What is a church? What can or should
be classified as a "church?"   When is it appropriate to use the term
"congregation" or "gathering of believers," or "assemblies?" Does it
really matter?

We want to look at what we mean when we talk about "Church"and "a
church" in the context of this book.There are many definitions and
descriptions of Church and a church today. When we are assessing a
city, and have a goal that includes churches, we need to have an understanding of what constitutes a local church. (Note: hereinafter an upper
case "C" refers to the corporate Church, the Body of Christ, and the
lower case for local gatherings of believers, e.g. churches.)

In most places, we have come to equate a church more with a service
and a building, than as a community. For the past several years there
has been a wave of new congregations emerging in many parts of the
world. There is a vigorous attempt to start churches in every people
group in every part of the city and nation. There is a healthy movement
of gatherings of new Christians ("new wine") not inhabiting the "old
skins." When do we count them as a church?

Background:
The New Testament speaks of the "ekklesia" or assembly. This refers
to a gathering of believers, or believers in community. In 1 Corinthians
11, Paul refers to three forms of church community: the *corporate
church* (v.22, also Acts 15:4), *churches* (v.16), and to a *church* (v.18).

The assemblies (ekklesia: "kaleo"-to call; "ek"-out from) is made up of
those called out from the world to become the people of God. Church
occurs when and where "called out ones" assemble, or congregate, or
gather together.

While our core tenets of the faith (e.g. Christ is the full revelation of God, and, the Great Commission to make disciples of all nations) are unchanging, the world is changing at an ever-increasing rate, and our methods of proclamation and our applications of *church* need to also change. We need to clarify and simplify the nature and purpose of church so it isn't carrying excess baggage that is defeating. We must stay flexible in our methods and forms without losing the purpose and nature of the church. (Monica Hill, Church Growth Digest[1])

Since Constantine, in AD 312, the Churchly structures have been highly institutionalized. This continued right through the Reformation with little impact on structure, although there were significant changes in doctrine. It has only been in the past 50 years that significant changes are occuring in "how we do church." This is a healthy and needful trend. We need a revolution, the old ways produce the old results.

Change is Needed
Yes, it is inevitable new, creative, contextualized *gatherings* are needed. People, "like birds of a feather," still gather together in an atmosphere friendly to their own culture. We need to reach people where they are. This is a need of crucial importance and the Church in America needs to take more heed in this area.

We must both change our model of *church*, and determine what *church* is in a changing culture. Fundamentally, we need to return to biblical principles that are not interpreted through the filter of current denominationalism or historical institutionalism. Many people today have rejected the church, but few of these have seen the true Church, only a caricature of it.

This is not advocating that organization is out, and randomness is in. The point is, we need to be very careful how we apply in practice biblical principles in a dynamic and diverse society. When we see gatherings of believers that do not fit the old mold, we can't dismiss them as not being a church. We would be foolish to look at our current structures and assume they alone are the contemporary and valid interpretations of biblical principles for our day. We must get to the nitty-gritty of soul-winning and maturing believers, in an atmosphere of community and fellowship, praise, instruction and worship without dictating the form this must take. We want to nurture health in the Body and in the city.

Current Situation and Challenge

Currently, the Body of Christ gathers (or assembles, or congregates) together in many different forms, and under many different labels.

Local churches
Organized churches
Unorganized churches
House churches
Store-front churches
Cell churches
Daughter churches
Worship centers
Chapels
Assemblies

Preaching points
Outreach small group Bible studies
Nurure small group Bible studies
Neighborhood prayer cells
Shepherding fellowship meetings

Note: All of the above down to and including "Assemblies" are descriptive labels for "local churches" today. These identifiers are helpful in describing some particular facet or distinctive of the church, but all are churches (ekklesia).

Each believer may meet in two or more settings. Preaching points are outreaches, and those who are involved are normally part of a local church. Bible studies, prayer groups and fellowship groups are groups having a special focus and are usually made up of people who attend local churches. There are some situations where some believers only attend the special focus groups, not what we are terming local church or congregation.

Some denominations and churches have a hard time accepting what others consider as a church. They feel their criteria is the right and logical one.

Minimal Criteria for a Local Church

It is needful that we set forth, from a New Testament perspective, the fundamental requisites for local *ekklesia* of believers that constitute a local *church* in order to determine which areas and peoples have been penetrated and occupied with a gathering of believers, and which ones have not.

Based upon passages in the New Testament, it appears (from direct statements, or strongly implied) the following five functions applied to the local "ekklesias":

Believers coming together (Heb. 10:25) regularly for:
* worship, praise, singing and thanksgiving (Eph. 5:19, 20; Col. 3:16; Heb. 12:28; 1 Cor. 14:26)
* prayer (Eph. 6:18; Ja. 5:16)
* instruction (1Tim 1:1-11; 5 & 6; Col. 3:16)
* communion (Lord's Supper) (1 Cor. 11)
* fellowship & encouragement (Heb. 10:24, 25; 1 Thes. 5:1)

(Regarding elders, the New Testament does not say specifically these were appointed for each local gathering or congregation, [although some interpret Acts 14:23 this way; however the context could speak otherwise] but for the broader Church in the city or area. (Titus 1:5, Acts 20:17, Phil. 1:1, etc.)[2]

Some denominations set standards for what they call "organized" churches. Often these include criteria such as:

* Meeting regularly
* Minimum number of believers
* Offerings are taken
* Must have a licensed pastor/leader
* One or more elders
* Communion

For those evaluating the penetration of the Gospel, this criteria (which varies from denomination to denomination) could be misleading. It is suggested the 5 points above be the basic criteria.

When evaluating the Church and local congregations, there are several criteria for determining effectiveness and impact:

1. Is the Body of Christ growing? If so, among which segments of society? Among which segments is it not growing or present?
2. Are the new Christians meeting with other Christians on a regular basis for: fellowship, worship, singing (Col. 3:16), prayer, communion, needs-meeting and burden bearing?
3. Do we understand the worldviews, cultural distinctives and views of the Church held by the unchurched?
4. Are there gatherings of believers that people will go to and can get to in the various segments of society?
5. Do the new believers feel they need to abandon or forsake their culture in order to become a Christian, or to meet with other believers? (Some things aren't wrong, they're just different.)
6. Are there new *wineskins* for the new *wine*? (The new wine is new believers that may be different socially and culturally from those in current assemblies.)
7. Are people accepting Christ, growing in Him, and walking with Him? (This is more important than upholding any of our traditions or practices. Some churches will not change, although their own youth [and their unsaved friends] don't want to attend because the "culture" of the services is so foreign to them.)
8. Are our structures more institutionalized and formal than those described in the New Testament?

Endnotes:
1. Monica Hill, *Revisiting the Church*, The Park (England): Church Growth Digest, Vol. 21, Number 1, Autumn 1999.

THE INFORMATION RESOURCE FUNCTION

Note: *Each city undertaking a citywide initiative needs to have an ongoing research and information resourcing function to obtain, manage and communicate the accurate, up-to-date data needed to support the initiative.*

A. **Coordinate research efforts within the city**. The IRF will *help facilitate needed research and information management* within the country through understanding the wide spectrum of needs represented, and initiating/coordinating appropriate action necessary to meet them.

1. There are a variety of types, kinds and levels of research that must be carried out within a city, each requiring careful *planning, coordination and mobilization of resources*. The IRF and its IRC (Information Resource Center) can be a key facilitator in this area.

2. A *summary* of strategic information is needed. Then holes must be filled via additional research and analysis. The IRF and leadership team will continually assess what information is needed and commission the necessary efforts to see the need met.

3. *Sharing information* is best accomplished when it conforms to certain commonly-held standards and definitions regarding criteria, format, coding, media, etc.. Through serving in this function, the IRF/IRC can help facilitate prudent and effective data sharing.

B. **Provide an information resource via a citywide Information Resource Center (IRC)**

1. Information is of little value if it doesn't get into the hands of those who need to make use of it. It needs to be in the right form and furnished in a timely manner. Having someone pay-

ing diligent attention to this is a valuable service for the city Church, and is a vital cog in the city reaching process.

2. Having a central information resource center provides a point of contact for sharing information-a place where information can be deposited for maximum exposure/use. It can also provide links to a variety of networks, and be the vehicle for seeing that the information is communicated and shared in usable formats and in a timely manner.

C. **Provide information management and analysis**

1. When a variety of information is brought together it requires careful management and analysis for it to be of value to those who need it. Huge amounts of data require special and skillful processing to make it readily available in usable form.

2. Analysis of information makes the data reveal its secrets, and helps provide the basis for how we'll do the ministry. Analysis is an ongoing effort. New and updated data feeds the analysis process. Various organizations or individuals may have a particular need for help in understanding their particular situation, and will call on the skills of the IRC.

The analysis inputs to the "prophetic message" what God is saying to the Church in the city regarding future vision, goals, and ministry.

D. **Coordinate/provide training in research and information management**. The IRF/IRC can help facilitate training to meet a variety of information-related needs.

1. <u>Training in how-to-do research and analysis</u> is a vital need in nearly every city. There are several research disciplines each having its own distinctives and unique skills. Performing interviews is an art, as is the design for good survey forms. The relative worth of the information available often relates directly to the process and quality of data gathering. Don't rely too

heavily on already published data. Much of it is based upon estimates and/or outdated.

2. Training in information management is essential. Today, at the national level, large amounts of information are becoming available from a variety of sources. Putting this into usable form requires good management skills and techniques.

Structuring of databases and spreadsheets, performing computerized mapping, developing graphic presentations, and preparing good reports all require special skills that require appropriate training. Hopefully the IRF/IRC will have people skilled who can train others. If the individual churches and organizations are skilled in data management, it will make the IRC's job much easier.

E. **Communicate the findings through a variety of media**. The IRF/IRC provides a vehicle for communicating information to a wide spectrum of the Body of Christ in the city.

1. Those that have accurate, up-to-date information have a responsibility for sharing it. This can be done effectively (and periodically) in a number of ways, and can be facilitated by the **Information Resource Center,** via:

a. **Publications**—excellent use is being made of publications in communicating research and analysis findings. Both **periodicals** and one-time reports play a strategic role in informing and motivating the Body in the city. Additionally, **atlases** (both geographic and ethnographic or a mix) can play a key role in helping leaders and others gain a valuable understanding and perpsective of the city and the Church. Maps provide a realm of intelligence not obtainable in any other format. Organizational, ethnographic and geo-political (city, MSA, counties, districts, etc.), and denomination and church **directories** and listings are necessary to provide a comprehensive picture of the city. Selecting atlases and directories published every five years will be a very valuable resource to the Body of Christ in the city.

    b. **Conferences and congresses**--these venues are strategic for getting the information into the right hands at the right time. In conferences information can be presented in a variety of "clothing" and good feedback received. In congresses the data and analysis form the basis for establishing projections and goals for new churches, believers, etc., and should be held every 2-3 years to provide both status and challenge.

F. Share information with others

1. When a central body of information is maintained, it has great potential value when it gets shared with the right people, organizations, and ministries. Efforts must be taken to assure that the information can be shared effectively and efficiently. This requires management and adhering to certain standards.

2. Part of sharing information is making your information and information needs known, and being prepared to send and receive the information. The Internet is a boon for today's researchers and analysts. Security must be considered in data sharing.

3. Each ongoing research function and Information Resource Center must be conscious of the fact that is a part of two or more information networks. One is the network of other information sources *within* the city. The other is the linking with *external* networks. Each city is part of a larger context and needs to give and receive vital information.

G. Process and Structures

1. Form a "research oversight committee" made up of key leaders and research/information management persons. The committee should have broad organizational and ecclesiasti-

cal representation to provide guidance to, and stewardship over, the IRF and IRC. This committee/team will interface with the citywide initiative leadership team.

2. Establish an Information Resource Center (IRC) that will help coordinate information gathering, management, training and communication. The IRC should also provide stewardship over certain information/information management and networking to assure needed data in an easy-to-use form is available in a timely manner.

The IRC should also maintain an area for displaying, in visual form, the distribution and status of the Harvest Field and Harvest Force, including spiritual diagnostics. Wall maps and graphs, in addition to other visual materials, provide a powerful and informative means for painting the picture of the city and the Church, their status and distribution. Each IRC should have their own Web Page.

In summary, the Information Resource Center should:
   A. Have qualified staff, adequate facilities, adequate equipment, adequate financial support
   B. Have an ongoing, methodical, reliable system of gathering and updating data and analysis. Identify key data sources.
   C. Prepare and publish reports containing data and the results of data analysis.
   D. Publish a periodical that provides: information (and hopefully motivation) to the various ministries and Christian entities in the city, selected data, ongoing status of church growth and church planting, information about resource availability, case studies, instructional articles, event announcements, etc..
   E. Establish a local information-sharing network. Linkup to other relevant and vital information resources.
   F. Sponsor/lead workshops, seminars, forums and consultations for the purpose of sharing and obtaining information, and for providing training and instruction.

Contents

1. Chronological Steps for a Citywide Survey
2. Things to Understand About a Citywide Survey
3. Additional Survey Guidelines.
4. Common Pitfalls of Research and Analysis

1. Chronological Steps for a Citywide Survey

1. Establish the purpose and parameters of the survey.
2. Organize survey committee under auspices of leadership team.
3. Draft survey plans and timeline.
4. Draft budget.
5. Design survey forms.
6. Solicit involvement, commitment and support by key churches and parachurch groups. (Leadership team has main role.)
7. Train "library" and "field" workers.
8. Conduct library and field research.
9. Initiate information management. Enter data into database or spreadsheet. Store and analyze data by zone or district, and total urban area. Utilize tables, maps and graphs in the analysis.
10. Arrange for consultations and workshops with various churches and groups for sharing the data.
11. Utilize information in a citywide congress where new goals will be set and commonly owned for new believers, churches and other entities and activities.
12. Initiate ongoing surveys and analysis to: a) obtain further information needed to answer questions arising from the initial reports, and b) provide ongoing, up-to-date status assessment of both the Harvest Field and Harvest Force needed for planning and strategy development, mobilization and allocation of resources, and ongoing evaluation of effectiveness.
13. Initiate a periodical which will give an ongoing picture of the status of evangelism and church planting, and also the extent to which the city is being transformed by the various ministries. The periodical should include: highlighting unchurched areas and peoples, case studies of successful methods, calendar of pertinent events, instructional articles and editorials, and a bibliography of relevant reference materials.

2. Things to Understand About a Citywide Survey

1. *The importance of looking at the total picture and not just parts of it.*
    Each part is a significant part of the whole, and what is learned in one area does not necessarily apply to any others. Caution and care need to be exercised in doing any kind of sampling survey. Use these for verification but not for primary data acquisition. Urban dynamics are tricky and challenging.

2. *The importance of clear, limited objectives for research.*
    Know why you are gathering what you are. Too often we try to do too much when we need to think in phases. Research should take a step at a time for several reasons. One is you only want to gather information for which you know the specific reason and application. Another is if you do the first phase well others may contribute to further work.

3. *The importance of collecting firsthand, factual data by trained field workers.*
    Having the facts dispels error and darkness. It takes people trained especially for the task at hand to obtain the desired results. Don't assume any data is accurate just because it is in print. In library research, check the sources and how the data was gathered, and when.

4. *The importance of dissemination of information in a variety of formats to all levels of Church leadership - from the leadership team to the grass roots lay activist.*
    Everyone involved in the process should have the same information base, otherwise there can be division and confusion. The leaders may not need the detail the grass-roots mobilizer does, but it needs to be from the same foundation and source.

5. *The motivation power of well-presented, factual information.*
    Factual information when well-presented can be a key to motivation and mobilization if it shows clearly the current status and what

yet needs to be done.

6. *The quality of the raw data is the crucial thing.*
   The accuracy and relevance of the raw data is of primary importance. Too often the Church has done business on estimates and
   derivations to its peril. And just because it's well presented doesn't
   mean it is accurate.

7. *Some initial data can get key people on-board and get the balance of the needed research and analysis sponsored.*
   Too often people get discouraged because the task is too great and
   too expensive. Wise planning starts the process small and then
   increases in increments as it gets people on board by demonstrating
   the need and power of the information. Throwing money at a project
   may not be the wisest use of resources. Having a clear understanding of what data is needed, and having appropriately trained
   people in the process, are prerequisite to wise stewardship and
   success.

3. Additional Survey Guidelines

*(These guidelines were adapted from a paper by John Dawson of YWAM
written in the 80's)*

1. Be in an attitude of intercession, hearing His voice and sensing His
   heart. Spiritual insights for a city can come suddenly, connecting
   thoughts, words and pieces of information.

2. Think in terms of "keys" that could open up people's understanding
   to the Gospel. Analyze the spiritual implications of the information
   gathered, while at the same time being careful not to overspiritual-
   ize, seeing every negative thing as demonic. Be aware of patterns
   of reccurring sin. For example, there are some obvious patterns
   throughout the history of New York City that are indicative of de-
   ception, injustice, greed and murder.

3. A simplified attitude toward researching cities can be detrimental.
   Too casual a look will give the feeling that cities can be easily bro-

ken down into ethnic and minority group while missing the more complex, non-residential communities (e.g. the "health-spa yuppies," the "professional (career) mothers," or the "nightshift janitors in the city").

4. There are no shortcuts to good research. On the other hand, it's important not to be overwhelmed by a deluge of statistics, facts and details, missing the overall picture and vision for the city.

5. Keep the main reason for your research at the forefront. Cities tend to produce a desire to specialize because they can be so overwhelming. Initial research should provide a clear general status picture. Leave more specific research for specialized teams after a ministry center has been well established.

6. Be considerate of any other Christians in the city who are involved in research. Our purpose is to serve and not alienate ourselves from others. Work together wherever and whenever feasible.

4. Common Pitfalls Regarding Research and Analysis

1. Gathering data for prideful, sinful purposes
    * promotional vs analytical
    * "Come to me, I have the answers"
    * information yields power-temptation to control

2. Misinterpreting the data
    * can result in making the data say what we want
    * can come from not being aware of correct definitions or criteria
    * results in the information not truly representing the situation
    * can result in improper or hasty diagnosis
    * can result in "form" overriding "function" (judged by appearance rather than purpose and function)

3. Overreliance on data

* can cover up and obscure other problems
* can be too gullible (false assumptions re data)
* data is just part of the overall picture and/or formula
* can miss inaccurate and incomplete data

4. Making decisions with incomplete data (samples and causes)
   * filling in the blanks improperly
   * incomplete and/or erroneous description of society and the
     Church
   * Joshua and the Gibeonites (Joshua 9)
   * bad conclusions and decisions
   * used too small and/or unrepresentative sample

5. Inadequate definitions and/or descriptions (samples and causes)
   * end up accidently mixing apples and oranges
   * definitions don't accompany data
   * irresponsible or not accepted definition
   * definitions too complicated, nebulous or unmeasurable (ex-
     ample: an Unreached People)

6. Inadequate preparation and utilization of the data for communication and application
   * not having the potential audiences in mind
   * arrangement of the data is illogical and/or hard to follow
   * didn't make wise use of maps and graphics
   * have data in a unique and/or non-communicable format
   * inappropriate or inadequate utilization of appropriate media (e.g.
     computer slide shows, Internet, overhead transparencies, flip
     charts, radio, TV, videos, periodicals, publications, newspapers,
     etc.)

7. No responsible person responsible

Bob Waymire 1998

SAMPLE SURVEY FORMS

These sample forms are provided for your assistance and consideration. You may well find that none of the forms herein exactly fit your situation. However, several of them are tied to other data item listings in this book. We have tried to provide samples of many of the various basic types of forms (and tables, maps and graphs) you will need to capture the data and perform the analysis as outlined in the various chapters and appendices.

Most all of the forms have found application in cities or countries around the world. However, the Church is in a new era and it is incumbent upon those involved in research and analysis to monitor those "cause and effect" situations relevant to today, whether or not they have been utilized in the past.

Enlarging the Forms
As they exist in this book, the forms are probably too small for your use. We suggest you enlarge them on a copier. If you find the binding does not facilitate this, full sized forms are available via www.discoveryourcity.com. There is also a **Discovering Your City CD** that will contain full-size copies of these forms (i.e. 8.5 by 11).

Cross-Reference Help
In regard to the tables included in some of the forms you may want to see if similar forms are included in Appendix-I (Sample Tables). There are some notes there regarding software that may be useful to you in your situation.

Sample Forms Included

1. Local Church Survey
2. Individual Survey Questionnaire
3. Urban Locality Survey
4. Pastor-Leader Questionnaire
5. Denomination Survey
6. Urban People Group Questionnaire

Local Church Survey

A.   General Church Information   **Survey date:** _____

(mandatory)

1. Church name:_____

2. Church Street Address: _____

3. Church Mailing Address: _____

4. City: _____District: _____ Zip: _____

5. Phone: _____ Fax: _____ Email: _____

6. Pastor's name: _____ Began here: _____

7. Pastor's address: _____

       City:_____ Zip: _____

8. Pastor's phone: _____ Email: _____

9. Year church begun: _____ Same site (Yes or No)? _____

10. Languages spoken in services/classes: _____

11. Main ethnic orientation: __ Anglo; __ Black; __ Hispanic;

     __ Asian; __Other (specify): _____

12. Denominational affiliation: _____

++

B. Current status information

1. Number of worship services held each week: Sunday___; Other___.

2. Average (past month) weekly attendance of all above services: _____

3. Baptized members:_____

(Current Status - continued)

4. Weekly home/neighborhood prayer cells (lighthouses, etc.): _____

5. Weekly small group believer's "home" Bible studies: _____

6. Weekly small group outreach Bible studies: _____

7. Weekly/semi-weekly home outreach "fellowship" meetings: _____

8. ("Cell" churches only-with stand-alone cell/daughter churches)
   If a "Mother" church with "Cell <u>churches</u>", number of cell churches:___

   Are you: a.   "Mother" church; b. ___ Cell church

+++

C. Ten Year History

Please provide as much of the following data as possible. Use year end statistics. Possible sources: records, annual reports, etc. Leave spaces blank if data not available.

Church Diagnostic Period Table

	10 Year Diagnostic Period										Last Year
	-10 yrs	-9 Yrs	-8 Yrs	-7 Yrs	-6 Yrs	-5 yrs	-4 Yrs	-3 Yrs	-2 Yrs	-1 year	
Year											
Weekly services											
Avg. Attendance											
Baptized members											
Baptisms-believer's											
Prayer cells(weekly)											
Weekly Bible studies											
Outreach meetings											
Daughter/cell ch's											
Pastors											
Staff - full time											
Missionaries-in city[1]											
Missionaries-ext.[2]											
Overall gen. budget											

1. "Missionaries-in city" = cross-cutural ministry-sent to work in this city.
2. "Missionaries-ext." = cross-cultural ministry - "sent" to work **external** to this city

D. Ministry Information (Local Church Survey - continued)

Identify the ministries which your church is involved in on a regular basis.

a. ☐ Neighborhood evangelism h. ☐ Community Development
b. ☐ Media evangelism i. ☐ Bible school
c. ☐ Mass evangelism j. ☐ Benevolence/social service
d. ☐ Shut-in k. ☐ Television
e. ☐ Seniors l. ☐ Radio
f. ☐ Singles m. ☐ Family counseling
g. ☐ Drug/alcohol rehabilitation n. ☐ _____

Other Involvement:
o. ☐ Have participated in March for Jesus. Years _____
p. ☐ Have been involved in "prayer walking."
q. ☐ Some men have attended Promise Keepers.
r. ☐ Have initiated "Lighthouses of Prayer." (ref. Mission America)
s. ☐
t. ☐

+++

E. Goals

Category	Identify owner-ship: 1. Board 2. Congregation	Goal (number)	By (Year or number of years)
1. Attendance			
2. Baptisms			
3. Small group Bible studies			
4. Prayer cells (Intercessory)			
5. New church starts			
6.			
7.			

Local Church Survey (Continued)

F. Other Data

1. Main auditorium/sanctuary seating capacity: _____

2. "Alternate" services held (Y/N): _____ When?_____

3. What do you feel is the church's most effective method of evangelism?

   _____

4. What is the greatest hindrance to growth or expansion? _____

   _____

5. What is the predominant age group in your church? _____

6. What is the most predominant occupational group(s) in your church?

   _____

7. Does the church keep weekly records of attendance for (Y/N)?

   a. ___Worship service;   b. ___ Sunday School

8. Do you have an educational institution associated with the church?

   a. Type: _____

   b. Number of students last year?

9. Have you targeted any areas or neighborhoods for ministry? _____

   a. Target area _____ Ministry_____

   b. Target area _____ Ministry_____

   c. Target area _____ Ministry_____

++

Name of person providing this information: _____

Position: _____ Date: _____

Date data entered: _____ By whom? _____

Individual Survey Questionnaire

Objective: To understand the needs of our community spiritually, socially and personally in order to facilitate more effective help and support of our neighborhoods. (Please identify the local area where you live at end of questionnaire).

1. How long have you lived in the neighborhood? ___ Years and ___ Months

2. What are three concerns you have heard others express about living in your neighborhood?

3. What are your and/or your family's main concerns?

4. What do you think are the three most important things in life?

5. What would you say are people's greatest concerns for the future?

6. What age group seems most prevalent in your area?__1-5; __6-12; __7-18

7. What religious affiliation or exposure do you have (e.g. Christian, Muslim, Humanist, etc.)?

8. Do you attend church? a) ___ regularly; b) ___ not regularly; c) ___ don't attend at all.

9. Why don't people attend church?

10. What is one way a church could be of help to families like yours?

11. Should church be formal or casual? ___ Formal; ___ Casual; ___No pref.

12. Do you believe in God? ___Yes; ___No; ___Don't know

13. Do you believe the Bible is from God for today?___Yes; ___No; ___Don't know

(continued - Indivudual Survey)

14. Do you believe in life after death? ___Yes; ___No; ___Don't know.

15. Do you believe you are on earth for a spiritual purpose? ___Yes; ___No: ___ Don't know. Any comments? _____
_____

16. The last question is about your household. Which one of the following most closely describes your household?

     ___ Married with children at home;
     ___ Married with no children at home;
     ___ Single, no children;
     ___ Single Parent-children at home; Ages: _____;
     ___ Other

17. Any other comments you would like to make? Please feel at liberty to express yourself.

_____
_____
_____

+++++++++++++++++

Name of person completing form:

_____Date: _____

Address:_____ District: _____

Phone: _____ Email address: _____

Urban Locality Survey

1. Area name/identifier: _____

     Next larger area: _____

2. Description (zone, district, neighborhood,etc.-specify):
     _____

3. Predominantly: a) ___ industrial; b) ___ residential; c) ___ profes
     sional; d) ___ other.

4. Population/pop year: _____ (data year____)
     a)__ published; b) __ estimate.

5. a) Ethnic majority: _____ b) minorities:
     _____

6. Schools (enter number): a) ___ elementary; b) ___ middle;
     c) ___ high schools; d) ___ Jr. colleges; e) ___ 4 yr. college;
     f) ___ university; g) ___ trade schools; h)___ Christian schools.

7. Neighborhood activities: a) ___ Neighborhood Watch; b) ___
     Block parties; c) ___ other (describe): _____
     _____

8. Where do <u>most</u> of the people work?: a) ___ in the subject area;
     b) ___ outside the area; c) ___ industry; d) ___ office workers;
     e) ___ professional; f) ___ blue collar.

9. Crime and violence - number in past year: a) ___ murders;
     b) ___ armed robbery; c)___ rapes; d) ___ assaults;
     e) ___ robberies; f) ___ other-describe:_____
     _____

10. Pornography and bars: a) ___ adult book stores; b) ___ strip
     joints; c) ___ hard liquor bars.

(continued - Urban Locality Survey)

11. Churches/worship centers: a) ___ Protestant; b) ___ Catholic;

    c) ___ JW's; d) ___ LDS/Mormon; e) ___ Synagogues;

    f) ___ Muslim mosques; g) ___ Buddhist temples; h) ___ other.

12. Prayer activity/centers: a) ___ Houses of Prayer; b) ___ Light

    houses; c) ___ other-describe: _____

    _____

13. Total attendance (approx.): a) ___ Protestant churches;

    b) ___ Catholic; c) ____ other.

+++++++++++++++++++

Name of person completing form:

_____   Date: _____

Organization:_____

Phone: _____   Email address: _____

Pastor - Leader Questionnaire

1. Name:_____ Position: _____
                                  (pastor, parachurch leader, etc.)

2. Number of years you have been in this position at this location: _____

3. Name of church/organization:_____

4. Denominational or organizational affiliation:

   _____

5. Address: _____Email:_____

6. City/Town_____ District:_____

7. State: _____ Postal code: _____ Phone:_____

8. Year church/organization began in this place (month/year):
   _____

+++
PLEASE FURNISH THE FOLLOWING INFORMATION FOR THE PAST
YEAR UNLESS OTHERWISE STATED:

A. Languages spoken in church services: _____

B. Which of the following characterizes the majority of attendance: 1) ___ under

   35; 2) ___ 25-50; 3) ___ over 50; 4) ___ unsure.

C. Which of the following characterizes the majority of attendance: 1) ___ White;

   2) ___ Afr Amer.; 3) ___ Hisp.; 4)___ Asian

D. Average attendance for past month of main service(s): _____

E. Total active baptized members: _____

F. Number of believer baptisms in past year (do not include babies/infants)

(continued - Pastor - Leader Questionnaire)

G. Describe those segments of society you are most effective in reaching:

_____

_____

H. Number of new members (or attendees) in past year: _____

I. Number of new churches your church started in past year: _____

J. What are the greatest areas of need for your church (check the most urgent two):

1) ___ building; 2) ___ training materials; 3) ___ worker training;

4) ___ evangelism; 5) ___ additional staff; 6) ___ revival; 7) ___ more

prayer; 8) ___ starting a new church

Denomination Survey

A. General Information   **Survey date:** _____

(mandatory)

1. Denomination: _____

2. Street Address: _____

3. Mailing Address: _____

4. City: _____District: _____ Zip: _____

5. Phone: _____ Fax: _____ Email: _____

6. CEO: _____ Began here: _____

7. Title (President, Director, etc.) _____

8. CEO's address: _____

        City:_____ Zip: _____

9. CEO's phone: _____ Email: _____

10. Year denomination begun in this city: _____

11. Predominant ethnicity of constituents: __ Anglo; __ Black; __ Hispanic; __ Asian; __Other (specify): _____

12. Organizational membership (IFMA/EFMA/NAE, etc.)_____

    _____

13. National headquarters location:_____

    _____

Page 2   Denomination Survey (continued)

B. Statistical Data   (for latest data year: _____)

    1. Total - all churches (incl. house churches):   _____

        1a. Total churches w/ traditional buildings: _____

        1b. Total "house" churches (incl. cell churches): _____

        1c. Total "Cell churches[1]" (not incl. Mother ch.) _____

    2. Total average attendance: _____

        2a Total avg. attendance-"house" churches: _____

    3. Average church size: _____

    4. Total baptized members: _____

    5. Total "believer's" baptisms (last data year)   _____

    6. Total prayer cells (Lighthouses, n'hood, etc.)   _____

    7. Total small group Bible studies - nurture: _____

    8. Total small group Bible studies - outreach: _____

    9. Total pastoral staff - full and part time: _____

        9a. Total full time pastors: _____

    10. Total full time denominational staff: _____

    11. Total income-all sources and designations $_____
            (per Annual Report)

Footnote:
1. "Cell churches" are stand-alone churches, but related to a Mother church.
    These are not the same as cells that are small group meetings.

Page 3 Denomination Survey(continued)

C. Five Year History
Please provide as much of the following data as possible. Use year end statistics. Possible sources: records, annual reports, etc. Leave spaces blank if data not available.

	5 Year Diagnostic Period					
	-5 years	-4 Years	-3 Years	-2 Years	-1 year	Last Year
Year>>>						
Churches (Total)						
Churches (House)						
Avg. attendance (Total)						
Avg. attend.- house churches						
Baptized members						
Baptisms ("believer's")						
Average church size						
Prayer cells (weekly)						
Bible studies - nurture (wk)						
Bible studies - outreach (wk)						
Other outreach meetings						
Pastors - full time						
Church staff - full time						
Denom. staff - full time						
Missionaries - external to city						
Missionaries - internal to city						
Overall income						

Note: Five years are utilized at the denominational level for diagnosis, however for local churches the period is ten years. The reason for the difference is because many churches are less than 10 years old. This causes complications when performing projections at the denominational level. Projections for denominations (churches and attendance) should be based upon growth over the past five years.

Page 4   Denomination Survey(continued)

D. Ministry information

1. Please check all of the following **organized** ministries or activites that
   currently apply to your denomination/churches in this city:

a. ___ Church-planting	b. ___ Bible school
c. ___ Seminary	d. ___ Counselor training
e. ___ Substance abuse counseling	f. ___ Food/shelter provision
g. ___ Medical/health care	h. ___ Shut-in care
i. ___ Mass evangelism	j. ___ Media evangelism
k. ___ Sports	l. ___ Music/drama
m. ___ Children's	n. ___ Teen's
o. ___ Inner-city evangelism	p. ___ City gov't evangelism
q. ___ Prayer evangelism	r. ___ "Lighthouses of Prayer"
s. ___ Concerts of prayer	t. ___ Prayer Renewal Ministries
u. ___ Missions conferences	v. ___ Missionary training
w. ___ Evangelism training	x. ___ Family counseling

2. Which of the following applies to this denomination?

   a. ___ Leaders cooperate in an organized, citywide strategy initiative.
   b. ___ Leaders are involved in regular meetings in the city with other:
      1) ___ denom./parachurch leaders; 2) ___ pastors/leaders.
   c. ___ There is a focus on unreached areas in the city:
      1) ___ for evangelism; 2) ___ for starting new congregations
   d. ___ There is a focus on the unreached people in the city:
      1) ___ for evangelism; 2) ___ for starting congreg. among.
   e. ___ Searching for innovative ways to reach the unchurched ages
      and cultures.
   f. ___ Are currently spending enough of the annual budget on evan
      gelism and church planting.
   g. ___ Some churches have "alternative services" as a means to
      reach a broader spectrum of society.
   h. ___ Want to vigorously cooperate with other groups in a meaning-
      ful way to reach this city with the riches of Christ.
   i. ___ Consider it a priority need to obtain an accurate, up-to-date
      picture of the Harvest Force and Harvest Field in our city.

Urban People Group Questionnaire
Page 1 of 3

City or Area: _____

A. General Description

1. People Group:

2. Country(ies) of origin:

3. People still emmigrating to this city/area?____ If yes, from what countries?

4. Why was this city/area chosen to locate?

5. What is causing them to leave their home country?

B. Socio-Cultural

1. Do your people find it difficult or easy to live in the American culture?

2. What is particularly offensive to you about America or this city?

3. What are the most important social or cultural customs an American should know when visiting your homes?

4. What are your most important holidays (list dates)?

5. Does your people group have your own cultural center(s) in this city? Location(s)

6. Which American holidays do your people group like to celebrate?

7. In what ways do you want to preserve your own culture in America?

8. Do you have places where your people's art/music/culture are displayed?____ Identify:

Page 2 of 3

C. Family and Community

1. How would you describe your people group's view of family?

   a) ___ extremely important;   b)___ important.

2. Who has final authority? a) ___ father; b) ___ mother;

   c) ___ grandfather; d) ___ grandmother.

3. Does the wife usually work or stay home?

4. How important is higher education to your people group?
   a) What level of achievement is important?

5. Who are the leaders of your people group?

   a) What are their ages?

6. With what other people groups in this city do your people mix?

7. Does your group maintain strong ties with your homeland(s)?

8. What are the main occupations your people are involved in?

D. Youth

1. What is the predominant age group in your youth? a) ___ 10 and

   under; b)___ 10-15; c) ___ over 15.

2. What schools do most of them attend?

3. What are their favorite sports and activities?

4. Where do the teen-agers congregate after school and on weekends?

5. What is the greatest social concern you have for your group's youth?

6. What are the greatest factors influencing your group's youth?

7. Who are the leaders among your youth?

E. Media

1. List the periodicals, radio and TV programs, videos focused upon your group. Give the publishers, stations broadcasting, frequency, etc.:

2. Is there any Christian programming produced by, or aimed at your group?

3. What media materials are being planned by your group?

G. Statistics

1. Total population for your group in this city: _____ Data year:_____

2. List population by country (ies) of origin for your group: _____, _____, _____

3. List the main zones or districts your group lives in:

4. What percent of your group are Christians? _____

5. What percent of your people speak English fluently?_____

6. What is their "mother tongue"?

H. Religion

1. What is the primary religion of your group?_____ What percent adhere to this religion? _____

2. Three most important beliefs of your people's religion?
    a.
    b.
    c.

3. Your people's attitude to Christianity? a) __ receptive; b) __ some what open? c) __ opposed.

+++

The respondent was: __ a man; __ a woman; __ under 20; __ 20-39; __ 40-59; __ 60 or higher.

__ White; __ Hispanic; __ Asian; __ Afr. American; __ Other

__ cooperative; __ hesitant; __ unwilling; __ hostile.

Person filling out this form: _____

INTERVIEW GUIDELINES

1. Select your interviewees with care. Try to select those that are the
    most knowledgeable in the area of your survey. Have realistic
    expectation levels regarding the information they will give. If at all
    possible, do not rely solely upon one source.

2. Be prepared. Do as much homework as you can regarding the
    subject area of the interview ahead of time. This will aid you in
    asking the most profitable questions, and prepare you for recogniz-
    ing evasive and not-too-accurate answers. In one interview Carl
    did for Native American information, he spent months studying the
    culture and the difficulty of reaching the Native American. He then
    wrote a paper, and finally set up an interview with a leading Native
    American for editing the paper. The resulting project gave him dra-
    matically new insights on why 14,000 Native Americans in Port-
    land have no church.

3. Become very familiar with your interview questions and the final
    information that you are after. Make yourself a checklist. People
    will think you are organized and prepared. Don't be afraid to use it.
    They will not think lesser of you. In fact it may well prompt them to
    be more responsive and responsible in their response because of
    your objectiveness. Another alternative is to memorize the inter-
    view questions, then take the interviewee through the questions
    informally.

Note: *In the above we are concerned with the "formal" interview.
When doing informal investigative surveys, and you are
interviewing people that are not aware of what you are doing,
or what you are after, in these cases using a written checklist
will probably be counterproductive. You will need to carefully
prepare a "mental" checklist.*

4. Many interesting facts and factors can be revealed in your conver-
    sations. Do not be too concerned about the sequence, but keep in
    mind the various areas needing to be covered so that you cover

them all. In many cases you will be increasing the interviewee's knowledge base, and doing some seed sowing just by the questions you ask.

Notes:

   a.   If you later discover you missed some important information, call back and state that there are some other important things you need to know. You may want to mention what they are, and a) get them answered on the phone, or b) make an appointment with whomever the person might suggest, or c) have the information mailed to you.

   b.   This is one of the more important privileges and responsibilities that a researcher has. He is face-to-face with someone who may be a key mobilizer, church planter, evangelist, etc. This is a key strategy of research. The opportunity afforded the researcher to penetrate various segments of society is a privileged and strategic one. As you meet with key people you are in a position to help facilitate networking in the Body of Christ.

5.   When carrying forth Harvest Force research it is a good idea to interview more than just the denomination or parachurch leader. Make appointments with regional superintendents, pastors, treasurers, et alia, in order to get a balance of perspectives, and to "calibrate" the data.

6.   Don't allow yourself to enter, or be drawn into, discussions about doctrinal differences or problems. Many will try to do this, but do not offer any opinions. It may seem then and there that you are helping your cause, but it will always backfire somehow, someplace, sometime. Your interview will also lose its credibility for their opinion of you will not be that you are an astute, impartial and objective researcher.

If they ask if you are also including data about "so and so organization or individual" in the survey (some won't even talk to you if you are), make the honest reply that you are (if you are), with the explanation that the survey is for all groups/religions in the area irregardless of their stance. Mention you are just gathering the data at this point, not making any judgements.

7. When engaged in Harvest Field survey/interviews/observations, you will need to have some familiarity ahead of time with the culture in order to correctly interpret what you see and hear. In a culture strange to your own, just your presence can influence any response.

Try to be very objective in documenting the situation. Don't make value judgments too early. What may seem wrong to you, may only be different. Don't be fooled by failing to detect differences between form and function. Try to detect the function, the "why," the motivation. Separate this from the form, the "how."

Many a surveyor has been fooled by making deductions from what they saw, instead of learning "why" it was being done. For example, in some countries small group Bible studies are the most effective growing edge of the Church. This does not mean that small group Bible studies will be equally effective in every culture and situation. What felt need was being met? What dynamic was taking place? Why is that important in this culture?

8. Don't take too long in your interview. Be considerate. Being on the short side is better than being long. You have a better chance of going back if you keep it short. Rarely should an interview exceed one and one-half hours, and often can be less than one hour.

9. *Try not to schedule interviews so back-to-back* you do not have time to catch up on your note-taking in between. This is very important. The time you spent will lose its value if you do not immediately tend to your notes. After you've had your second interview the details of the first will fade or you'll get confused between the two.   (This is the voice of some frustrating experiences.)
    Even if you have recorded the interview, there will be insights you need to document. So take a break and "catch up with the paperwork."

10. Often it will be good for TWO people to carry forth the interview. It is an interesting phenomenon how the interviewee will often reply to the second person (not the primary one carrying forth the interview) elaborating on a point not directly asked to make sure they are understood.

Additional Guidelines

George Otis of Sentinel Group provides these guidelines for preparation for the interview:

1) Locate a knowledgeable source.
2) Develop an explanatory introduction.
3) Arrange for an interview.
4) Familiarize yourself with key subject matter through background research.
5) Make a list of specific questions.
6) Review the list and delete repetitive or unnecessary questions.
7) Obtain and check recording equipment.

The following should also be helpful:

a) Be prepared to answer why you want the information and how it will be used. Many will want to know, and the answer to this question will play a big role in what answers you will receive.

b) Give yourself sometime between interviews to get all your notes in order. If using a recorder, you may still need to take some time to record some observations before your mind gets busied with the next interview.

c) In many instances it will be good for two of you to be in attendance for the interview. This provides the "witness factor," which, in some cases, will decrease careless and erroneous statements, and increases the scope of observations and interaction. In this situation, one person should be the primary interviewer.

HARVEST FORCE DATA DICTIONARY

This appendix correlates with **Chapter 5 "Harvest Force Data."** This is an expanded data description list and much of the data will be gathered in various phases of a citywide initiative. Chapter 5 contains suggestions for where to find the data.

At the end of this listing there is the **Harvest Force Data Table** categorizing the data (without description) according to phases, ie. Initial (Phase 1), Primary (Phase 2), and Extended (Phase 3). See **Chapter 3 "Spying Out the Land: Part 1"** for a description of Phases and Levels.

Data Summary Outline
I. Basic Administration and Ministry Descriptions
   a. Basic Identity
   b. Goals and Programs
   c. Ministries description
      1) Evangelism
      2) Missions
      3) Benevolence
      4) Community Development
      5) Media
      6) Education and Training
   d. Target Peoples
   e. Target Areas
   f. Stance on Socio-Cultural Issues

II. Churches and Related Statistical Data
   a. Churches (English speaking)
   b. Churches (non-English speaking)
   c. Small Groups (by age and purpose)
   d. Average Weekly Attendance (worship or main service(s))
   e. Active Baptized Members
   f. Baptisms-Believers and Infant
   g. Pastors and/or Staff

III. **Other Harvest Force Data**
   A. Local churches - information not included above-unique to local churches.
      1. Predominant ethnic orientation
      2. Seating capacity
      3. Number and Types of Services
      4. Five-Fold Ministry presence and status
      5. Weekly meetings/services
   B. Parachurch groups
      1. Organizational Affiliations
      2. Index of Non-profits
   C. Other corporate Church data
      1. Identification of Special Efforts and Groups
      2. Identification of Key Christians in Special Posts

I. Basic Administrative Data and Ministry Descriptions

In this category you are identifying the various Harvest Force organizations in the city (or region) and what each of these do. This can be used for a ministry/church directory.

Basic Identity
- Organization Name
- Mailing address, site/street address (for mapping), phone and fax numbers, Email address
- Pastors and/or officers names, titles and tenure
- Ecclesiastical tradition
- Founding date (in the city)
- Predominant ethnic orientation - Is the church or organization majority white, African American, Hispanic, Chinese, Korean, Japanese, Filipino, Native American, etc.? (Later you will be asked to record the ethnicity and language of other services held by each church or organization.)

Goals and Programs
Record measurable goals of the church or organization. Document programs relating to these goals, listing target year(s), target peoples, areas, etc.

- New churches (types, locations)
- New believers
- Baptisms
- Membership (church size)
- Small group Bible studies
- Missions/missionaries
- Outposts/preaching points
- Budget (administration, evangelism, missions, etc.)

Ministry Descriptions

- Evangelism
  Evangelism is one of the key 'health giving' aspects of the Church in that it keeps the Church and churches from being ingrown and stale. It also provides both a quantitative and qualitative growing edge for the Church/churches. Perhaps the biggest problem facing the Church is equipping and obtaining involvement in *effective* evangelism in the various segments of society. Obtaining the right information here can provide crucial help in leading the Church in the city out of its lethargy and ineffectiveness in evangelism.

  Identify, describe and status the involvement in the following categories of evangelism as they apply. Record statistics for the past year, 3,5, and 10 years. Provide information regarding number, frequency, audience and response as applicable.

  Mass evangelism (newspapers, radio, TV, films, crusades, rallies, revival meetings, literature, drama, mime, dance, concerts, videos, stage plays, etc.)
  Neighborhood evangelism (block parties, prayer walks, prayer cells/houses, sports, Bible studies)
  Personal evangelism (house-to-house, friendship, visit jails, prisons, juvenile halls, other)
  Children evangelism [1-12 yrs] (backyard clubs, vacation

Bible schools, child care, sports)
Youth evangelism [12-18 yrs] (sports and recreation, Bible studies, music, drama, campus ministry, other)
College and careers [19-30 yrs] (campus ministries, sports, drama/stage, concerts, special conferences (Promise Keepers, Planning, career seminars)

- Missions
Measurement is needed of the extent the City Church (including parachurch) and churches are involved in missions, missions training, and missions mobilization and sending.

Missions giving (dollar amount per year, distribution of dollars by missionary ministry category [e.g. training, evangelism, medical, etc.], annual missions budget past 5 years)
Missions education, orientation and training (description of each category and target audience (e.g. congregation, missionary candidates, etc., number involved per year in missionary training)
Missionaries sent (number of foreign missionaries and domestic [inside this country or city] sent: by target area/country, by target peoples/language - per year for past 5 years.

- Benevolence (Love in Action)
Note: This and the next category ("community development projects") are closely related, but there are some distinguishing features. It would be good to read both before doing any planning.

Identifying the needs in a community, and determining how and to what extent the Church is meeting these needs is very fundamental to the city-reaching strategy. Needs should not only be met because Christ's love demands it, but because they also provide a bridge for evangelism and meeting the real need, which is Jesus Christ and His righteousness.

Food and clothing (local, foreign disaster)
Shelter (emergency, temporary, permanent, homeless care)
Counseling (family, unmarried mothers, single parent, youth, abuse victims, substance abuse, abortion)
Health (clinic, nurse, doctors, education and training, emergency)
Job placement (counseling, placement)
Shut-in care (visitation, professional, food)
"Rescue missions"-jails-prisons-juvenile halls (visits, services, counseling, financial help)

- Community Development Projects

  Describe the various current and planned projects, obtaining the goals, budgets and locations, sponsors and participants, target areas and target peoples for the following (these are examples, there will be others):

  Municipal improvements (e.g. parks and recreation)
  Arts and entertainment related projects
  Housing projects
  Medical clinics projects
  Family counseling center projects
  Youth recreation projects
  Volunteer work force mobilization projects
  Rehabilitation center projects
  Neighborhood watch projects
  Etc.

- Media

  Identify for each media:
  Titles and type of media
  Stated purpose and target audiences
  Organizational identity and information
  Hours per week of programs (TV and radio)
  Frequency of publication or broadcast
  Summary of response and/or impact

- Education and Training
  Obtain the following information as applicable, identifying the location, organization and/or church or churches involved plus the statusing data indicated.

  Christian schools (grade range, e.g., K-12, # students)

  Bible schools (# students, curriculum categories)

  Seminaries (# students graduate and postgraduate, majors/ degrees offered)

  Special training classes (small group "shepherd" leaders, evangelism, parenting, counselor training, Bible study leaders)

  On-the-job-training (types, # trainees involved by type)

  Non-formal education (types, # involved, curriculum description, degrees available, etc.)

Target Peoples

Identify the ethnic, ethnolinguistic (language), and socio-cultural groups which are targeted for planned entry and ministry. Also identify those groups among which there is current ministry and/ or church attendance. Identify the type of ministry(ies) for those being targeted. *Note*: The descriptive information relating to the group's distinctives, locations, populations, etc. is outlined in the next chapter-Harvest Field Data. Some of the target people category possibilities are:

Hispanics	Spanish speaking Hispanics	Native Americans
Middle East Arabs	Senior Citizens	Shut-ins
Widows	South-East Asians	African American
Baby Boomers	Busters	Upper Middle Class
Generation-X	Dock workers	Taxi Drivers
Single Moms	Gang members	Business CEO's
Homeless	Government employees	Caribbean Creoles
Anglo Pastors	Women in Shelters	Prostitutes
Pre-school children	Street People	

Target Areas

Identify the areas (regions, zones, districts, neighborhoods, etc.) in which the organization is targeting for further presence and ministry, note the year when entry is anticipated, and identify the form

of the planned presence or ministry. For example:
- New churches or church planting
- Outreaches
- Lighthouses (neighborhood houses) of prayer
- Social services or benevolence work
- Youth outreach

Stance on Socio-Cultural Issues
There can be several issues that can be sensitive or divisive in terms of impacting the overall citywide initiative. Some organizations, in particular, may have a nonpolitical or related clauses as part of their policy statement. Others may be involved in campaigning or demonstrating on some issues.

> *Note:* When the survey is being carried forth, some of this kind of information might appear in the organization's annual or special reports, and therefore can be obtained at the same time as statistical or statusing data.

There may be several controversial social-cultural issues in the city. Record the majority and minority positions held by denominations, churches and parachurch groups. Some examples of possible issues are:
- "Right to life"
- Capital punishment
- Pornography
- Position regarding homosexuals
- Homeless

II. Churches and Related Statistical Data
The purpose of this data is to not only get the current status of the Church, but also a dynamic picture of how this is changing. Obtain the following statistical data for past year, and 3, 5 and 10 years ago. Additionally record the number of churches in the city every 5 years starting as far back as records have been kept.

Guidelines:
1. Record source and date for every piece of data.

2. Try to collect data for ten years. Ten years is considered the "diagnostic period", and it is preferable if data is obtained for every year. However the high priority is for the last year, 3 and 5 years ago. This is the minimum needed for contemporary growth analysis and projections, and to correlate with other data for similar periods. If data for some other years are available in this range that will prove useful also.

3. Think in terms of the eventual tables you will create. Eventually the following data will need to appear in tables. Constructing these tables early may save you from doing it twice. See **Appendix "I"** for sample tables. Also chapter 8, "Painting the Picture." Looking there now should prove helpful.

4. Avoid duplication. There needs to be care taken that there is not a duplication of statistical data between denominations and parachurch groups. That is, you don't want to double count churches, members, etc.. There is some duplication in ministries, but this is not a problem as far as analysis is concerned. A problem arises when parachurch groups and denominations both furnish numbers of affiliated churches and double counting occurs in the statistical summary.

Churches data - Primarily English speaking.

Identify every form of the Church in the city and every component, or entity, of that form. See Appendix-A for guidelines regarding definitions and descriptions of a church.

Obtain the mailing and physical address of each church, identifying those that are House Churches, Cell Churches (this is not the same as churches with cells, or small cells. See "small groups/cells" below), and other congregations that *gather for worship, prayer, teaching and communion.*

· Classify the various types of congregations and provide the number for each (including traditional, House Churches, Cell Churches and other congregations).

· Record the number of churches that closed their doors for

each data period (last year, 3,5, and 10 years past).

· If data is available, note total church seating capacity, and the percent filled or not filled.

· Record the number and language of the non-English services and Sunday School classes (in the primarily English speaking churches).

Churches data - Primarily other than English speaking.

In addition to the above, record the language of the worship services, Sunday school, and any other services (list type) for those other than English. Provide:

a. Total number of churches in each language category
b. Attendance and members for each language service.

Small Groups (includes cells, but not Cell Churches)- Record the number and location of: any small groups,

> Note: *There are fundamentally two different types of cells. Typically, churches have some percent of their congregation meeting in small groups for prayer, Bible study, fellowship and/or evangelism. These are often referred to as cells and this is the data field addressed here. "Cell Churches" should be identified and recorded under churches above.*

Average Weekly Attendance

Attendance data is preferred over membership; however, this data may not be available in all cases and definitions may vary among denominations. Do not mix *attendance* and *membership* data, unless you have no other data. Where *attendance* data is spotty, and you have more complete *membership* data, make your calculations using *membership*.

Record the average attendance that includes all the services primarily attended by Christians for corporate worship and teaching. Try to avoid double counting. When not automatically supplied, obtain data for the average attendance for the last month or months of the statistical period.

Obtain the age breakdown for attendance if the denominations have maintained this data. This is important to see who is being reached or churched. This could be very powerful and useful information for bringing attention to least-reached generations.

- Identify attendance in major age (generational) groups, e.g. 0-12, 13 to 18, 19 to 30, 31 to 50, 51-65, over 65.
  The Barna Research group uses the following groups:

Generation	Birth Years	
Builders	1927-1945	
Boomers	1946-1964	
Busters	1965-1983	
Mosaics	1984-2002	(or Millenials)

- Obtain breakdown of attendance for ethnic or other language service. Some organization's year-end is not the same as the calendar year. This doesn't present a problem as long as it is consistent year after year.

  Note: *Do not accept or record "roll" or "membership" data as a substitute for "attendance." Record and identify these separately. If the denomination does not keep attendance data, note so this can be taken into consideration during analysis. Attendance data is desired over "roll" or "members" as it provides a more realistic barometer into the life and dynamics of the church. There is a wide variety of practices pertaining to membership/rolls. (Some are on the "roll called up yonder," but haven't been purged from the earthly records.)*

Membership - This is not the same as "attendance" (see note above). This would usually be those on the "roll" providing the roll is purged for those that depart for whatever reason, e.g. transfer or death.

Baptisms (adult "believer" and "infant") - for each of the data years. Keep statistics for infant baptisms separate from adult or believer's baptism. Adult or *believers* baptisms usually applies to any 9 to 10 years-of-age or older, but different denominations and/or churches may have other criteria.

Record the ages of those baptized (needed to determine where conversion growth is occurring from an age/generation standpoint).

> **Note:** *A record of baptisms (except infant) is needed to help determine conversion growth, versus transfer growth. Infant baptism is a helpful measure of biological growth.*

Pastors and/or Staff - Record the number of full time pastors (and type: senior, youth, mission, etc.), part time pastors, full time staff and part time staff. Also note the number of "home missionaries" of this denomination/church working in this city.

III. Other Harvest Force Data

In addition to those data items pertinent to local churches mentioned above, the following data should be gathered for each local church:

A. Other Church Data

Predominant Ethnic Orientation - Note whether the church is majority white, African American, Hispanic, Chinese, Korean, Japanese, Filipino, Native American, etc.. Record the ethnicity and language of other services held by this church.

Seating Capacity of the Church
- for worship service
- for Sunday school

Number and Type of Services – Identify each type of service and record the number of times held each week, e.g. traditional Sunday worship service, Saturday night worship service, mid-week prayer meetings, youth service, other language service, etc.

Five-Fold Ministry - Identify which of the five-fold ministries listed in Ephesians 4:11 (apostle, prophet, evangelist, pastor, teacher) are present and being administered for "equipping the saints" from within the church, and also from outside the church.

Weekly meetings/services- Record the type, purpose, and day of week for each service held.

Note: *There are getting to be so many different types and styles of services (many new wineskins) that you can't lump them all together, for this will prevent you from determining the distinctives and effectiveness of each, and who are being reached by each type and location of service.*

B. **Parachurch Data**

Most of the needed parachurch data is listed above and should be completed for each organization/group.

• Identify organizational affiliations, e.g. denominations, other city organizations, national organizations (e.g. Evangelical Foreign Missions Association [EFMA], Interdenominational Foreign Missions Association [IFMA]), international organizations (e.g. World Evangelical Fellowship [WEF], World Council of Churches, etc.)

• Obtain or build an index of Christian nonprofit groups (501c3) carrying forth social services, e.g. crisis pregnancy centers, family counseling centers, drug rehab, health care, community development.

C. **Other Corporate Church Data**

• Identify and describe special efforts and groups. For example: fellowships of pastors, churches, united prayer efforts, and other citywide and Body-wide movements or fellowships that are meeting regularly.

• Identify key Christians in special posts: government, public media, and in arts and entertainment (including sports) in the city.

++

Harvest Force Data Table - Phased

The following data table is set forth in phases to help facilitate a citywide initiative as described in this book. See Chapter 3, and Figure 4-1 on page 4-11 of Chapter 4. You may want to make some changes to accommodate your particular needs. A common problem is to try to gather too much data too soon. Not only is the task (and usually the cost) much greater, but there is a danger of some information sitting around, not being used.

For a broader treatment of "phased" data (including many spiritual mapping variables) obtain the *City Survey Data Guide*[1].

Endnotes:
1. Waymire, Bob. *The City Survey Data Guide-USA Edition.* Etna, CA: LIGHT International, 1999. To order contact LIGHT International at 530-467-5373 or bwaymire@sisqtcl.net, or PO Box 368, Etna, CA 96027. (Treats both Harvest Force and Harvest Field data. 32 pages, $5 each including postage. Credit cards OK.)

Initial-Phase 1 Data	Primary-Phase 2 Data	Extended-Phase 3 Data

A. Index of local churches
Only data for the past year is requested and this data may already be available via an existing directory, or can be compiled from the Yellow pages and minimal additional research. Also, other data may be readily available and it should be recorded if it is, such as attendance, members, baptisms, etc., although these would normally be Phase-Two data.
 	
1) name and address
2) denominational affiliation (or identify if independent) (optional)
3) predominant ethnic orientation
4) language of services (primary and secondary)
	A. Denominations & Parachurch Organizations
	Note: The following data is needed for each denomination and each parachurch organization-as applicable.
	
	Record the following data for the past year, 3, 5 and 10 years ago. Often denominations and parachurch groups produce annual reports that will contain much of the following data.
	
	1) Basic administration - denominations & parachurch
	  a. Identity-name, address, phone number, email address
	  b. ecclesiastical tradition
	  c. founding or begin date (in city)
	  d. Predominant ethnic orientation(s)
		A. Denominations & Parachurch Organizations
		Note: The following data is needed for each denomination and each parachurch organization-as applicable.
		
		1) Churches and related statistical data
		  a. number of pastors-full and part time
		  b. number of full-time staff (in addition to pastors)
		  c. number of weekly small groups (such as Lighthouses of Prayer, Bible studies, etc.-note type)

B. Index of denominations
Obtain data from denominational offices or headquarters. Group independent churches as a denomination.
 	
1) denomination name and address of office in this city
2) number of churches
3) number of cell churches and number of total cells (avoid double-counting).
	2) Churches and related statistical data - *denominations & parachurch*
	  a. number and location of churches (primarily English speaking)
	  b. number and location of churches (primarily other than English speaking)
	  c. average weekly attendance (main worship-type services)
	
	  d. members
		2) Goals – denomination/parachurch. *Note year(s) for which goals apply.*
		  a. outpost/preaching points
		  b. missionaries (domestic and foreign)
		  c. prayer ministry and involvement (incl. united prayer movements)
		  d. budget (administration, evangelism, missions, church planting, etc.)
		
		3) Ministry descriptions - denominations & parachurch.
		
		<u>missions</u> - describe missions program for both domestic and foreign missions.
		
		  a. missions

Harvest Force Data Table

Initial-Phase 1 Data	Primary-Phase 2 Data	Extended-Phase 3 Data

C. Index of parachurch organizations
 	
1) name and address of city office
2) classification of primary ministries-e.g. evangelism, education, training, service, media, literature, inner-city, benevolent, consulting, planning, mobilizing, etc...
	e. baptisms-infant and "believers"
	
	3) Goals - denominations & parachurch. *Note year for which goals apply.*
	  a. new churches
	  b. new believers
	  c. baptisms ("believers")
	  d. attendance
	  e. small group Bible studies
	
	4) Ministry descriptions - denominations & parachurch. *Provide a short description of the various ministries carried forth by the organization. Describe the ministry target areas and people groups.*
	
	  a. prayer (including "neighborhood houses of prayer," "lighthouses of prayer," participation in united prayer, prayer evangelism, etc.)
	  b. evangelism - describe various types employed in this denomination
	
	5) Target people - denominations & parachurch
	  a. identity of ethnic or socio-cultural groups targeted for churches, gatherings, or churches
	  b. expected date of initial engagement
	  c. anticipated entry method or ministry
		b. community development (including energy, shelter, health, etc.)
		  c. social service/benevolence (including health care, drug rehab, food, clothing, family counseling, crisis pregnancy/counseling center, job placement, child care, etc..)
		  d. media - produced or sponsored by organization-TV, radio, video, newspaper, etc.
		  e. education and training (including Bible schools, seminaries, K-12 schools, trade schools, specialized training, etc.
		  f. five-fold ministries - identify which of the 5-fold ministries listed in Ephesians 4:11 (apostle, prophet, evangelist, pastor, teacher) are present within the denomination and are being actively engaged in "equipping the saints."
		
		(Note: it is not necessarily expected that all denominations or churches will have all five (5), or are even intended to do so. However, this information is helpful when looking at the City Church for identifying presence of biblically-specified roles and resources.)

Harvest Force Data Table

Initial-Phase 1 Data	Primary-Phase 2 Data	Extended-Phase 3 Data
	6) Target areas - denominations & parachurch a. Identity of areas in the city being targeted for churches, gatherings or other ministry. b. Expected dates of engagement c. Anticipated entry method or ministry **B. Local Church Data** *The following data will normally be gathered using one or more "local church survey" forms. Nowadays, it also pays to check the WorldWide Web to see if a church has a Web Page, and if so, what information is it making available. In any event, you will probably have to make a personal contact with the church to either obtain missing information, or to authenticate data you have already obtained from one source or another. In this case we suggest you refer to the book, Discovering Your City, and review the appendices on interviews and forms.* 1) Administration - local church a. identity/name b. address (street and PO Box) c. denominational affiliation (or independent)	**B. Local Church Data** 1) Administration - local church a. Full-time staff - titles and responsibilities b. Budget - annual (provide departmental breakdown e.g. general, missions, evangelism, music, etc.)

Harvest Force Data Table

Initial-Phase 1 Data	Primary-Phase 2 Data	Extended-Phase 3 Data

	d. ecclesiastical tradition
	e. phone, email and/or Web address
	f. pastor(s) names, titles and responsibilities
	
	2) Statistical data - local church. Obtain statistics for past year, plus 3, 5, and 10 years ago.
	
	  a. main service(s) attendance (average attendance for last month of data period
	  b. worship-type services - avoid duplication as much as possible)
	  c. Sunday School attendance - ditto but for Sunday School
	  d. members - preferably active baptized members. *Members on roll ok if attendance data not available.*
	  f. services - number and type all services
	  g. ethnic groups - number of ethnic minority groups represented in the church, and approx. population of each major group in the church
	
	3) Non-statistical data - local church
	  a. main ethnic orientation of church - identify main ethnic groups attending services, identify services, also include country of origin and whether
		2) Statistical Data
		  a. seating capacity - number of seats in building(s) for main services
		  b. pastors, staff - number of all pastors and full-time staff
		  c. missionaries - number of domestic (US) and foreign missionaries (those sent to minister in other cultures)
		  d. languages - number of languages used in services (identify languages), number of speakers of each language
		  e. small groups - number of small groups, including "cells" but not Cell Churches (include Bible studies, home/neighborhood fellowship meetings, "home" prayer meetings, outreach meetings, etc.) Where data is available record the number attending the gatherings.

Harvest Force Data Table

Initial-Phase 1 Data	Primary-Phase 2 Data	Extended-Phase 3 Data

	or not there are small groups avail.)
	b. <u>languages/translations</u> - list all languages spoken in services. Identify which are being translated into or from English.
	c. <u>types of services</u>, purpose/target audience, services per week, meeting locations
	
	4) Ministry descriptions - local church
	  a. <u>prayer</u> (including "neighborhood houses of prayer," "lighthouses of prayer," participation in united prayer, prayer evangelism, etc.)
	  b. <u>evangelism</u> - describe various types employed by this church
	
	C. Citywide Harvest Force Information
	
	1) Prayer
	  a. describe citywide united prayer effort (include coordinator(s), key leaders, committee, frequency of meetings, level of participation, etc.)
	  b. describe citywide prayer special events over past 2 years (including conferences, special seminars,
		3) Ministry descriptions - local church
		  a. <u>missions</u> - describe missions program for both, domestic and foreign missions
		  b. <u>community development</u> (including energy, shelter, health, etc.)
		  c. <u>social service/benevolence</u> (including health care, drug rehab, food, clothing, family counseling, crisis pregnancy counseling/ center, job placement, child care, etc..)
		  d. <u>media</u>
		  e. <u>education and training</u> – describe types and location of schools/training.
		  f. <u>five-fold ministries</u> – (see description under "denominational data" above: A) 1. a.)
		
		C. Citywide Harvest Force Information
		
		1) Image of the Church in the city
		  a. What Church news attracts the most attention?
		  b. Does the city have the sense the Church is truly interested in its problems? How so? (e.g. city leader statements, etc.)
		  c. Has there been public mockery of the

Harvest Force Data Table

Initial-Phase 1 Data	Primary-Phase 2 Data	Extended-Phase 3 Data

	convenors, speakers, etc.)
	 c. describe the significant changes or transformations which have occurred in the city that can be attributed directly to prayer.*
	 d. identify/describe areas of the city where prayer seems to be difficult.*
	
	 2) Church mobilization initiative
	   a. describe initiative - vision, goals, objectives, process, coordinators, participants
	   b. current status vs. goals and objectives
	   c. describe and status research and analysis to date and what is planned for next 1, 3, 5 years.
	   d. describe major events to date (e.g. conferences, workshops, seminars, congresses, etc.)
	
	 3) Church health
	   a. describe causes if community faith was strong but has given way to permissiveness.*
	   b. describe where reconciliation within the Body is needed.
	   c. describe the current specific strongholds in the city that are obviously points of resistance to growth and/or vitality of the Church.*
		Church?
		
		 2) Evangelistic activity and progress
		   a. What are recognized, mature intercessors hearing from God concerning the city?
		   b. Has a "prophetic message" been spoken forth regarding the city? What is it? By whom? When?
		
		   c. Identify key figures who have been converted. What has changed in their lives and work? Do they have influence with the city leaders? Within the Church?
		
		 3) Church Health
		   a. What is the history of church splits in the community? What are they attributed to?
		   b. Are there recognized apostolic leaders in the area who have made public commitments to the community? If yes, what is the reason they give for doing this?
		   c. Is there a sense of hopeful

Harvest Force Data Table

Initial-Phase 1 Data	Primary-Phase 2 Data	Extended-Phase 3 Data
	d. describe the current areas in the city of needed focus and action by the Church. e. describe the extent to which the Church represents all the social classes in the city.* f. describe the attitude of the community leaders toward Christian morality and ethics.* g. describe the ways the Church is actively involved in city government. (*) describing spiritual mapping oriented situations	expectancy among the ranks of the believers? Much discouragement?

Harvest Field Data Dictionary

This appendix correlates with **Chapter 6 "Harvest Field Data."** This is an expanded data description list and much of the data will be gathered in various phases of a citywide initiative. Chapter 6 contains suggestions for where to find the data. **Appendices "H" thru "K"** contain many examples of ways you can format the data.

At the end of this listing there is the **Harvest Field Data Table** categorizing the data (without description) according to phases, ie. Initial (Phase 1), Primary (Phase 2), and Extended (Phase 3). See **Chapter 3 "Spying Out the Land: Part 1"** for a description of Phases & Levels.

A note regarding maps

Early on in your research you will do well to obtain a variety of maps of the city depicting the various geo-political entities, such as: county boundaries, incorporated city boundaries, zones, districts, regions, census tracts, postal (zip) codes, etc.. Look for maps that have major highways and roads, schools, parks, churches, government buildings and other landmarks. Determine which computerized mapping systems are being used by local map publishers and city offices.

Data Summary Outline
    1. Population and Demographics
    2. People Groups
    3. Arts, Media, Culture and History
    4. Social Concerns, Religions and Worldview
    5. Economics, Industry and Commerce, Gov't and Politics

I. Population and Demographics
    A. Population, population density (as applicable), and population growth rate - for basic geo-political entities included in the initiative-past year, 3, 5 and 10 years ago.

1) MSA-Metropolitan Statistical Area (encompassed by the initiative)
2) county(ies) if applicable
3) incorporated city(ies) - there may be more than one incorporated city in the MSA
4) census tract or census block group
5) city zones or regions (as designated by the city and for which data is available)
6) by age group (e.g. Builders (born 1927-1945), Boomers (born 1946-1964), Busters (born 1965-1983), Millenials (born 1984-2003)
7) by ethnicity - ethnic/ethnolinguistic
8) by gender
9) number of households
10) average number per household

B. Vital Statistics (per geo area where data is available)
1) birth and death rates
2) life expectancies (male and female)
3) numbers and rates of:
   a) violent and nonviolent crimes and locations
   b) divorces
   c) abortions
   d) births out of wedlock, age of mother
   e) single-parent families (male and female)
   f) unemployed
   g) those below the poverty line
   h) juvenile delinquents

II. People Groups
A. Ethnic/Ethnolinguistic Groups
1) identity and country of origin (national heritage)
2) number of immigrants this group-last year, 5 years ago
3) population by census tracts, and by zones, districts or regions
4) religious affiliations, and number and/or percent of adherents
5) primary and secondary language or particular dialect (e.g. dialects of Chinese would be Mandarin, Cantonese or Hakka),

number of speakers of each language/dialect
6) description of each group's physical, social, and economic
   condition and needs
7) identity of government or other non-Church sponsored programs to help the group

B. Socio-Cultural Groups
Identify as many of the groups as possible in this category in
addition to the ethnic groups. These will have distinctives other
than race or ethnicity, such as economic class and/or occupations, generational culture, students, etc. These groups would
be candidates for tailor-made evangelism, church planting, prayer
and other ministries. Record the following data where possible
and practicable:
1) identifier/category
2) approximate number in this group
3) location in the city (census tract, zip code, zone, district or
   region) where there are concentrations of these people
4) identify/record known physical, social, economic and spiritual needs

College students	School teachers
University professors	Senior Citizens
Senior citizen shut-ins	Female Sr. Citizens
Baby Boomers	Busters
Upper Middle Class	Generation-X
Preschool children	Taxi Drivers
Single Moms	Gang members
Business CEO's	Homeless/street people
Government employees	Actors/actresses
Anglo Pastors	Women in Shelters
Prostitutes	Pastors-churches >500
Poverty class	Attorneys
Law enforcement personnel	Dock workers
Unwed pregnant teen-agers	Drug abusers
Criminals (violent crimes)	Professional athletes

III. Arts, Media, Culture and City History

A. Arts and Entertainment

Identify which are present in the city, and provide a thumbnail description of the groups, rating their popularity (based upon audience attendance) on a scale of 1 to 3 (1 = mildly popular, 2 = moderately popular, 3 = very popular).

1) Actors and actresses guild, playhouses, opera houses, theaters, etc.
2) Entertainment centers, game parks, etc.
3) Sports teams and sports, e.g. football, hockey, basketball, baseball, skiing/snow- boarding, gymnastics, soccer, track, auto racing, horse racing, etc.

B. Media

The media makes a tremendous impact for good or evil upon individuals, segments of society, and the entire city. It is incumbent upon those involved in citywide transformational ministries to have accurate, up-to-date information relating to the presence, quality and impact of the media.

1) Identify the various media producers and publishers, and their products. Rate them according to their alignment with Christian ethics, values and issues.
Include:
   a. television
   b. magazines
   c. radio
   d. pornography publishers/retailers (TV, videos, films, magazines, literature, etc.)
   e. newspapers
   f. videos and video stores/retailers (include the Internet/ Web)
   g. movies and movie theaters
   h. public mass meetings
2) Identify which media groups and companies are producing, publishing, and/or broadcasting material considered to be: a) deleterious to the moral fiber of the individuals and seg-

ments of society in the city, and b) that which is uplifting and morally excellent.

3) Identify which producers and publishers are pro-Christian in their ethics, and/or are sympathetic to Christian causes and platforms. Which do this openly, and which do not?

C. Cultural Events

Understanding the cultural traditions and events is needful to understand the personality and functions of the city. This information, coupled with that disclosed by spiritual mapping (Layers 5 and 6), can lead to determining why things are the way they are in the city, and also will lead to a deeper understanding of the forces for good and for evil. Document the following:

1) Celebrations - annual citywide celebrations such as: parades, special city holidays, rallies, rodeos, fairs, Native American events/celebrations, etc., the sponsors and the history. Also document any accompanying rituals.
2) City themes, mascot(s), slogan(s), etc.
3) "Sister City" - many cities have a "sister" city somewhere in the world.
4) Museums, zoos, other public attractions.

D. City History
1) Year founded
2) Founder(s) of the city
3) Reasons city was established where it is
4) Major historical events in city's history (year and purpose)

IV. Social Concerns, Religions, and Worldview
A. Social Concerns and Needs
Many areas of social concern and need exist in every city. Identify, describe and status the prevalent concerns and needs. Some categories to consider are:

1) Health and medical care
2) Alcohol and drug abuse
3) Homeless and destitute care
4) Single parent family care
5) Teen pregnancy
6) Gangs, mob and riot control
7) Religious killings and burnings
8) Good water, energy, shelter
9) High school dropouts/attendance
10) Child and parent abuse
11) Violent/non-violent crime
12) Abortion/crisis pregnancy
13) Pornography
14) Immoral and violent TV/videos
15) Family counseling
16) Job training and placement

B. Religions

Provide data for past year, 3, 5 and 10 years ago. Include all religions and religious cults: Christian, Muslims, Hindus, Buddhists, Animists, Spiritists, Atheists, Humanists, etc.. Give breakdown of Christians by Catholics, Protestants, Orthodox, and the estimated percent evangelical of each. Also include all cults, e.g. Moonies, Mormons (LDS), Jehovah Witnesses, New Age, etc.. Include number of Sikhs, Punjabis, Bahai, Jains, etc. Gather the following information:

1) Name/identity
2) Number and percent of population of adherents or community.
3) Number of active communicants
4) Immigrants for each of the above data years (city planning office may help here-but data will probably lag a year or two). Give country of emigration if known.
5) Identify any concentrations in the city. Census data may help here.

C. Worldview of the Unchurched

It is incumbent upon researchers and analysts to monitor which generations and peoples are minimally churched and to put their finger on why. We usually wait until it reaches the "disaster" level before we pay attention to the Barnas and Gallups. Determining and understanding the worldview of the unchurched is a fundamental necessity in reaching them with the Good News.

Obtaining answers to the following questions is a first step in understanding the worldview of the unchurched. For the most part this will require a special survey. Contact should be made with those experienced in these kinds of surveys to determine the best methods. The knowledge provided is worth the effort, providing it is done in a professional manner. This kind of data can be used effectively in waking up the Church to some stark realities. George Barna in several of his books has included questionnaire questions related to the following. Contact Barna Research Group, Ltd located in Oxnard, California for more information.[1]

1) Do most people in the community believe in God? How do they define Him? About what percentage? Do they believe in any Supreme Being?

2) What percentage of people believe in an actual heaven and hell? Of these, what percentage believe they will go to heaven because of the way they lived their lives?

3) About what percentage of the community believe in the devil (or demons)? How do they define him/them? Do most college students believe in the devil?

4) What is the size and influence of the New Age Movement?

5) What are the predominant secular philosophies (worldviews) in the area? Humanism? Rationalism? Enlightenment? Materialism? Anti-establishmentarianism? What is the level of their influence?

6) Are Native Americans practicing their native religions? What percentage?

7) Are there any Voodoo or other spiritist religions being practiced in the city? About how many? Where in the city? Do any offer animal or other sacrifices?

8) What are the main reasons the unchurched do not attend any church? Do they feel the Church has any worthwhile purpose? Do they feel they can be good Christians and not attend *church?*

V. Economics, Industry & Commerce, Government & Politics

A. Economics

1) Per capita income
   a) number in each basic economic category/levels (per census).
   b) by geo area-census tract/block, or zones/regions
2) Housing values-by census tract, zone or district.
3) Land values-by census tract, zone or district.
4) Percent and distribution of population for several different income levels (at least 5).
   Note: the distribution needs to match either the zones, census tracts, zip code areas, or other geo area for which population data is also available.

B. Industry and Commerce

1) Identify 6 leading industries. Note annual earnings, number of employees, annual sales/income, products, services, annual exports.
2) Major trade partners for city industries. Major exports and imports.
3) Transportation: airports (annual traffic), harbors/ports (annual traffic/tonnage), major trucklines headquartered in city (tonnage per year), municipal bus lines and rapid transit (passengers per year).

C. Government and Politics

Those involved in surveying and analyzing the city should become first-hand familiar with the government of the city, especially the planning office, law enforcement offices, and the office of social services. Not only can these be rich storehouses of needed information, they can play a strategic role in assisting the Church in the transformation process of the city. It should be a priority for those involved in research and analysis, plus other key persons in a citywide initiative to get acquainted with the city government. Document: names, date entered office, phone numbers, and office addresses:

1) Mayor
2) Chief of police
3) Fire chief
4) City attorney
5) City administrator
6) Other major department heads
7) Political party leaders

Harvest Field Data Table-Phased

The data table on the following pages is set forth in phases to help facilitate a citywide initiative as described in this book. See Chapter 3, and Figure 4-1 on page 4-11 of Chapter 4. You may want to make some changes to accommodate your particular needs. A common problem is to try to gather too much data too soon. Not only is the task (and usually the cost) much greater, but there is a danger of some information sitting around not being used. Thus the phases.

For a broader treatment of phased data (including many spiritual mapping variables) obtain the *City Survey Data Guide*[2].

Endnotes:
1. Barna Research Group, Ltd., Oxnard, California. George Barna has written several books based upon surveys aimed at determining the health and relevancy of the Church in America. We recommend you avail yourself to: *Evangelism That Works, Generation Next, and Turning Vision Into Action.* (Ventura, CA, Regal Books) Web addr: www..barna.org
2. Waymire, Bob. *The City Survey Data Guide-USA Edition. Etna, CA: LIGHT International, 1999.* To order contact LIGHT International at 530-467-5373 or bwaymire@sisqtel.net, or PO Box 368, Etna, CA 96027. (Treats both Harvest Force and Harvest Field data. 32 pages, $5 each incl. postage. Credit cards OK.)

Harvest Field Data Table

Initial-Phase 1 Data	Primary-Phase 2 Data	Extended-Phase 3 Data

A. Population, population density (as applicable), and population growth rate - for basic geo-political entities included in the initiative-past year, 3, 5 and 10 years ago. (Much of the data is available via census projections.)
 	
1) MSA-Metropolitan Statistical Area (encompassed by the initiative)
2) county(ies) if applicable
3) incorporated city(ies) - there may be more than one incorporated city in the MSA
4) census tract or census block group
5) city zones or regions (as designated by the city and for which data is available)
6) by age group (e.g. Builders (born 1927-1945), Boomers (born 1946-1964), Busters (born 1965-1985), Millenials (born 1986-2005)
7) by ethnicity - ethnic/ethnolinguistic
8) by gender
9) number of households
10) average number per household
 	
B. Socio-economic data (census or city report) (past year, 5 years ago)
 	
1) per capita income
  a) number in each basic economic
	A. Vital Statistics (per geo area where data is available)
	
	1) birth and death rates
	2) life expectancies (male and female)
	3) numbers and rates of:
	  a) violent and nonviolent crimes and locations
	  b) divorces
	  c) abortions
	  d) single-parent families (male and female)
	
	B. Ethnic/Ethnolinguistic Groups
	
	1) identity and country of origin (national heritage)
	2) number of immigrants this group-last year, 5 years ago
	3) population by census tracts, and by zones, districts or regions
	4) religious affiliations, number and/or percent of adherents
	
	C. Social Concerns and Needs
	Many areas of social concern and need exist in every city. Identify, describe and status the prevalent concerns and needs. Some categories to consider:
		A. Vital Statistics (for each significant geo area where data is available)
		
		1) births out of wedlock, age of mother
		2) unemployed (age, race)
		3) those below the poverty line
		
		B. Ethnic/Ethnolinguistic Groups.
		
		1) primary and secondary language or particular dialect (e.g. dialects of Chinese would be Mandarin, Cantonese or Hakka), number of speakers of each language/dialect
		2) description of each group's physical, social and economic condition and needs
		3) identity of government or other non-Church sponsored programs to help the group
		
		C. Socio-Cultural Groups. *Identify as many of the groups as possible in this category in addition to the ethnic groups. These will have distinctives other than race or ethnicity, such as economic class, occupations, generational culture, students, etc. Record the following data where possible and practicable:*
		(Note: you may desire to gather some of this

Harvest Field Data Table

Initial-Phase 1 Data	Primary-Phase 2 Data	Extended-Phase 3 Data

category/levels (per census)
b) by geo area-census tract/block, or zones/regions
	1) Health and medical care
	2) Alcohol and drug abuse
	3) Homeless and destitute care
	4) Abortion/crisis pregnancy
	5) Teen pregnancy
	6) Child and parent abuse
	7) Violent/non-violent crime
	8) Pornography
	9) High school dropouts/attendance
	10) Main sources of pain e.g. injustice, poverty, corruption in government, discrimination, etc."
	
	D. Media
	The media makes a tremendous impact for good or evil upon individuals, segments of society, and the entire city.
	
	Identify the various media producers and publishers, and their products. Identify which media groups and companies are producing and/or broadcasting material considered to be: a) deleterious to the moral fiber of the individuals and the community, and b) uplifting and morally excellent. Include:
	
	   a. Television
	   b. Radio
	
	E. City History
		data during Phase-Two for illustration or case-studies.)
		  1) identifier/category
		  2) approximate number in this group
		  3) location in the city (census tract, zip code, zone, district or region) where there are concentrations of these people
		  4) identify/record known physical, social, economic and spiritual needs
		
		The Internet/Web may be of help. Some examples of groups are:
		
		College students School teachers
		Univ. professors Senior Citizens
		Sr Citizen shut-ins Fem. Sr.Citizens
		Baby Boomers Busters
		Upper Middle Class Generation-X
		Dock workers Taxi Drivers
		Single Moms Gangmembers
		Business CEO's Homeless
		Gov't employees Actors/actresses
		Anglo Pastors Women in Shelters
		Prostitutes Preschool children
		Attorneys Poverty class
		Pastors-churches >500 attendance
		Law enforcement personnel

Initial-Phase 1 Data

Primary-Phase 2 Data

1) Year founded
2) Founder(s) of the city
3) Reasons city was established where it is
4) Major historical events in city's history (year and purpose)
5) City slogan or motto. What is their meaning or significance? *

F. Economics

The economic distribution needs to match either the zones, census tracts, zip code areas, or other geo area for which data population data is also available. Census data often includes this data.

1) List percent and distribution of population for several different income levels (at least 5 and as many as 10).

G. Industry and Commerce

1) Identify 6 leading industries. Note annual earnings, number of employees, annual sales/income, products, services, annual exports

H. Religions

Provide data for past year, 3, 5 and 10 years ago. Include all religions and religious cults: Christian, Muslims, Jews, Hindus, Bud-

Extended-Phase 3 Data

D. Social Concerns and Needs

Many areas of social concern and need exist in every city. Identify, describe and status the prevalent concerns and needs. Some categories to consider are:

1) Single parent family care
2) Immoral and violent TV/videos
3) Family counseling
4) Job training and placement
5) Religious killings and burnings
6) Good water, energy, shelter
7) Gangs, mob and riot control
8) High school dropouts/attendance

E. Arts and Entertainment

Identify which are present in the city, and provide a thumbnail description of the groups, rating their popularity (based upon audience attendance) on a scale of 1 to 3 (1 = mildly popular, 2 = moderately popular, 3 = very popular).

1) Actors and actresses guild, play-houses, opera houses, theaters, etc.
2) Entertainment centers, game parks, etc.
3) Sports teams and sports, e.g. football, hockey, basketball, baseball, skiing/ snow-boarding, gymnastics, soccer, etc.

Harvest Field Data Table

Initial-Phase 1 Data	Primary-Phase 2 Data	Extended-Phase 3 Data
	theists, Animists, Spiritists, Atheists, Humanists, etc.. Give breakdown of Christians by Catholics, Protestants, Orthodox, and the estimated percent evangelical of each. Also include all cults, e.g. Moonies, Mormons (LDS), Jehovah Witnesses, New Age, Satanist groups, witches covens, etc. Include number of Sikhs, Punjabis, Bahai, Jains, etc. Gather the following information: 1) name/identity 2) number and percent of population of adherents **I. Worldview of the Unchurched** *Note: The following data items are also found in Phase-3, L. For the congress you well may want to have some of the following information available to help paint the picture of the context in which the Church finds herself.* 1) What are the predominant secular philosophies (worldviews) in the area? Humanism? Rationalism? Enlightenment? Materialism? Anti-establishmentarianism? What is the level of their influence? 2) Are Native Americans practicing their native religions? What percentage? 3) Are there any Voodoo or other Spiritist religions being practiced in the city?	track, auto racing, horse racing, etc. **F. Media** *The media makes a tremendous impact for good or evil upon individuals, segments of society, and the entire city. It is incumbent upon those involved in citywide transformational ministries to have accurate, up-to-date information relating to the presence, quality and impact of the media.* 1) Identify the various media producers and publishers, and their products. Identify which media groups and companies are producing, publishing, and/or broadcasting material considered: a) deleterious to the moral fiber of the individuals and the community, and b) uplifting and morally excellent. Include: a. Magazines b. Pornography publishers/retailers (TV, videos, films, magazines, literature, etc.) c. Newspapers d. Videos and video stores/retailers (include the Internet/Web) e. Movies and movie theaters f. Public mass meetings

Initial-Phase 1 Data	Primary-Phase 2 Data	Extended-Phase 3 Data
	4) What are the main reasons the unchurched do not attend any church? Do they feel the Church has any worthwhile purpose? Do they feel they can be good Christians and not attend Church?	**G. Cultural Events** *Understanding the cultural traditions and events is needful in understanding the personality and functions of the city. This information, coupled with that disclosed by spiritual mapping can lead to determining why things are the way they are in the city, and also will lead to a deeper understanding of the forces for good and for evil. Document the following:* 1) Celebrations - annual citywide celebrations such as: parades, special city holidays, rallies, rodeos, fairs, Native American events/celebrations, etc., the sponsors and the history. Also document any accompanying rituals. 2) City themes, mascot(s), slogan(s), etc. 3) "Sister City" - many cities have a "sister" city somewhere in the world 4) Museums, zoos, other attractions **H. Economics** 1) Land values-by census tract, zone or district 2) Housing values-by census tract, zone or district

Harvest Field Data Table

Initial-Phase 1 Data	Primary-Phase 2 Data	Extended-Phase 3 Data
		I. Industry and Commerce 1) Major trade partners for city industries. Major exports and imports. 2) Transportation: airports (annual traffic), harbors/ports (annual traffic/tonnage), major truck lines headquartered in city (tonnage per year), municipal bus lines & rapid transit (passengers per year). **J. Religions** *Provide data for past year, 3, 5 and 10 years ago for Muslims, Hindus, Buddhists, Bahai, Sikhs, etc.* 1) Number of immigrants for each religion for each of the above data years (city planning office may help here-but data will probably lag a year or two). Give country of emigration if known. **K. Government and Politics** *Document: names, date entered office, phone numbers, and office addresses for the following:* 1) Other major department heads (See Phase 2 - provide title & responsibility information) 2) Political party leaders (provide party, role and candidacy if applicable)

Harvest Field Data Table

Initial-Phase 1 Data	Primary-Phase 2 Data	Extended-Phase 3 Data
		L. Worldview of the Unchurched *See note under Phase Two, item I.* 1) What are the predominant secular philosophies (worldviews) in the area? Humanism? Rationalism? Enlightenment? Materialism? Anti-establishmentarianism? What is the level of their influence? 2) Are Native Americans practicing their native religions? What percentage? 3) Are there any Voodoo or other Spiritist religions being practiced in the city? What is their identity? Where in the city? Do any offer animal or other sacrifices?* 4) What are the main reasons the unchurched do not attend any church? Do they feel the Church has any worthwhile purpose? Do they feel they can be good Christians and not attend church?

Painting the Analysis Picture

This appendix contains information on how to display the data you will need for a comprehensive analysis of the city. You will find an array of sample graphics including maps in Appendices "I", "J", and "K". You may want to generate formats tailored to your particular application.

With today's computers, converting tabular data into graphics is fairly straightforward. This will greatly enhance the communicability and understandability of the data. This is not to sell tables short. Tables in themselves are very helpful, and often insightful observations can be made from them, especially tables of growth rates. Bar, line and pie graphs each have their applications and different types of graphs optimize the picture of the data for analysis and communication. Maps are vital for any spacial relationships, and can depict a wide variety of compound themes. Color is very helpful, but not mandatory.

In this section we look at the *two general data categories* and how to display them using basically *three data formats* .

Categories	**Formats**
1. Harvest Force	1. Tabular (tables)
2. Harvest Field	2. Graphical
	3. Cartographical (maps)

(Note: The actual statistical and factorial analyses processes are treated in Chapter 9.)

Although you may not feel it is necessary to generate every table, graph and map specified in the following pages, each one has been listed to provide a comprehensive analysis, and to provide insights into growth cause and effect relationships. Many are needed for comparison and to provide further interpretation of other tables, graphs and/or maps. It is important to differentiate between the apparent and the real. An example of this would be in searching to know, of the growth measured, what portion is biological, transfer or conversion. The answer to this question then leads into a whole new realm of analysis. Some sample tables and graphs are provided to give you an idea of how they could be constructed. Most of the samples herein have been constructed using the Microsoft Excel spreadsheet.

NOTE!! *When making tables and graphs, give them the identity specified to aid for cross-referencing.* <u>*Some samples are provided.*</u>

Harvest Force-Mathematical Analysis

Before you move into formatting the data, and on into Factorial Analysis you need to review the following calculations (they are essential to further analysis and painting the final picture). You should have already performed most if not all of these calculations as you were formatting your data as outlined earlier. In that case, this will just be a good review. Appendix-M, Growth Rates may be of assistance.

You should make the calculations for each of the following conditions. Some exceptions may apply.

1. For last year, 3,5, and 10 years ago where data is available.
2. For each selected area or areas (e.g. zones, districts, tracts, etc.); each ethnic and/or other identifiable group for which data is available.

A. *Identify and status churches*

1. Define total number of churches (Protestant, Catholic, Orthodox, Other, cell, house, organized, unorganized, etc.)
2. Define the number of churches for each of the above specified years, and for each geo and ethnic entity
3. Calculate the growth rates (AGR, AAGR, DGR)
4. Calculate the "population per church ratio"
5. Calculate the average church size (based upon attendance. Where attendance data not available, use membership.
   - # of churches in each of 4 ranges->1000, 500-1000, 150-500, <150 (for major areas and groups)

B. *Attendance (and/or membership).* Attendance data is preferred over membership; however, this data may not be available in all cases, and definitions may vary among denominations. Do not mix *attendance* and *membership* data, unless you have no other data. Where *attendance* data is very spotty, and you have more complete *membership* data, make your calculations using *membership*.

Calculate the following for, and in addition to, the attributes outlined at the beginning of this *Mathematical Analysis* section, e.g. rates, distribution, etc..

1. Growth rates-Annual (AGR), Average Annual (AAGR), and Decadal (DGR)
2. Age groups (0-12, 13-18, 19-30, 31-50, 51-65, >65) if and where data is available

C. *Baptisms-number by type*

1. "Infant" - in the first four years of their life. (Low priority.)
2. "Believers" - those who have been baptized as the result of a profession of their faith in Jesus Christ as Lord and Savior.

D. *Small groups or "cells" - Nurture.* Include Bible studies, neighborhood prayer cells, shepherding groups, etc. those groups attended mainly by Christians for nurture and fellowship. Calculate the following for, and in addition to, the attributes outlined at the beginning of this *Mathematical Analysis* section, e.g. rates, distribution, etc..

1. Number of Small Group Studies or Cells. (Identify those cells formed exclusively for prayer.)
2. Attendance

E. *Small groups - Evangelistic.* Include: "outposts," preaching points, evangelistic home Bible studies, i.e. groups that are primarily evangelistic in purpose and function. Identify the following for, and in addition to, the attributes outlined at the beginning of this *Mathematical Analysis section*, e.g. rates, distribution, etc..

1. Number of Evangelistic Small Group Studies

2. Attendance
3. Decisions for accepting Christ as Lord and Savior

Harvest Force-Denominations

A. **Statistical Tables - Denomination.** (Note: *There are several table samples in Appendix I*).

1. **Basic Data Tables-Tables D1 & D2.** You will need two tables: Table D-1 depicting the following data for each denomination; Table D-2 depicting basic data for all of the denominations. In the latter, list denominations in decreasing order according to attendance. These two tables should include:
   - churches *
   - attendance*
   - members *
   - baptisms (believer's)*
   - average church size *
   - cell/small groups (nurture)
   - cell/small groups (evangelistic)
   - neighborhood prayer cells/houses of prayer
   - new churches started past year

            * = priority/fundamental data

DENOMINATION DATA				
Denomination:				
		Basic Data		
	Last year Yr.	3 yrs ago Yr.	5 yrs ago Yr.	10 yrs ago Yr.
Churches				
Attendance				
Members				
Baptisms ("Believer's")				
Average church size				
small groups-nurture				
small groups-outreach				
Prayer cells				

Table D-1 Sample

2. **Denominational *Growth Rate* Table-Table D-3.** List

churches and attendance for: most recent data year, previous year, 3, 5 & 10 years ago. List growth rates for both, (a) churches and (b) attendance for each period.

Notes:
1. *Formulas and instructions for calculating growth rates, as well as sample growth rate graphs, are found in Appendix-M.*

2. *Small group/cell data and rates can be very meaningful data pertaining to the "growing edge" of the Church. However, at the denominational level there may not be many groups maintaining the data. Nevertheless, depict whatever data is available.*

3. **Denominational *Growth Projection* Table-Table D-4**. This table shows the growth rates for the past 5 years and makes projections for the next 5 and 10 years based upon: a) the same growth rate, b) increased rate of 2.5%, c) increased rate of 5%, and d) increased rate of 7.5%. Both, churches and attendance or members should be depicted for each denomination.

B. **Bar Graphs – Denomination.**
1. Utilizing data from Table D-2 you previously prepared, construct the following *horizontal* bar graphs:
   a. Descending order of denominations by number of churches
   b. Descending order of denominations by attendance (or members)
   c. Descending order of denominations by baptisms

2. Prepare the following *horizontal* bar graphs:
   a. Descending order by rate of growth of churches (5 year AAGR)
   b. Descending order by rate of growth of attendance (5 year AAGR)

3. Prepare the following *vertical* bar graphs:

a. Growth *rates*-aggregate of all denominations-for past year, 3, 5, and 10 years based on churches.
b. Growth *rates*-top 10 fastest growing denominations based on churches.
c. Growth *rates*-top 10 fastest growing denominations based on attendance (or members)

Note: *see Appendix "M" for how to use Standard and Semi-log graphs for depicting rate comparisons.*

B. Denominational Pie Graphs
1. Percent of denominations in each basic ecclesiastical tradition, e.g. old mainline (United Meth., Episcopal, etc.), evangelical, pentecostal, charismatic, holiness, Catholic, Orthodox, etc.
2. Percent of denominations in each of 6 size groupings based upon average church size (attendance or members). (i.e. <50, 51-100, 101-200, 201-350, 351-500, >500

C. Denominational Line Graph (Depict for as many years as data is available.)

1. Construct line graphs of the following entities. Restrict number of denominations per graph to approximately ten for readability. Utilize data for all previous years available.
a. Churches
b. Attendance (or members if attendance data too sparse)
c. Attendance projections for same rate, +2.5%, and +5.0% rate increases for next 20 years for top 10 denominations.
2. Construct aggregate line graph including all denominations for each of the above entities.

D. Maps-Denominations
1. Location of denominational offices and related churches

Harvest Force-Local Churches
Note: *For most local church data it will be helpful to have*

*tables and graphs by region, district, or zone (in addition to
the overall city tables/graphs) for these will be useful in analysis,
planning and strategy development, especially to those involved
in the overall citywide strategy initiative.*

A. Statistical Tables - Local Church

Note: In each situation where church size is the issue, *attendance*
data is preferred over *members*. However in some situations
attendance data may not be available, and in those situations
members can be used.

1. **Basic Data Tables-Table C-1 & C-2**. You will need two
   data tables. Table C-1 for each local church, and Table C-2
   listing all the churches in decreasing or increasing order by
   attendance (or members if attendance data not available). Data
   should be recorded for: last year, and 3,5, and 10 years previous.

   Each table should contain the following data (as a minimum):
   - Attendance
   - Members
   - Baptisms (believer's vs infant)
   - Baptisms per attendance
   - Small groups (nurture-Christians)
   - Small groups (Evangelistic outreach))
   - Prayer cells/houses of prayer (specifically for intercessory
     prayer)
   - Worship services per week (not just Sunday)
   - Full-time staff

#	Church	Year Began	Data Year	Ave. Attend.	Memb.	Believer's Baptisms Data Yr.	Bapt. per Attend. Ratio	Small Groups Nurture	Small Groups Outreach	Prayer Cells/Houses of Prayer	Full-Time Staff	No. Worship Services-/Wk
	New Hope Church	1983	1998	4000	4,850	328	1:122	260	94	285	16	5
	Central Foursquare	1947	1998	2000	2,244	78	1:26	86	14	85	11	3

Table C-2 Sample

Note: *Attendance. This statistic would be average attendance for last month of data period, not for the entire year, nor just the final week of the period.*

2. **Growth Rate Table-Table C-3**. List churches in decreasing order by number of attendance (or members if attendance data not available). Data will need to be depicted for 1, 3, 5 and 10 years previous, and rates (AAGR) for 3, 5, & 10 years. See Table C-3 below.

Churches Growth Rate Data Table							
Church	**Attendance**				**AAGR**	**AAGR**	**AGR**
	1988	**1993**	**1997**	**1998**	**88-93**	**93-98**	**97-98**
New Hope	1475	2660	3630	4000	12.5%	8.5%	10.2%
Central Foursquare	1530	1790	1805	2000	3.2%	2.2%	10.8%
Living Waters Fellowship	640	925	1120	1200	7.6%	5.3%	7.1%
Westside Church of God	620	840	900	925	6.3%	1.9%	2.8%
First Baptist	500	575	605	650	2.8%	2.5%	7.4%
Trinity Lutheran	475	560	565	575	3.3%	0.5%	1.8%
Hillside Presbyterian	395	430	450	450	1.7%	0.9%	0.0%
Rose Hill Nazarene	270	360	395	425	5.9%	3.4%	7.6%
First Adventist	340	355	380	400	0.9%	2.4%	5.3%
Grace Epsicopal	340	355	365	375	0.9%	1.1%	2.7%
United Methodist	460	375	315	300	-4.0%	-4.4%	-4.8%

Table C-3

3. **Growth Projection Table-Table C-4**. List churches in decreasing order by number of attendance. In one column list attendance for latest year. In next column list AAGR for last 5 years. Add four columns and calculate projected attendance for next 5 years based upon: a) rate for past 5 years, b) increase rate of 2.5%, c) increase rate of 5.0%, and d) increase rates of 7.5%. (See Table C-4 sample below.)

Church Projection Table

Church	Attendance		5 Year AAGR	Attendance Projections 5 Years			
	1993	1998	93-98	Same	(+)2.5%	(+)5%	(+)7.5%
New Hope	2660	4000	0.085	6015	6741	7535	8402
Central Foursquare	1790	2000	0.022	2235	2522	2837	3184
Living Waters Fellowship	925	1200	0.053	1554	1747	1959	2191
Westside Church of God	840	925	0.019	1019	1150	1294	1453
First Baptist	575	650	0.025	735	829	932	1046
Trinity Lutheran	560	575	0.005	590	668	753	846
Hillside Presbyterian	430	450	0.009	471	532	600	674
Rose Hill Nazarene	360	425	0.034	502	565	635	712
First Adventist	355	400	0.024	451	508	572	642
United Methodist	300	240	-0.044	192	218	248	280
Totals	**8495**	**10625**	XXXXXXXX	**13762**	**15480**	**17365**	**19429**

Table C-4 Sample

Note: *the vertical bar graph below shows the number of increased attendance over a 5 year period for the above rates.*

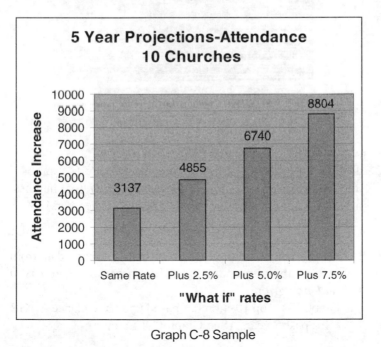

Graph C-8 Sample

B. Bar Graphs - Local Church (See **Appendix "J"** for additional samples.

   1. Bar Graph-Basic-Graph C1 & C2. Utilizing data from Table C-2 (sample on page 7) prepare the following *basic **horizontal** bar graph*s for the churches:
   a. Graph C-1. Attendance in descending or ascending order. See sample above:
   b. Graph C-2. Baptisms in descending or ascending order.

Graph C-1 Sample

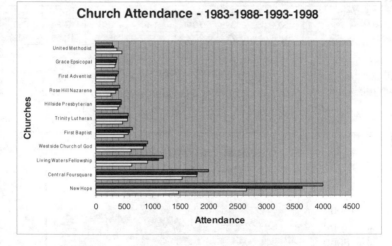

   2. Bar Graph-Rates. Utilizing data from Table C-2 prepare the following ***horizontal*** *growth rate bar graph* for churches:
   a. Graph C-3. Growth rate of attendance (or members) in descending or ascending order.

   3. Bar Graph-Rate Comparison-churches. Utilizing data from Table C-3 above prepare the following *rate comparison **vertical** bar graphs*:
   a. Graph C-4. Top 10 churches based upon attendance AAGR for past 5 years. (See Graph C-4 Sample)

    b. Graph C-5. Aggregate of top ten growing churches – last year, 3 and 5 years ago – based upon attendance (or members) (see sample)

    c. Graph C-6. Median ten churches - (same)

    d. Graph C-7. Ten slowest growing churches - (same) (same)

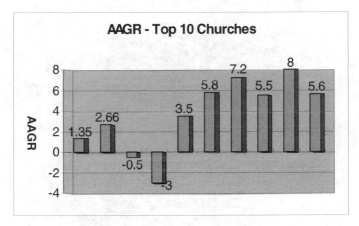

Graph C-4 Sample

4. **Bar Graphs-Projections** Utilizing data from Tables C-4 above prepare the following *vertical bar projection* graph:

    a. Graph C-8 (see sample on page H-9). Using as a base the last year's attendance for the top 10 churches, add columns depicting the projected attendance *increase* for a 5 year period for each of the following rates:

      ♦ latest year rate

      ♦ latest year rate +2.5%

      ♦ latest year rate +5.0%

      ♦ latest year rate +7.5

C. **Pie Graphs - Local Church** – construct the following *pie* graphs from local church and denominational summary data tables (See below and **Appendix "J"** for samples):

1. Graph C-9. Number of churches in each of the following nine

size grouping as percent of total churches:
  less than (<) 50, 50-100, 101-200, 201-350, 351-500, 501-750, 751-1000, 1001-2000, >2000 – based upon Attendance (or Members if Attendance data not available or in majority).

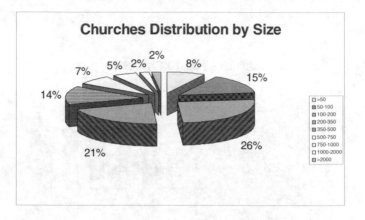

Graph C-9 Sample

2.. Graph C-10. Based upon five year average annual growth rates (AAGR) of Attendance or Members, the number of churches (expressed in % of total) experiencing the following six rate groups: <0, 0-2.5, 2.6-5, 5.1-7.5, 7.6-10, >10

3. Number of churches or worship centers (expressed in % of total) in each of the following categories:
  a. Graph C-11. Old mainline (United Presbyterian, United Methodist, Lutheran, Episcopal) Congregational, Pentecostal, Holiness, Baptist, Independents
  b. Graph C-12. Protestant, Catholic & Orthodox, No Affiliation (Independents), "Other" world religions and cults.

4. Graph C-13. Distribution of age group of Attendees or Members

C. Line Graphs - Local Church (plot as many data points for as many years as you have data) (See **Appendix "J"** for samples.)
  1. Graph C-14. Make a history graph based upon attendance (or

members) for the top five largest churches.

2. Graph C-15. Make a history graph based upon attendance (or members) for the five fastest growing churches with last data year's attendance 100 and over.

3. Graph C-16. Repeat #2 above for churches less than 100 attendees (or members).

4. Make a *projection* line graphs for: (Graph C-17) largest two churches, and (Graph C-18) two fastest growing churches with attendance >100. On graphs depict attendance growth history for past 10 years, and then projections for 10 years based upon the AAGR for the past 5 years. Show past AAGR's for each church. Also plot projected attendance for one or more of the following rate increases: +2.5%, + 5.0%, and 7.5%.

   See previous projection tables (Example: Table C-4 Sample) and Appendix "M" for how to determine projected numbers. A spreadsheet such as Microsoft Xcel or Corel Quattro Pro can automatically do the calculations.

D. Maps – Local Church You will want to construct maps for displaying primarily church location data in relation to other data, including possibly a variety of geopolitical entities, e.g. Zip Code or Census Tract, zone, district, etc. See **Appendix "K"** for sample maps.

Notes:
*1. See **Appendix "L"** for suggestions for constructing maps, and **Appendix "N"** for suggestions for mapping software.*
*2. You may find it beneficial to get familiar with the Mapping Center of Evangelism's **tailor-made Kingdom Combine**$_2$ city mapping system that is available for every major city^2.*
3. See Maps-Composite later in this chapter for additional church-related map listings.

   Construct the following maps. Using a variety of combinations of icon shapes and sizes, you can create attractive maps that

    communicate well.
1. Distribution of Churches – a basic map plus the following variations:
    a. Tailor icon size or shape to indicate church size (use size grouping in C.1. above)
    b. Tailor icon to indicate churches having particular characteristics. For example: Churches involved in prayer-walking, those with evangelistic small groups, neighborhood houses of prayer (or lighthouses), benevolent outreach ministries, counseling centers, etc.
2. Distribution of church membership. The membership of several churches in an area can be mapped using a different icon for each church. This map can then be used for visitor follow-up and cell group planning.
3. Church benevolent ministry distribution.

Parachurch Groups

A. Tables – Parachurch. Construct the following tables:
1. List parachurch groups in alphabetical order. Include the following data: denominational affiliation, type (education, youth, literature, media, church planting, research, mobilization, sports, benevolence, etc., etc..), year begun in city, full-time staff, part-time staff, target areas, target peoples, annual budget.

B. Bar Graphs – Parachurch
1. Horizontal stacked bar graph-organizational list ranked in descending order by full-time staff,and showing part-time staff.

C. Pie Graphs – Parachurch
1. Primary ministry type groups – number of organizations as percent of the total: evangelism, church planting, benevolence, youth/college, education, media, social services, counseling, other.

D. Line Graphs-Parachurch
1. Number of parachurch groups in the city – over past 50 years

E. Maps-Parachurch

    1. Location of parachurch groups offices and ministries (e.g. Rescue Missions, counseling centers, food and clothing distribution points, Christian bookstores, etc.

Harvest Field

A. Tables - Harvest Field

    1. **Basic geopolitical/demographic table**. This table(s) provides the summary for the greater city area, and for the major geopolitical subdivisions. More than one table may be required in order to accommodate different geographic and/or geopolitical subdivisions, such as districts, zones, neighborhoods, census tracts, zip codes, etc..

    The column headings are the various data variables, and the rows will be the geopolitical entities. The column headings should include:

    *geo entity * population * pop. year * % of total pop * pop. growth rate *pop. density, *area –sq. miles, *area-sq. km, *majority race or ethnic group & % of pop., *age groups (builders, boomers, busters, gen-x, millenials, and youth [13-18], and children [12 and below]), *socio-economic (unemployed, lower/middle/ upper, number on welfare), *civil status (married, single, divorce, single parent, widowed, etc.),*

    Where information is available you should also record the above population data for the preceding 3, 5 and 10 years (needed to correlate with church data for several different calculations).

    2. **Ethnic or people group summary table**. This table lists basic data for the various ethnic groups in the city, and summarizes them. The data depicted would include:

    *population *pop. year *pop. growth rate *percent of population *per capita income *majority religion *percent*

Christian *percent evangelical *immigration rate (past year, and/or past 5 years) *native language *number of speakers *number bilingual with English *crime rate (violent and nonviolent) *major occupations

3. **Other vital statistics table.** This table lists the various vital statistics pertinent to the city. This data may not be available for geopolitical subdivisions, but only for the entire city or MSA. Where there is data for some second or third order geo entity the table should reflect this.

   The table should include the following:
   - *crime rates (violent and nonviolent),*
   - *homeless (male/female),*
   - *abortions (by age),*
   - *gangs,*
   - *accidental deaths (list causes),*
   - *number of pornography points (adult bookstore, strip joints, etc.)*

B. Bar Graphs – Harvest Field

1. **Horizontal Bar Graph.** Construct the following horizontal bar graphs-descending order-for the major geopolitical entities used for displaying data (such as district, zones, or neighborhoods):
   a. Graph S-1. Population
   b. Graph S-2. Population density
   c. Graph S-3. Crime (show number of violent and non-violent stacked on same line)
   d. Graph S-4. Average Income
   e. Primary Needs and Concerns

2. **Vertical Bar Graph**
   a. Graph S-5. Population growth rate for city – every 5 years for 50 years
   b. Graph S-6. Population growth rates for each major geopolitical entity-latest data available
   c. Graph S-7. Major ethnic group populations

C.   Pie Graphs – Harvest Field Construct the following pie graphs:
1.   Graph S-8. Age groups - Percentages of population (use grouping found in 2.C.4 above)
2.   Graph S-9. Religious adherents - Breakdown of the various religions in the city (as percentage of total population)
3.   Graph S-10. Christians – Protestant (with Evangelical subdivision if data available), Catholic, Orthodox, Cults – for latest data year available
4.   Graph S-11. Major ethnic groups (top eight) as percent of population.
5.   Graph S-12. Socio-cultural groups distribution (See Graph S-X)
6.   Graph S-13. Economic distribution - Five levels from Census data (latest update).
7.   Graph S-14. Occupation distribution – By major occupations (if data available)
8.   Graph S-15. Industry distribution – Census data or other source

D.   Line Graphs – Harvest Field - Construct the following line graphs:

1.   Graph S-16. Population history - past 50 years or more (sample next page)

Graph S-16 Sample

2. Graph S-17. Population – total, African American, Native American, Asian, Hispanic, Middle East, Other-for past 50 years (and/or 25 years)

E. **Maps – Harvest Field.** Note: *Color maps are most effective, but with foresight you can make maps by using various griddings, icon/point shapes and sizes, and variation in lines that will be effective if printed in black and white.*
Construct the following maps:
1. Basic street map showing main streets, freeways, parks, rivers, railways, and major public buildings.
2. Population distribution by Census Tract, zone and/or district
3. Population density by Census Tract, zone and/or district
4. Ethnic group distribution-majority group for each geo entity (use Census or other data)
5. Economic distribution by Census Tracts (or blocks)
6. Murder and robbery locations
7. Porno points and crime rates (violent and nonviolent)
8. Distribution of single parent families
9. Senior citizen distribution by Census Tract
10. Location of cult headquarters and meeting points. Identify Mason headquarters and meeting places. Identify high point in city.
11. Social-economic mapping (Lifestyle mapping, Percepts)
12. Primary needs and concerns (Percepts)

Composite Harvest Force/Harvest Field

Prepare combinations of Harvest Force and Harvest Field data into the following formats.

A. **Tables - Composite**
1. Table B-1. Population per church ratio-geo. Depict: geo entities, population, population density, number of churches, population per church ratio.
2. Table B-2. Population per church ratio-ethnic. Depict: ethnic groups, population, number of churches, population per church ratio.

B. Bar Graphs – Composite
  1. Horizontal Bar Graph – Construct the following:
      a. Population per church by geo entities (same entities as used in Harvest Force and Harvest Field data) – descending order
      b. Population per church by ethnic minorities

C. Pie Graphs - Composite
  1. Number of churches by ethnic minorities
  2. Population per church by ethnic minorities

D. Line Graphs – Composite
  1. Church attendance (or members) and population growth history

E. Maps - Composite
  1. Church locations and crime points or porno points (adult book and video stores, strip joints, etc.)
  2. Church locations and majority ethnic (largest ethnic minority for that geo entity)
  3. Population per church.

Summary and Conclusions

Now that you have your data into these various formats you have probably discovered the following:
  1. You see some very interesting results or trends you think will make good case studies.
  2. There are some holes in the data that need to be filled.
  3. There are some apparent anomalies that need to be explained, and require further explanation and investigation.
  4. You can now see some obvious areas where specific work needs to be done.
  5. You have indications there are some very effective ministries being carried forth; and some not so effective.
  6. You now have a preliminary measurement for evaluating against the basic saturation church-planting goals.

You should realize this emerging picture will be of utmost importance to many pastors and other leaders, including those leading the citywide initiative, if one is operational. Many others will also be vitally interested in the information, once they get exposed to it, or know it exists. It will be very helpful if you have the graphics in a program from which it is easy to print in color. If you do not have access to a color printer, take your disk to the nearest service shop, such as Kinkos. They can handle most software, and can readily make overhead transparencies.

You can import your graphics into presentation programs, such as PowerPoint or Corel Presentations and organize them into slide shows, or use these to print from. You can communicate the graphics over the Internet to those whom you want in your audience (of course, with the proper authorization and precautions).

You will be able to generate very informative and attractive reports. By utilizing the right software you can make your reports easily updateable.

If you have been able to generate a good share of the foregoing analysis, you are probably the most knowledgeable person around. Now the task is to get the right information into the right hands at the right time.

TABLES

This appendix contains samples of tables for a variety of applications. Some of them have appeared in other settings, mainly in Appendix "H".

In many current computer applications, making these tables can be very straight-forward. Rather than constructing a blank table and then filling it in with data, whenever you have your data in a database and spreadsheet program, most all of them can generate tables similar to those shown.

Database software such as Access, Paradox and dBase contain "report" functions to help you format the data into a tabular and graphic formats. This is also true of spreadsheet programs such as Excel and Quattro Pro, which also have good graphic capabilities.

Tables samples included are:

1. "District" Church Data
2. Denominational Data
3. Ethnic Group Data
4. Organization - People Group Data
5. Church Data -A
6. Church Data -B
7. Local Church Diagnostic Period
8. Churches Growth Rate Data Table
9. Attendance Projection Table
10. Diagnostic Period Table and Graph

DISTRICT' CHURCH DATA

Zone/District Census District, etc.	Zone ID	Pop.	Churches	Average Attend.	Memb.	Average Ch. Size	Believer's Baptisms	Houses/Cells of Prayer	Pop per Church

DENOMINATIONAL DATA

Denomination	Abbr.	Eccles. Tradition	Churches	Average Attend.	Memb.	Average Ch. Size	Believer's Baptisms	Houses/Cells of Prayer	Pop per Church

ETHNIC GROUP DATA

Ethnic Groups	Abbr.	Pop.	Churches	Average Attend.	Memb.	Average Ch. Size	Believer's Baptisms	Prayer Cells	Pop per Church

ORGANIZATION - PEOPLE GROUP DATA

Data Year:___	Page ___ of ___		People Groups										
People Group Name>>>													
Denomination/ Organization/ Church	Total Churches	Total Attend	Churches	Attend	Churches	Attend	Churches	Attend	Churches	Attend	Churches	Attend

Church Data - A

Data Year:_____

#	Church	Year Began	Data Year	Ave. Attend.	Memb.	Believer's Baptisms Data Yr.	Bapt. per Attend. Ratio	Small Groups Nurture	Small Groups Outreach	Prayer Cells/Houses of Prayer	Full-Time Staff	No. Worhsip Services-/Wk
	New Hope Church	1983	1998	4000	4,850	328	1:12.2	260	94	285	16	5
	Central Foursquare	1947	1998	2000	2,244	78	1:26	86	14	85	11	3

Church Data - B

Data Year:_____

#	Church	Year Began	Data Year	Ave. Attend.	Ave. Attend. -5 Yrs.	Attend. AAGR 5 Yr.	Memb. (Roll)	Believer's Baptisms Data Yr.	Small Groups (Nurture)	Small Groups (Outreach)	Intercess. Prayer Cells	Full-Time Staff	No. Worship Service-s/Wk
	New Hope Church	1983	1998	4000	2650	10.85%	4,850	328	260	94	285	16	5
	Central Foursquare	1947	1998	2000	1790	6.45%	2244	78	85	14	85	11	3

Local Church Diagnostic Period

	10 Year Diagnostic Period										
	-10 yrs	-9 Yrs	-8 Yrs	-7 Yrs	-6 Yrs	-5 yrs	-4 Yrs	-3 Yrs	-2 Yrs	-1 year	Last Year
Year											
Weekly services											
Avg. Attendance											
Baptized members											
Prayer cells (weekly)											
Weekly Bible studies											
Outreach meetings											
Daughter/cell ch's											
Pastors											

Growth Rate Table for Churches

Data Year:_____

Churches Growth Rate Data Table							
Church	**Attendance**				**AAGR**	**AAGR**	**AGR**
	1988	**1993**	**1997**	**1998**	**88-93**	**93-98**	**97-98**
New Hope	1475	2660	3630	4000	12.5%	8.5%	10.2%
Central Foursquare	1530	1790	1805	2000	3.2%	2.2%	10.8%
Living Waters Fellowship	640	925	1120	1200	7.6%	5.3%	7.1%
Westside Church of God	620	840	900	925	6.3%	1.9%	2.8%
First Baptist	500	575	605	650	2.8%	2.5%	7.4%
Trinity Lutheran	475	560	565	575	3.3%	0.5%	1.8%
Hillside Presbyterian	395	430	450	450	1.7%	0.9%	0.0%
Rose Hill Nazarene	270	360	395	425	5.9%	3.4%	7.6%
First Adventist	340	355	380	400	0.9%	2.4%	5.3%
Grace Epsicopal	340	355	365	375	0.9%	1.1%	2.7%
United Methodist	460	375	315	300	-4.0%	-4.4%	-4.8%

Attendance Projection Table

Data Year:_____

Church Projection Table							
Church	**Attendance**		**5 Year AAGR**	**Attendance Projections 5 Years**			
	1993	**1998**	**93-98**	**Same**	**(+)2.5%**	**(+)5%**	**(+)7.5%**
New Hope	2660	4000	0.085	6015	6741	7535	8402
Central Foursquare	1790	2000	0.022	2235	2522	2837	3184
Living Waters Fellowship	925	1200	0.053	1554	1747	1959	2191
Westside Church of God	840	925	0.019	1019	1150	1294	1453
First Baptist	575	650	0.025	735	829	932	1046
Trinity Lutheran	560	575	0.005	590	668	753	846
Hillside Presbyterian	430	450	0.009	471	532	600	674
Rose Hill Nazarene	360	425	0.034	502	565	635	712
First Adventist	355	400	0.024	451	508	572	642
United Methodist	300	240	-0.044	192	218	248	280
Totals	**8495**	**10625**	XXXXXXXX	**13762**	**15480**	**17365**	**19429**

Diagnostic Period Table and Graph

Diagnostic Period Table

Fill in the table below for every year data is available with the latest data year being on the right. Note there are places for 11 years of data. This is necessary to determine growth for past 10 years. Plot available data on graph using different symbols or line patterns for the different data categories.

Churches -- Attendance -- Other

(GRAPH PAPER GOES HERE)

Year	Yr	Yr	Yr	Yr	Yr	Yr	Yr	Yr	Yr	Yr	Latest Yr	AAGR Last 5 Yrs
Churches												
Attendance												

Sample Graphs

Note: This is a random sampling of graphs. There are other graph
samples in Appendix-H.

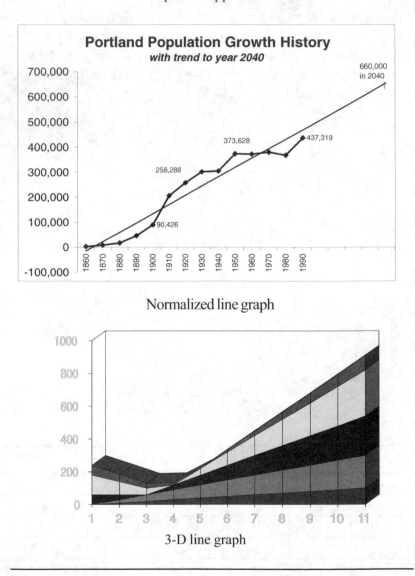

Normalized line graph

3-D line graph

Sample Pie Graphs (Charts)

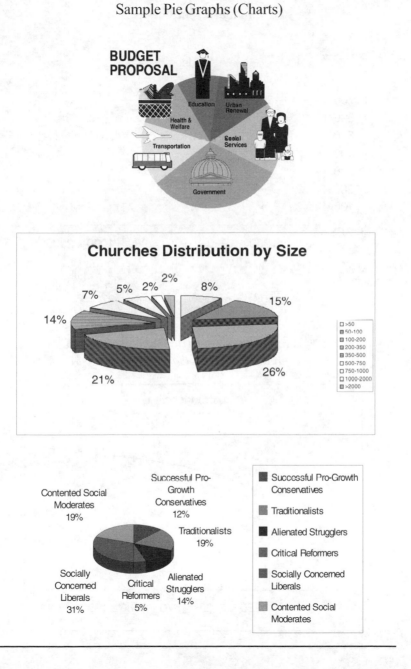

BUDGET PROPOSAL

Education
Urban Renewal
Health & Welfare
Social Services
Transportation
Government

Churches Distribution by Size

2%
5% 2% 2%
7%
8%
14%
15%
21%
26%

- □ >50
- ▣ 50-100
- ▣ 100-200
- ▣ 200-350
- ▣ 350-500
- □ 500-750
- □ 750-1000
- □ 1000-2000
- ▣ >2000

Contented Social Moderates
19%

Successful Pro-Growth Conservatives
12%

Traditionalists
19%

Socially Concerned Liberals
31%

Critical Reformers
5%

Alienated Strugglers
14%

- ■ Successful Pro-Growth Conservatives
- ■ Traditionalists
- ■ Alienated Strugglers
- ■ Critical Reformers
- ■ Socially Concerned Liberals
- ■ Contented Social Moderates

Standard Line Graph

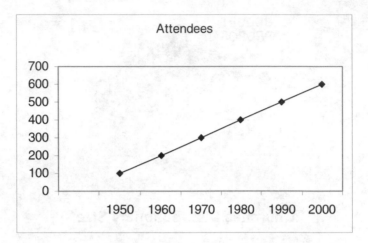

Semi-log Graph (rate sensitive)
(same data as above-also see Appendix-M)

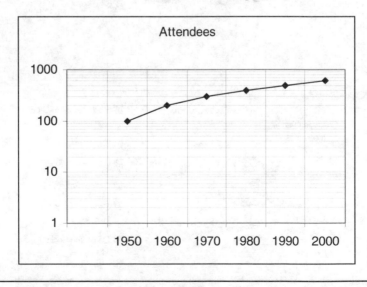

Vertical Bar Graph
(plus and minus)

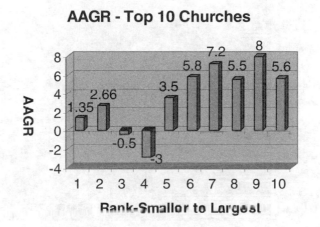

Vertical Bar Graph

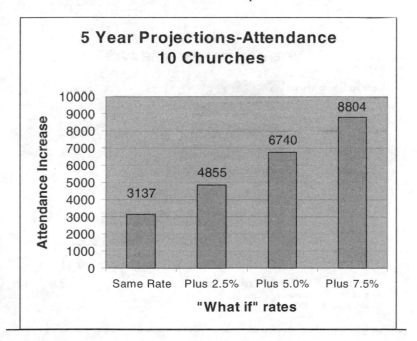

Horizontal Bar Graphs

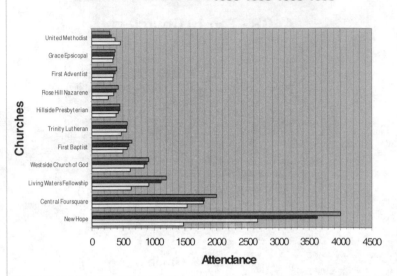

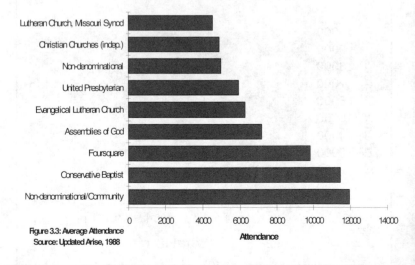

Figure 3.3: Average Attendance
Source: Updated Arise, 1988

Graph Ideas - Clip Art

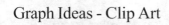

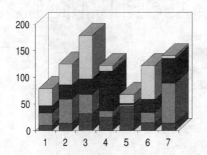

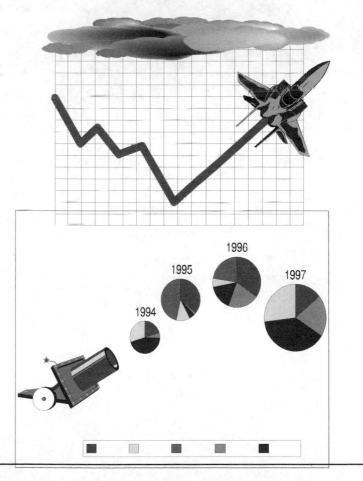

SAMPLE MAPS

This appendix contains a few samples of the dozens of meaningful maps you can make for your city. These maps were made using Atlas GIS mapping software available from Global Mapping International (www.gmi.org).

These maps and many others in color are available on CD. Contact www.discoveryourcity.com (or .org) for ordering details.

See Appendix-L for information regarding working with maps.

Map 1

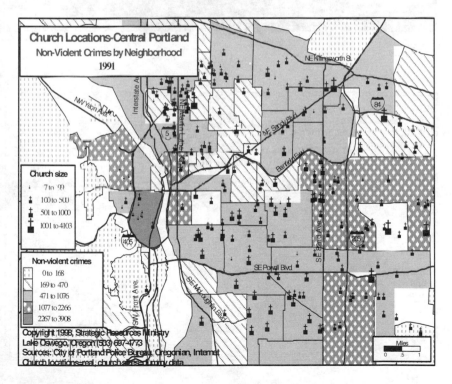

Map 2

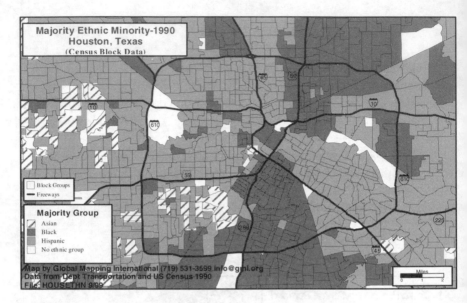

Map 3

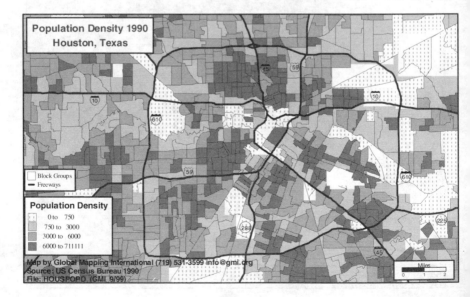

Map 4

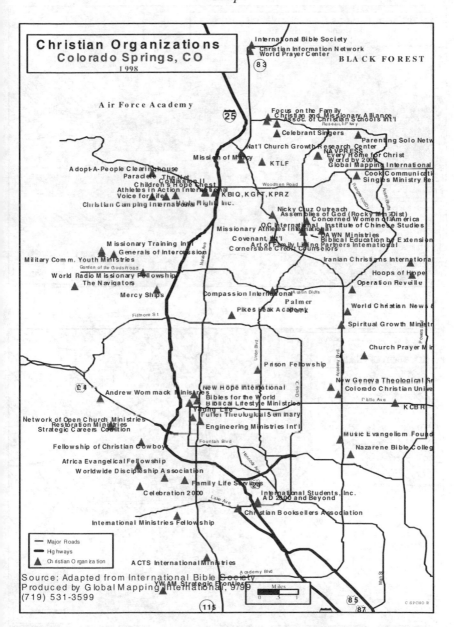

Christian Organizations
Colorado Spring, CO
1998

International Bible Society
Christian Information Network
World Prayer Center
BLACK FOREST
83

Air Force Academy
25

Focus on the Family
Christian and Missionary Alliance
Assoc. of Christian Schools Int'l
Research Pkwy

Celebrant Singers

Parenting Solo Netw

Nat'l Church Growth Research Center
NAVPRESS
Every Home for Christ
World by 2000
Global Mapping International

Mission of Mercy
KTLF

Cook Communicati
Singles Ministry Re

Adopt-A-People Clearinghouse
Paraclete
The Net
COMMISSION II
Children's Hope Chest
Athletes in Action International
Voice for Life
Christian Camping International Flight Inc.
KBIQ, KGFT, KPRZ

Woodman Road

Ranger (VOID)
North Bluffs

Nicky Cruz Outreach
Assemblies of God (Rocky Mtn Dist)
Concerned Women of America
OC International
Institute of Chinese Studies
Missionary Athletes International
Covenant Int'l
DAWN Ministries
Biblical Education by Extension
Art of Family Living Partners International
Cornerstone Credit Counselors

Missionary Training Int'l
Generals of Intercession
Military Comm. Youth Ministries
Garden of the Gods Road
World Radio Missionary Fellowship
The Navigators

Mercy Ships

Iranian Christians Internationa
Hoops of Hope
Operation Reveille

Nevada Ave

Compassion International
Austin Bluffs
Palmer
Pikes Peak Academy

World Christian New
Spiritual Growth Minist

Fillmore St

Union Blvd
Oriole Circle
Academy Blvd
Powers

Prison Fellowship

Church Prayer Mi

24
Andrew Wommack Ministries
New Hope International
Bibles for the World
Biblical Lifestyle Ministries
Young Life
Fuller Theological Seminary
Network of Open Church Ministries
Restoration Ministries
Strategic Careers Coalition
Engineering Ministries Int'l

Fountain Blvd

New Geneva Theological Se
Colorado Christian Unive
Platte Ave
KCBR

Music Evangelism Found
Nazarene Bible College

Fellowship of Christian Cowboy
Africa Evangelical Fellowship
Worldwide Discipleship Association

Family Life Services
Celebration 2000
Lake Ave
International Students, Inc.
AD 2000 and Beyond
Christian Booksellers Association

Hancock Ave

International Ministries Fellowship

- Major Roads
- Highways
▲ Christian Organization

ACTS International Ministries
Academy Blvd
Main St

Source: Adapted from International Bible Society
Produced by Global Mapping International, 9/99
(719) 531-3599
YWAM Strategic Frontiers

Miles
0   .5   1

115
85
87
C SPCHO R

Map 5

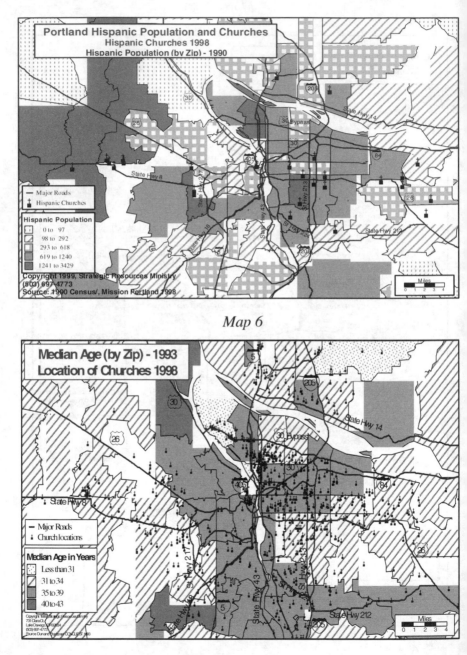

Portland Hispanic Population and Churches
Hispanic Churches 1998
Hispanic Population (by Zip) - 1990

— Major Roads
† Hispanic Churches

Hispanic Population
- 0 to 97
- 98 to 292
- 293 to 618
- 619 to 1240
- 1241 to 3429

Copyright 1999, Strategic Resources Ministry
(503) 697-4773
Source: 1990 Census/, Mission Portland 1998

Miles
0 1 2 3 4

Map 6

Median Age (by Zip) - 1993
Location of Churches 1998

— Major Roads
† Church locations

Median Age in Years
- Less than 31
- 31 to 34
- 35 to 39
- 40 to 43

Miles
0 1 2 3 4

Map 7

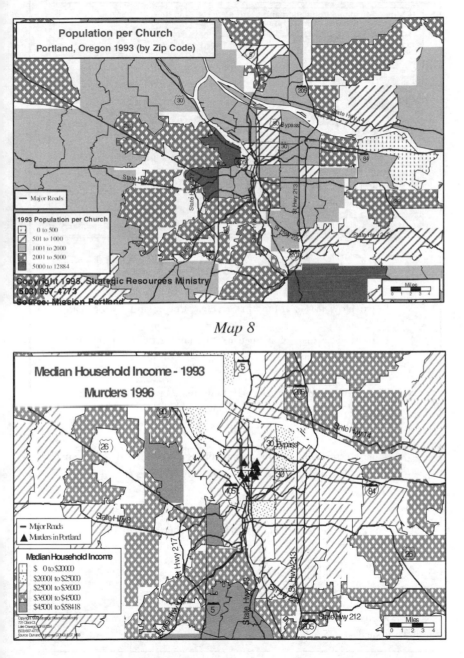

Map 8

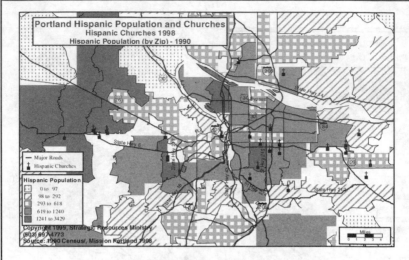

Portland Hispanic Population and Churches
Hispanic Churches 1998
Hispanic Population (by Zip) - 1990

— Major Roads
✠ Hispanic Churches

Hispanic Population
0 to 97
98 to 292
293 to 618
619 to 1240
1241 to 3429

Copyright 1999, Strategic Resources Ministry
(503) 697-4773
Source: 1990 Census/, Mission Portland 1998

CityMap CD-ROM!

√ Learn How to Use Maps in Strategic Prayer and Evangelism!

√ Explore how maps can be used in transforming communities
   spiritually, socially, economically, and politically!

√ View, print, and zoom over 100 city maps, primarily of the
   Portland, Oregon area. Also includes some maps of Houston,
   Minneapolis/St. Paul, and other cities.

√ This is essentially a course in mapping as applied to city transformation that can be used by city initiative leaders in any city.

Price: $24.95 ppd in US
Contact: Oregon Professional Microsystems
            731 Clara Ct.
            Portland, OR 97034
            (503) 697-4773

Note: Most maps are 8 1/2" X 11" and in color. They are from multiple sources
and vary in quality.

WORKING WITH MAPS
Carl Townsend

The basic purpose of our mapping a city or neighborhood is evangelism and transformation; that is, the Spirit of God covering the city as waters cover the sea. And the transformation of every level and aspect of society, including the Church, until it conforms and remains conformed to the righteousness of God.

Many tools exist for geographic mapping. In fact, this is the first generation in which Christians have had such a large array of tools to use. These tools will be examined in this chapter as we look at specific strategies and tasks.

Introduction to Mapping
Computer programs that support the construction and management of geographic maps and data are called GIS, or Geographic Information Systems. These programs give you the power to construct, visualize, explore, query and analyze data geographically. They permit you to see spatial (geographic) relationships that were previously hidden, gain new insights, solve geographic problems, and achieve new results – in the context of evangelization.

These programs exist with a variety of features and costs. For serious GIS, we recommend Atlas*GIS or ArcView GIS . Both are available from Global Mapping International[1] or Environmental Systems Research Institute.[2] For local church outreach programs (reaching everyone in the community with the Gospel), we recommend the Kingdom Combine (Turbo version) from the Mapping Center for Evangelism.[3]

What's Involved
For the moment, let's look at the commercial mapping programs mentioned above. You need two types of data for using these mapping programs:

- *Boundary data files define the basic attributes of the area that are used in all of your maps.*

For working with a particular area, such as a city, you need the geographic boundary data files to use with the mapping program for that area. Each individual boundary file could be considered as a layer in the map. Each layer can consist of polygons (such as counties, neighborhoods, zip codes, rivers), lines (highways, streets), or points (hospitals, airports). This base map, as it is referred to, is used for all area maps. Each boundary file is a separate layer in the map. You can turn off or on each of the various layers; for example, you don't need zip codes and census tracts turned on at the same time. Some of this boundary data will vary over time, such as streets.

You need to be aware that boundaries change and therefor must be updated. Other data doesn't change much with time. Census tracts, for example, change only every ten years.

- *Spatial data is the information you wish to map*: census data for different census tracts, church locations, crime data for different neighborhoods, etc. The data that you use depends on the specific goal or objective. This data (in general) frequently changes.

Two Basic Map Types
- *Thematic maps* show data mapped to specific areas, such as a map that shows the crime statistics by neighborhood or median income by census tract.
- *Datapoint maps* show data mapped as points based on the latitude and longitude of the points. An example would be a map showing the location of churches in an area.

In both cases you are actually mapping information by latitude and longitude. The polygons in the boundary files are actually a set of closed lines (point to point), with the endpoints of each of the lines defined by latitude and longitude. Streets are a collection of linked lines with the endpoints of each defined by latitude and longitude.

Geocoding

In most cases of datapoint mapping you have a data file (such as a church file or church membership file or some building or site) containing addresses you wish to map. Since the mapping is done by latitude and longitude, you have an additional process that involves converting the address to a latitude/longitude location if it is not already supplied. *Geocoding is the process of converting a street address to latitude/longitude coordinates.* The mapping program then automatically plots the point using this latitude and longitude. Let's look at three methods for getting this latitude and longitude.

1. One simple method, often used with inexpensive programs, is to use the nine digit zip code of the address. The geocoding program has a separate database and obtains the latitude and longitude from this database for the centroid of the nine-digit zip code. The point is then mapped to this centroid. This is not as accurate as actual street mapping, but does give an approximate map.

2. A second method is to geocode from the actual street address. This requires a separate program that reads the street address and zip code (5 digits is sufficient) and then attempts to match this in a database to the latitude and longitude. An example here is the StreetMap program from ESRI that can be used with the ArcView mapping program. This is a good approach and quick, but has two disadvantages. The first is that only about 85% of the points will be successfully mapped even in a good program, and in some programs this figure is much less. Second, the quality is only as good as the database file, which must be updated frequently. Since the streets change in most cities quite often, you are constantly updating this database file to insure a high match level. Each time you update, it costs money.

3. The best approach for getting the latitude and longitude is by using a GPS (Global Positioning System) to get the actual latitude and longitude from the satellites. (You can combine this "GPSing" with prayerwalking, which Steve Hawthorne defines as "praying on site with insight".) The GPS is a small device about the size of a cell phone. You stand at the physical location of the point to map and

read the latitude and longitude (and altitude) from the GPS. These devices cost in the neighborhood of $100 and give you a very accurate reading of the location for the mapping program. For a few additional dollars you can get the software to directly transfer the latitude and longitude to a laptop computer. We recommend using the GPS:

- It is more accurate than geocoding
- You insure that every point is mapped.
- You get a better idea of the point you are mapping; i.e., its context. You are not dealing with a remote analytic point, but a real location that has a spiritual context.
- You can really map any point. It doesn't need an address. Indian burial grounds, cemeteries, etc. can all be mapped with a GPS.

You'll make many additional discoveries doing mapping with a GPS. The primary disadvantage is the amount of time it takes you to travel around with the GPS and get the exact readings. In areas of tall buildings it can be difficult to maintain the needed satellite fixes.

Types of Information to Map
There are basically two types of spatial data you can map: *Harvest Force and Harvest Field* data. Let's look at each of these. It's not either/or or one before the other. Both are integral to the task of evangelism. With either of these, you are building the map in layers.

Harvest Force Mapping
Harvest Force mapping consists of identifying and mapping all organizations actively involved in the Great Commission enterprise and their activities: churches, parachurches, as well as Christian bookstores and other places of business used for Christian purposes.

The Harvest Force mapping itself is in layers, with the layers defined and determined by the city (or church's) vision. Putting everything in one map can make the map too dense, and have a lack of focus. By creating multiple layers (on transparent acetate), you can selectively choose the information to display at a particular time.

For example, here are some possible layers at the city level:

- Churches
- Parachurch Organizations
- Christian Schools
- Christian Benevolent Organizations
- Denominational Headquarters or Offices
- Houses of Prayer, Lighthouses, etc.

Harvest Field Mapping

Harvest Field maps show the context and permits accurate targeting for evangelism. Examples in thematic maps show median income, densities of senior citizens or single mothers, ethnic groups and crime rates. Data point maps show locations of residents, spiritual quest sites (temples, mosques, cemeteries, Indian burial sites, etc.), crime locations, adult entertainment, city offices, etc..

As a general rule, contextual maps showing data points are generally more specific than thematic maps. For example, a map showing specific locations of burglaries is more meaningful than a map showing burglaries per neighborhood. The burglary datapoints will have certain cluster patterns that can be used to predict where future burglaries will occur.

The Mapping Process

In the rest of this chapter we will take you through the process of generating a base map and a variety of layers and themes.

The Base Map

When starting the mapping, you should have a set of boundary files already used to create various maps of the area using a variety of spatial data files. You may even wish to print a base map showing just the boundary file information. This is particularly useful if you are planning to put the spatial information in layers on transparencies. For overhead projections, the base map would also need to be on a transparency.

This base map is the starting point. Work with the leaders to define the boundaries and scale for this map. For a city, this is often the MSA, or

---

Metropolitan Statistical Area, as defined by the U.S.Census Bureau. This definition can change at the ten-year census point. A commercial Thomas map book for your area will probably define the counties for your MSA, or you can check with the U.S. Census Bureau. Since this can be a large area, you may wish to print regional base maps as well for local churches to use.

You may need to purchase boundary files for specific layers. In Portland, we obtained the census boundary files from the mapping program supplier, the neighborhood boundary files from the city's mapping center, and the street files from a special geocoding program we purchased. We also had a conversion program to convert each boundary file to the format needed for our mapping program. Notice the boundary files are a single set used for ALL city mapping of ANY data. They are dated (the street files generally going out of date first), but you can use them for all your mapping. If you are using the Kingdom Combine program from the Mapping Center for Evangelism, it will have a mapping program in it with the street files for your area.

Additional Layers
The next layers are created from a database containing data defining the layer. This means your next task is to define the layers you wish to use. Here are the datapoint layers used in our example:

- Churches
- Parachurch organizations/commercial
- Spiritual Quest Sites
- Benevolent organizations
- Schools

Each of the above can be actually a collection of layers in its own separate map. For example, the church "layer" is really a map with a layer for growing churches, another layer for new churches, and another for churches with no information. The one church database could be considered several databases when it is utilized to drive the mapping program for multiple church-related layers.

In this example, the first "layers" *database* contains all the churches in the area. The actual church data could be obtained from one or more sources, including a field survey, library research such as using a telephone book, state or city offices (since all churches are registered), or a commercial source. In depicting the churches in multiple layers you could show growing churches with green points, and declining churches as red points using one or two layers. Or you can use different icon shapes to signify the size of the church, the kind of a church, the age of a church, etc.. Another idea is to use separate layers for each ethnic church group.

In the same way, you can create additional layers. In one project the school layer, a list of local preschools (and the vision statement of each) was obtained from the Internet. These were loaded to a database and geocoded (as with the churches). Other schools were shown in the commercial Thomas map guide. A single GPS trip through the area queried for both preschool, private and public schools. These were all mapped, with the preschool, elementary, Middle, High and Adult schools in separate layers with individual symbols and colors.

Spiritual Quest Sites
The spiritual quest site layer is one of the more challenging layers, as it can require extensive research. To do this layer, you need to know some of the spiritual history of the area. Some spiritual mapping research is needed. Cemeteries, temples and alternative religion centers are easy to map, but it takes more work to find Indian burial sites. To find locations for cultic activities check with the local police. This composite layer would use one symbol/color for Buddhist temples, another for Indian burial sites, another for cemeteries, another for occult sites, etc.

Thematic Maps
Thematic maps show data as it relates to areas, such as crime statistics by neighborhood or median income by census tract. These layers are also driven by databases, but no geocoding or GPS work is needed, as the input data file is linked to the boundary file by a polygon ID, such as a zip code or census tract code.

You can also combine a datapoint file with a thematic map, such as creating a map that shows Hispanic population by zip code and, in another layer, the location of Hispanic churches. When overlaid this assists you in determining where to plant new Hispanic churches. You can also, with not much additional work, map the Hispanic population to Hispanic church ratio for each area.

Layout Design

Each map will need a layout design. This includes the legend, scale, compass points indicator, title, and any notes you wish to add, such as a copyright notice. Strive for consistency here. The user doesn't need to try to re-figure how to read the map each time a new map is printed. Use the same scale, notes, color coding (where practicable), etc. and be sure the title communicates what the map is all about.

Printing the Maps

Finally, you can print the composite map and see if it is what you wish, editing as necessary. Special print versions can help tailor the map to a variety of needs. E.g.

- Transparency to use with the basic map to show correlations, such as a transparent layer with only the churches shown.
- Muralling. With most print dialog boxes, you can choose to print the map as a set of 8 ½ X 11 pages. For example, you might choose to print a city map on a set of pages three wide and four high (33 inches X 34 inches). These can then be cut and pasted together as a single composite or used, much like a Thomas map set, as a collection of maps for the area.
- You may want to use a local quick-print shop to print a large composite map, such as 3' X 4'. To do this, first call the print shop and ask if they have a printer for large pages (such as a Tektronix 600) and ask them prices and policy. Determine what software and printer drivers they require to print your map. Install that same printer drive file to your Windows system (Control Panel->Printers) from the Windows CD-ROM and set the output to file. Now print the map to the disk with that printer selected. Windows will prompt for a file name. Take the disk to the print shop, and they should be able to print it directly with no fuss or muss.

Other Mapping Resources

The object is to see geographical/spacial relationships for the purpose of evangelism and transformation. You don't have to stick with just your own mapping program – use other mapping resources. Some to consider are:

* City planning offices often have computerized mapping systems and generate a variety of maps. Take some time to get acquainted. It can bring good rewards over time.
* The Thomas maps are good for locating parks and other features, and are now available electronically.
* See the "endnotes" for the suppliers listed there. They may have just what you need.
* See local mapping companies. Many of them are doing special mapping for clients that may prove very useful for your needs. (In Knoxville, TN the local Superior Mapping Company produced a large wall map of the metro area depicting churches, major buildings and other landmarks. It had all the administrative districts identified.)

Some Basic Guidelines

* Maps should have a single message. Putting too many points on a map will make the map too dense to read and the central message will be lost. Break the points to layers. For example, if you wish to show on the map where an area of Hispanics live that are unchurched, use a thematic map showing the population with the churches as datapoints on the map. You could also code the datapoints to show the size of the churches. Nothing else needs to be on the map. Then use a title that summarizes the message.

* If a certain area of the map communicates something of importance, make sure the eye is drawn to this area first. For example, a map showing the Hispanic population/church ratio for each zip code could use red to show significantly high ratios where churches need to be planted.

- All maps of a given area should use the same scale and boundaries. This is particularly significant when overlaying overhead transparencies.

- On each map, include a date and the source of the spatial information. Include scaling information and compass directions.

- Choose your color scheme for thematic maps carefully. A map has a good color scheme when: a) it communicates the main point without having to study the legend, and b) if the color mix is pleasing to the eye. Many organizations develop standard color schemes. Patrick Johnstone, a prolific mapmaker, author of Operation World, and Director of the International Research Office for Worldwide Evangelization Crusade, always uses green for Muslims, brown for Hispanic, red for Buddhist, and so on.

- Some maps show areas without values or gradients, such as a map identifying city zones, etc., where no legend is used. In this case you can repeat colors as long as adjacent areas do not have the same color.

Endnotes:
1. Global Mapping International, Colorado Springs, Colorado " www.gmi.org"
2. Environmental Services Research Insititute, Redlands, California "www.esri.org"
3. Mapping Center for Evangelism, Lenexa, Kansas "www.map4jesus.org"

Growth Rates

Calculations:

Annual growth rate. If you are computing the growth rate for any succeeding years the calculation is fairly straightforward. Subtract the earlier year's number from the latest. (Note that your figures must be one year apart and not more). Divide your answer by the earlier year's number. Then multiply this answer by 100 to give you percent.

The formula is: L-B/B X 100=AGR in %.

Average Annual Growth Rate (AAGR)

Please note that you do NOT get the AAGR by dividing the growth over a certain number of years by the number of years. This would be like simple interest, and AAGR is like compound interest. The AAGR must take into consideration the new additions (churches, members, baptisms, etc.) each year. AAGR is also helpful in comparing the growth of your church or group of churches with the population in your community.

Calculating AAGR is a little more involved mathmatically. It is used to find the average rate for periods more than one year. The calculation is the same as for figuring compound interest. Accounting programs, such as Quicken, can be used if you are not using a spreadsheet that has the formula available. If it is available, you can put the formula in the respective cells and it will automatically perform the calculations and depict the rates.

The formula for AAGR is: $(E/B)^{(1/n)}-1$ where E is the end year, B is the beginning year, and "n" is the number of years. Using a scientific calculator, the calculation can be made as follows:

		Display
1.	Clear the calculator	0
2.	Enter the data for latest year (ex. 700)	700
3.	*/* Press "divide by"	700
4.	Enter the data for the beginning year (ex. 500)	500
5.	=	1.4
6.	Y^x	1.4
7.	6 (number of years)	6
8.	1/x	0.16666
9.	=	1.05768
10.	-1	1
11.	=	0.05768
12.	x100	100
13.	= (answer in %)	5.76 (%AAGR)

Decadal Growth Rate (DGR):

To continue and calculate the Decadal Growth Rate based upon the same beginning and ending amounts, after step 9 you would do the following:

10.	Y^x	1.05768
11.	10 (for ten years)	10
12.	= (wait until answer shows)	1.752
13.	x100	100
14.	–	175.2
15.	100	100
16.	= (answer is DGR)	75.2%

Note: See Chapter 8, Figure 8-1 to see how various rates rank growth-wise.

Displaying Growth Rates Graphically

Growth rates can be shown graphically to good advantage. There are two useful types of graphs which aid the analyst: standard graph and semi-log graph.

When looking at a *standard graph (Graph 1)*, you get an accurate and proportionate numerical picture of the growth of churches or members. On the *standard graph*, a straight line indicates constant *numerical* increase or decrease.

However, it is important to note that a constant numerical increase represents a decreasing growth rate. Although you are adding the same number of churches or attendees each year, the actual percent of increase is less. This is readily seen on the semi-log graph (Graph 2). Here the slope of the line is steadily decreasing.

Standard Graph
Constant Numerical Increase

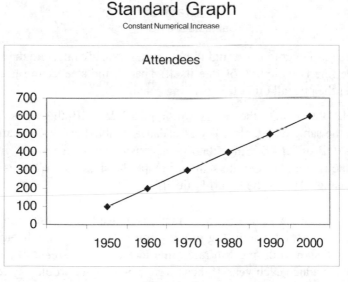

Graph 1

Semi-Log Graph
Constant Numerical Increase

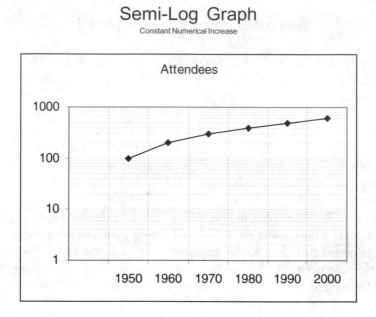

Graph 2
(Same data as Graph 1)

On a semi-log graph, a straight line denotes a steady rate, and the slope of the line is indicitive of rate itself. That is, the steeper the line the higher the rate, all other things being equal.

Graphs 3 & 4 show the reverse of Graphs 1 & 2. Both graphs come from the same data table. The attendance doubled every 10 years for an AAGR of 7.17%. Since the rate is constant on the semi-log graph, the line is straight. On the standard graph the slope of the line is ever increasing. This is the logarithmic effect.

When you see a standard graph that has a steady increase, you will want to construct a semi-log graph to provide a true growth picture. This will show a drop off in rate. In effect, a fewer *percent* of people are being added each year. If these were converts, we would say fewer people are leading people to the Lord each year on the average. The church leaders need to know this.

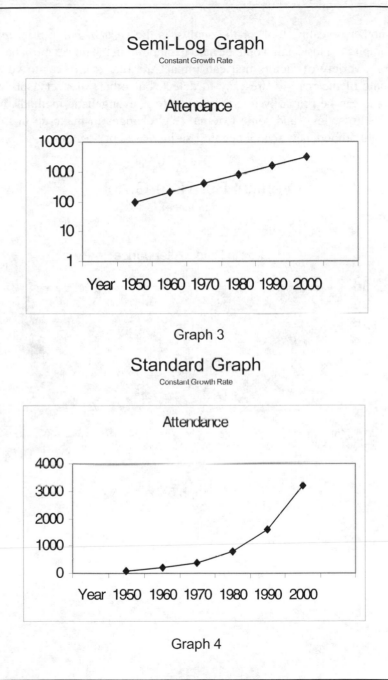

Semi-Log Graph
Constant Growth Rate

Attendance

Graph 3

Standard Graph
Constant Growth Rate

Attendance

Graph 4

Another revealing tool for the analyst is the *vertical bar rate graph* (Graph 5). This detail would be hard to pinpoint in the line graph. There are a variety of factors that can impact the rate from year to year. Some of the reasons are easy to detect, but others are very subtle. Some can be primarily internal factors (e.g. evangelistic methods, or worship styles) and some external (e.g. changes in make-up of the neighborhood, new school opening, or increased persecution).

Vertical Bar Rate Graph
(Attendance)

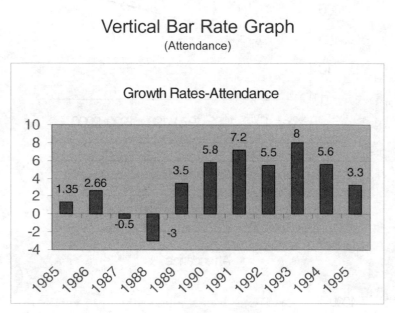

Graph 5

Additional Notes

(Thanks goes to John Gilbert of the Southern Baptist Research Department for the following.)

1. Doubling Time. A useful formula in church growth that gives the number of years it takes to double the membership at a given AAGR.

The formula is: $DT = (\ln 2)/(\ln(AAGR+1))$ where: "ln" is the natural logarithm.

2. Reliability of Linear Regression Analysis. In calculations of linear regression (putting the best straight line through a bunch of data points), a term is usually calculated called the "variance" or "R-squared." The variance is the number between 0 and 1, and can be expressed as a percentage. For example:

$$r^2 = 0.957 \text{ (can also be expressed as 95.7\%)}$$

Thus, a variance of 0.957 means that 95.7% of the variance of y (membership) is accounted for by differences in x (year). That is, 95.7% of the variance of membership is related to the change in the year. A high variance means that the straight line fits the data very well. A low variance means that "differences in x do not affect y." That is, the data is badly scattered and the line is the best that can be done, but it is not very reliable.

3. Biological Growth Rate. In the U.S., the biological growth rate of a church has been estimated to be about 25% per decade, which is an AAGR of about 2.2%. That is the growth from baptizing the children of its members. Thus, a church should have an AAGR of more than 2.2% if it is reaching outside its own membership.

You can make this same calculation for the whole Church in the city vs the population growth in the city, to see if the church is broadening its impact proportionately within the city.

Hardware/Software

Let's take a look at the computer-related tools you should have at a fully functional research center. Especially one that will be involved in ongoing research, analysis and publication. There is often the tendency to save money by using inexpensive tools or tools that are given to the center. In the long run, however, this will hurt you and you will find yourself working with non-standard files (such as word processing or database files) that can't be read by others networking with you in the city or with other cities. You will also find that many of the up-to-date programs, because of their size and capabilities, require more memory and speed.

The following hardware and software are considered adequate for a fully functional Information Resource Center.

Hardware

Pentium II Processor (or higher), at least 366 mhz, 64MB RAM.
10 GB of disk space
Scanner
Color and black and white printers
Backup tape or other media
Zip drive or other removable disk storage
Presentation projector
CD-ROM (write/rewrite)
Monitor 17" 1024x768 pixels graphics

Software

Microsoft Office 2000 or higher containing: Microsoft Access,
PowerPoint, Word and Excel (or equivelant)
Windows 98 or higher
Atlas*Gis or ArcView mapping software. Available via:

- Global Mapping International
  7899 Lexington Drive, Suite 200A
  Colorado Springs, CO 80920
  1-719-531-3599

mapsupport@gmi.org
www.gmi.org

Or:
- ESRI
  380 New York Street
  Redlands, CA 92373
  1-909-793-5953
  www.esri.com

Map-related materials:
Tiger Boundary Files for Target Area (Zip, Census Tract,
    Block Group)
Tiger Street Files (such as ESRI StreetMap)
Other Boundary Files (such as neighborhood boundary files,
    school districts, etc.)
Census Data Files for Target Area
Other Data Files for Target Area (from city or commercial
    sources)
ESRI Spatial Analysis Program (ESRI or GMI)
Kingdom Combine (Turbo Version) $450 (1999). Available
    via:

- Mapping Center for Evangelism
  P.O. Box 14945
  Lenexa, KS 66285
  1-888-627-7997 or 1-913-438-7301
  www.map4jesus.org

Other recommended but optional software:
Drawing and Painting Tools
    Adobe Photoshop (For creating and editing bit-mapped
        images)
    Corel Draw (For creating and editing vector graphic
        images)
    Statistical Analysis software (shareware at http://
        www.westernseminary.edu – click on MRP)

Spiritual Mapping Data

The following are some of the basic data points to get you started on your own spiritual mapping of your community, city or region. Anyone serious about understanding in-depth spiritual mapping of their city needs to obtain the book *Informed Intercession* by George Otis Jr. (Ventura: Renew Books, 1999). Much of the following is adapted from this book.

Gathering the information will require astute and insightful observation plus interviewing a variety of individuals. Otis outlines the following basic steps in way of preparation:

1) Locate a knowledgeable source.
2) Develop an explanatory introduction.
3) Arrange for an interview.
4) Familiarize yourself with key subject matter through background research.
5) Make a list of specific questions.
6) Review the list and delete repetitive or unnecessary questions.
7) Obtain and check recording equipment.

The following should also be helpful:
1) Be prepared to answer why you want the information and how it will be used. Many will want to know, and the answer to these questions will play a big role in what answers you will receive.
2) Give yourself some time between interviews to get all your notes in order. If using a recorder, you may still need to take some time to record some observations before your mind gets busied with the next interview.
3) In many instances, it will be good for two of you to be in attendance for the interview. This provides the "witness factor," which, in some cases, will decrease careless and erroneous statements, and it increases the scope of observations and interaction. In this situation, one person should be the primary interviewer.

---

4) In many situations (but certainly not all) asking questions from a written list will make the interview more objective, and will give the impression you are asking many the same questions.

Spiritual Mapping Harvest Field Data

Note: Some of the following data items are marked with (**). These items/variables are those considered as minimal candidates for the "pre-congress" phase (Phase 2) of a citywide initiative. These phases are described in Chapter 3 *Spying Out The Land, Part 1.*

A. Founding History of the Community (City)
1) (**)Who were the people who founded the community? Where did they come from and when? What were their beliefs, philosophies and religion?
2) What were their personal or corporate reasons for founding the community?
3) What was the significance of the names or popular designations for the community?
4) Who were the designers who designed the city? Were any Freemasons?
5) Have any of the early Christian leaders been Freemasons?

B. Later History of the City
1) What significant immigration has occurred? How have they been treated? How are the minorities treated?
2) (**) Does the community have a slogan or motto? What is its meaning?
3) Have any wars directly affected the community? Were any battles fought in the community? Was there bloodshed?
4) (**) Is there known gross immorality in the city (abortion clinics, homosexual prominence, pornography shops, etc.)?
5) (**) Who are the most prominent leaders in the community? Why? Are they religious? What religion?

C. History of Non-Christian Religion in the Community
1) What were the religious views and practices of the people who inhabited the area before the community was founded?

2) What secret orders (such as Freemasonry) have been present in the community?
3) (**)What witches' covens, Satanist groups, New Age groups, and other such cults and cultists have operated in the city? Were there any known curses placed upon the city?
4) (**)Has there been conflict between religions in the community? How is it manifested?

D. Physical Research

1) What is the background and possible significance of the statues and monuments of the community? Do any reflect demonic characteristics or glorify the creature rather than the Creator?
2) Is there any significance in the architecture, location, layout or positional relationship of the central buildings, especially those representing political, economic, educational or religious powers? Did Freemasons lay any of the cornerstones?
3) What are the locations of the "high places," altars, temples, monuments or buildings associated with witchcraft, occult, fortune telling, Satanism, Freemasonry, Mormonism, Eastern religions, Jehovah's Witnesses and the like? Do these form any noticeable patterns when plotted on a map?

E. Social Bondages

1) What is the most prevalent form of suffering in the community (outside of alcohol and drug abuse)? Why is the condition so prevalent?
2) (**)What kinds of pain (or negative conditions) exist within the community (such as: injustice, poverty, discrimination, disease, corruption in government, etc.)
3) How widespread are these problems? How long have they existed?
4) Is there legalized gambling in the city? How many city people are involved?
5) What role, if any, does media have in promoting spiritual darkness in the city?
6) Are there any new alliances emerging between groups and institutions that want to promote righteousness?

These are a few samples of many that could provide a foundation for the spiritual mapping of the Harvest Field, or non-Christian aspects of the city. So much has occurred in this area over the past few years case studies are multiplying rapidly where spiritual mapping and simultaneous and subsequent intercessory and warfare prayer having resulted in strategic spiritual breakthroughs, victories and transformations.

Spiritual Mapping Harvest Force Data

This category contains Harvest Force data not covered in previous phases/levels (with some exceptions). This data coupled with the other Harvest Force data provides a fairly comprehensive historical, qualitative, and quantitative picture of Christianity and the Church in the city. When combined with all other data a comprehensive "prophetic message" will result. This message can then guide the Church in effecting significant transformation of the societies in the city and the Church.

This information, however, will need to fall into the hands of faithful, humble and obedient men and women who look to God for guidance, provision and protection (as Nehemiah did). Then the righteousness of God can steadily pervade every element and aspect of the city. Many of the following data items have been adapted from Informed Intercession by George Otis Jr. (previously referenced). In many instances specially prepared survey forms and questions will need to be drafted.

> **Note:** Some of the following data items are marked with (**). These items/variables are those considered as minimal candidates for the "pre-congress" phase (Phase 2) of a citywide initiative. These phases are described in Chapter 3.

A. Size and Nature of the Church
1) What percent of the community considers itself Christian?
2) What percent of the community considers itself Evangelical?
3) How does this compare with surrounding areas?
4) (**) Have any of the early Christian leaders been Freemasons?
5) Is Christianity in the community/city growing, plateauing, or

declining?

6) Are the local churches in the community/city actively refuting immorality, e.g. abortions, pornography, homosexuality, drugs and alcohol, etc.?

7) (**) Who are the Christian leaders who are considered as the "elders" of the city?

8) What is the sense of hope for the future within the Church? Is it bright? Is it dull?

B. Public Image of the Church

1) What kind of Church news seems to attract the most attention?

2) (**) Who are the primary public representatives of the Church? Are they Evangelical? Are they liberal?

3) Does the community have the sense that the Church is truly interested in its problems? If yes, what kinds of programs reinforce this idea?

4) How has the city received God's messengers?

5) (**) What are the most difficult areas in the city in which to pray?

6) (**) What is the view of community leaders toward Christian morality?

C. Health of the Church

1) What is the history of church splits in the community? To what were they attributed?

2) Are there recognized apostolic leaders in the area who have made public commitments to the land/community? If yes, who are they, and what do they say is the reason for this?

3) Is there a sense of hopeful expectancy among the ranks of the believers? Of discouragement? Of complacency?

4) (**) If community faith was strong in the past, has this given way to permissive, lukewarm Christianity? To what is this attributed?

5) Has there been conflict between Christians or churches?

6) (**) Where is reconciliation within the Body of Christ needed?

D. Evangelistic Activity and Progress

1) Is this an area where the Gospel has never really taken root, or is it part of a "Bible belt?"
2) (**) Is the Church actively involved in city government? In which ways?
3) Have all geographic sectors of the community been evangelized? Do they have churches?
4) (**) Is the church representative of all social classes in the city?
5) What are recognized, mature intercessors hearing from God concerning the community?

E. Spiritual Opposition

1) Is there tangible opposition to the Gospel in the community?
2) Has there been public mockery of Christianity?
3) Do any judges, politicians, bureaucrats or police officials go out of their way to obstruct the Gospel? What is motivating their behavior?
4) (**) Has there been any physical persecution of Christians? Any damage to Christian property?
5) What kind of opposition has come from militant secularists?
6) Is there any verifiable evidence that local witches or shamans have placed curses on Christian personnel, property or activities?

Spiritual Mapping Combined Harvest Field and Harvest Force Analysis

Make observations regarding:

a. The general spiritual condition and status of the city and the unchurched.
b. Areas and peoples of the city where there are causes for real concern, such as: racial strife, poverty, crime, homeless, etc..
c. The attitude of the city and area governments toward Christianity and the Church.
d. The identity of the people in city government leadership who are most vocal against Christianity and/or Christians, and those who are vocal in support of Christianity and Christians.
e. (**) Significant changes or transformations within the city,

and/or the Church that can be directly related to united inter-cessory and/or warfare prayer.

f. (**) Identification of current specific strongholds in the city that are obviously points of resistance to the growth and/or vitality of the Church.

g. The correlation between events, people, groups or structures in the city's history, and periods of growth and non-growth of the Church.

h. Areas of effectiveness (highlights) and ineffectiveness (lowlights) of the Church impacting transformation of various segments of society and government.

i. (**) Areas of needed focus and action by the Church.

j. The extent of unity or disunity and cooperation of the Church in the city.

k. The relevancy of the Church to the unchurched (as observed by church attendance, surveys, interviews, and/or the Church's culture vs the current generation's cultures).

l. Identity and role of key figures that have been converted or reverted.

m. Whether or not the secular media has made any comments, or carried any programs, addressing Divine activity, or changing moral attitudes, values or allegiances within the city.

n. The willingness in the city to accept/adopt broader social limits (i.e. alternative lifestyles, abortion, pre-marital and teen sex, drug use, etc.).

o. (**) Significant decisions reached through elections, council meetings, or other forms of public decision-making that have impacted the spiritual life and character of the community.

SAMPLE PUBLICATION PAGES

The following pages contain sample pages from a variety of publications aimed at providing the Body of Christ in a city or nation, status of the Harvest Force and Harvest Field, pertinent information, and challenge. They have been selected to provide ideas for content and format considerations for your publication.

Every citywide (or broader) initiative should seriuosly consider publishing periodically information and status pertinent to the initiative and the Church in the city. This can start with one page, and then grow as the initiative grows and more information becomes available.

Sample pages that follow are from:

1. *Discovering Our City* by "Mission Etna".
   (this is a mock-up-not real data)

2. *DAWN Report* by DAWN Ministries
   (a global monthly publication)

   DAWN Ministries   719-548-7460
   5775 N. Union Blvd.
   Colorado Springs, CO 80918

3. *Church Planting Canada* by Outreach Canada
   (a nationwide monthly publication)

   Outreach Canada   604-272-0732
   #16-12240 Horseshoe Way
   Richmond, B.C. V7A 4X9 Canada

4. *The BridgeBuilder* by BridgeBuilders International
   (an area-wide [Phoenix, AZ] monthly publication)

   BridgeBuilders International Leadership Network
   PO Box 31415
   Phoenix, AZ 85046-1415
   602-789-1111

Comparing the Generations

If you were to stop and think about the differences between the past three generations, you would probably agree they were different alright, but may find it difficult to verbalize why.

In February a forum of Church leaders and sociologists was convened to study the inability of the Church to significantly attract current generations. The results were quite revealing. These generations portray significant cultural distinctives, which when not adequately understood or considered, result in the Church's inability to draw and/or keep them.

The following chart is a comparison of some of the defining generational

Comparing the Generations

Builders (b. 1927-1945)	Boomers (b.1946-1964)	Busters (b. 1965-1985)
Formal	Relational	Spontaneous
Programs	People	Community
Responsibility	Fulfillment	Challenge
Reverence	Participation	Energy
Hymns	Hymns-Praise	Praise-Alternative
Expository	Topical	Issues
Missions	Missionaries	Causes
"Be sure!"	"Let's do it!"	"Whatever!"

differences observed by the forum.

Their report contains several recommendations of innovative ideas for reaching the various generations. It also suggests some things churches might want to consider in structuring their services. The report is available at www.etnaforum.html.

Distribution of Churches by Size

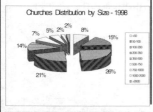

Churches Distribution by Size - 1998

Tabulation of God's Faithfulness

Shortly after the Mission Etna citywide initiative was formed in mid 1997 the Information Resource Center (IRC) was established to provide periodic assessment of both the Harvest Force (the Body of Christ) and Harvest Field (the Church's secular context) in the city.

The results just published in the annual report for calendar year 1998 are a strong testimony of God's faithfulness, and should be very heartening for all of us. However, it does highlight some challenges as well.

Over the past three years there has been healthy increases in several categories, including the number of new church starts, overall church attendance, baptisms and neighborhood houses of Prayer.

Lighthouses

Of special significance is the marked increase in the number of churches participating in forming Lighthouses of Prayer. This local neighborhood intecession effort is producing many wonderful testimonies of God's faithfulness, with many seeing their neighbors making professions of faith.

Another remarkable fact is the rate of growth for churches has nearly doubled over the past three years. Mission Etna leaders contribute this, and some of the other heartening increases, to the increased cooperation and partnering that is taking place among most of the churches in the area. There has been unprecedented cooperation among the various denominations covering a wide variety of doctrinal stances. It is reported that nearly 75% of the area's churches have ascribed to the Mission Etna vision statement and goals, which include marked increases in gatherings of believers in every segment of the area's population.

Some Areas of Need

The table below does not reflect one area of weakness which was revealed in the IRC report, and that is the church picture for some of the area's minorities. There are still some segments of society that need close attention, including Native Americans, Hispanics (due to the influx of farm and service workers) and those below the poverty line. This latter group is also candidate for health care, food and shelter and family counseling.

Increases in Evangelistic Bible Studies, and Lighthouses of Prayer have been credited for much of the increase in conversions (baptisms) and church attendance. Some of the new churches began as small group Bible studies.

It is estimated the following table represents approximately a 90% accuracy for those categories listed.

3 Year Assessment	1996	%Incr 96-97	1997	%Incr 97-98	1998
Total churches	187	6%	199	11.2%	224
New church starts	7	71%	12	58%	19
Baptisms (believers')	1,148	8%	1,248	11%	1,481
Total church attendance	14,645	6.5%	15,646	9.1%	17,212
Lighthouses of Prayer (neighborhood prayer cells)	180	43%	316	105%	656
Evangelistic Bible studies per church (average ratio)	3.2 to 1	22%	4.1to 1	34%	6.2 to 1

IRC April 1999

In this Issue: MINISTERING WITH POWER

ISSUE NO. 28 OCTOBER 1996

DAWN REPORT

Covering The 'Discipling a Whole　　　　　Nation' Movement

When 110% of the City All Came to Church!

by Myron Steeves

One of the most exciting aspects of the DAWN movement is seeing how the discipling of nations is so intertwined with prayer. Discipling goals lead the church to pray. But the reverse is also true. United prayer for a geographic area leads the Church to discipling that area.

Nowhere is this more clearly illustrated than in the inspiring story of the little town of Jefferson, Oregon, told by Terry Dirks of international Renewal Ministries (IRM).

In this town of 1,700 people, a Baptist church had maintained a Sunday morning attendance of 200 for many years. After attending an IRM city-wide "prayer summit," the pastor committed himself to spend an extended time in prayer every day.

This so inspired his congregation that the poorly attended Wednesday-night prayer meeting soon expanded to enthusiastic prayer meetings three evenings and five mornings each week!

Within one year, Sunday morning attendance grew to 300, and six years later average attendance was up to 700 - in a town of 1,700!

God's blessing spilled into other congregations as well when the incredible mix of neighboring Episcopal, Methodist and Assemblies of God pastors joined the Baptist pastor in weekly prayer for their community.

These churches also began to grow so that last Easter total church attendance in Jefferson was greater than the population of the whole town!

Jefferson is just one of 260 prayer summits IRM has facilitated since its beginning less than 10 years ago. It began when Dr. Joe Aldrich, president of Multnomah Bible College and Biblical Seminary in Portland, OR, started asking colleagues what it took to attract God's blessing to a community.

When a group of pastors was gathered to study this question, it soon became obvious these men of God did not need another conference - they needed to pray.

As a result, Multnomah began to coordinate four-day prayer summits, and IRM was created to facilitate this ministry. For these prayer summits, there is no set agenda, no prominent speakers to draw a crowd no workshops, no bragging or complaining about each other's congregation: just prayer!

The results, as illustrated by the Jefferson story, have been remarkable. Walls are crumbling and unity among disparate churches in one city after another is becoming increasingly visible. Vision for the discipling of whole cities is emerging in virtually every case.

Recognizing the inseparable bond between powerful prayer and effective strategy, Dawn Ministries has entered into a covenant relationship with IRM "more powerful than the signing of a formal document, because our agreement is based on a relationship with no boundaries," says Dirks.

IRM believes that Dawn Ministries, with its vision, experience and process can provide the next step in the development of city projects that have been birthed in prayer but now need to move toward mobilization for discipling whole cities.

"Vision for DAWN-like strategies is emerging in cities throughout the nation," says Jack Dennison, Dawn Ministries Coordinator for North America. "It is clear God is so moving that we will eventually see a great conflagration for the re-discipling of the cities and peoples of the United States."

As Jim Montgomery says, "Church attendance, of course, will never reach 110% of all cities in the USA or in nations around the world. But the power unleashed when God's people get together in concerted, united prayer will continue to be the foundation for strategies for completing the Great Commission in our time."

(continued on page 2)

Volume 2, Issue 1

Transforming the Nation to be Released in June

An updated version of *Reclaiming a Nation* (1990) in preparation is expected to be released June 15.

The volume contains new chapters on Quebec, prayer, the DAWN (Discipling a Whole Nation) vision and process, unreached people groups, vital information based on 1996 census data, along with contributions by Gary Walsh, president of the EFC and Arnell Motz, Canadian coordinator of the AD2000 Movement.

The prophetic message sets out the vision, basis and challenge of mobilizing the whole church to reach the whole nation through saturation church planting.

A "pre-release" edition was made available to participants at the "Canadian Church Planting Congress '97." Advance orders may be placed by contacting Outreach Canada. The cost is expected to be under $15.00.

Updated Mapping and Demographic Now Available

By using Census Canada 1996 data Outreach Canada is now able to provide updated colour mapping to assist leaders in identifying key target locations and language groups for church planting. In addition, custom demographic studies are available for most areas of Canada.

Maps indicating the number of biblically orthodox churches per capita, (target: one church per 1000 people) and maps showing home language information have been updated.

In addition, map can now pinpoint the exact location for known churches (Evangelical, mainline and Catholic) in any given community.

Reasonable fees apply. Please contact Lorne Hunter for further information at (604) 272-0732 or **lhunter@outreach.ca.**

Check "Church Planting Canada' Website for Updates

The Church Planting Canada website can be accessed at **www.outreach.ca/cpc.**

Check regularly for resources and training events and email us about events you'd like to publicize.

Share Your Best Idea with Canadian Church Planters

Tell us your most effective idea, how you implemented it (action steps), costs, hours invested, and results for the Kingdom. We'll include one submission in each newsletter.

No Place Like Home

Many pastors find starting a new church right in their existing worship facility is a very practical way to go. See How to Start a New Service by Win Arn from Centre for Leadership Development (800) 804-0777.

Conference and Training Events

Church Planter Assessment Centre: April 27-29, 1998 at Camp Harmattan (outside of Olds AB). please contact Dr. Daniel Gales at 403-250-5181, **76644.2566@compuserve.com.** For information on the less involved **Planter Assessment System** please contact Pastor Arnie ter Mors at 403-250-5547.

Cell Church Conference: May 8-9, 1998, Saint John, NB.

Contact Pastor Barry Adams at 506-634-6996 or: **nuhope@nbnet.nb.ca** for info.

BootCamp for planters and Coaches: May 11-15, 1998 in White Rock includes 6 hours of coaches training. A two night BootCamp for pastors planning to daughter churches is available. (**Chinese BootCamp** also available, same dates.)

To register on-line:
www.cmtcmultiply.org or

contact Erma Schar at 719-531-6393 or **cmtc@iex.net.**

Church Planters Forum: August 31-September 1, 1998 Gary McIntosh is resource leader at the International Bible Society's annual church planter's forum in Colorado Springs, CO. Contact Vicki Ewy for details at 719-488-9200 or **vickie@ibs.org.**

NOVEMBER '99 NETWORK CALENDAR
Connecting the Church of the Valley of the Sun

Pastors' and Ministers' Networks

VISION '99
Providing opportunities for ministers to build relationships and develop effective principles for ministries of excellence. For information call AZUSA World ministries (602)269-6959.

CEP (Companerismo Evangelico pastoral)
Hispanic pastors meet monthly for the purpose of fellowship and information. For more information call Leroy Albo, (602)275-3191.

CEP - Evangelistic Fellowship of Hispanic pastors' Wives
Meet monthly for the purpose of building relationships, prayer and evangelistic outreach. For information call Matty Myers (602)336-9696.

Bridgebuilders International Leadership Network
Uniting pastors and Christian leaders for the purpose of building the local church, encouraging biblical unity, concerted prayer, and cooperative evangelization. Call Hal Sacks (602)789-1111.

Chandler Ministerial Association
Next Meeting: Chandler Christian Church, 1825 S. Alma School Rd., Chandler, noon - 1:30 pm, Thursday, November 11. (location changes monthly). Call (480)963-3997.

East Valley Association of Evangelicals
Next meeting: Brown Road Baptist Church, 6502 E. Brown Rd., Mesa, noon to 1:30 pm, Wednesday Nov. 17 (3rd Wednesday every other month). Call Bonnie for location, (480)985-6361.

Greater Phoenix Association of Evangelicals
Next meeting November 15 (every third Monday) from 9am to 10:30am at JB's Camelback at 35th Ave.

Sun City Ministerial Association
For information call Jerry Smith, (623) 584-2280.

Monthly Ministers' Gathering
Ministers, pastors, spouses, and church staff members meet with Iverna Tompkins, Judson, R.L. and Jim Cornwall. Scottsdale Worship Center (6508 E. Cactus), 10a.m.-12 noon, Tuesday, November 9 (2nd Tuesday each month). Call (480)951-0053.

CHIEF (Christian Hope Indian Eskimo Fellowship) Chief Shepherd Discipleship Center
For the purpose of providing short-term training sessions for Native pastors and leaders in the Fundamentals of Faith. The center is located at 1644 E. Campo Bello Drive. Call Huron Claus (602) 482-0828.

Pastors' Prayer Networks
Neighborhood pastors meeting together to pray for one another, their churches, communities and for revival in their cities.

Hispanic Pastors' Prayer (monthly)
Family of God Church, 2010 W. Sherman, 9am-noon, every 1st Saturday. Call Leroy Albo (602) 275-3191.

West Valley (weekly)
Skyway Church of the West Valley, 13419 W. Ocotillo, Bible study and prayer 9am - noon (every Tuesday.) Call Greg Brown (623) 935-4858.

Arizona Church Directory Coming to the Internet
arizonachurches.net, the valley's church informational site, is up. If you are already included, please go on-line and check all of the information in your listing. Let us know if there are any changes, mistakes or omissions.

Don't miss out on being included in www.arizonachurches.net. Send information to: BridgeBuilders, P.O. Box 31415, Phoenix, AZ 85046.

West Central Phoenix (weekly)
Covenant of Grace, 906 W. Peoria, Phoenix, 7am, (every Thursday). Call Leonard Griffin (602) 678-0999.

Arrowhead Pastors' Prayer (weekly)
New Life Community Church, 8155 W. Thunderbird Rd., Phx., 7:30 am (every Tuesday). Call Bill Phillips (623) 979-3514.

Central Phoenix Pastors' Prayer (weekly)
1st Evangelical Free Church, 498 W. Missouri Ave., Phoenix, 7am., every Tuesday. Call David Edgington (602)279-6011.

North East Phoenix (weekly)
Desert Springs Bible Church, 16215 N. Tatum Blvd., Phoenix, 8am (every Thursday). Call Gary Olander (602) 285-1885 or Rick Efird (602) 996-9000.

South Mountain (monthly)
Rotate churches each month, 12 noon, November 10, (every 2nd Wednesday). Call Andrew Cunningham (602) 243-1900.

Celebrate Jesus 2000...Caring for the Valley of the Son.
Celebrate Jesus 2000 is a call for the mobilization of the body of Christ to pray for and share the gospel with every man, woman and child in America by year-end 2000.

To connect with Celebrate Jesus 2000 Phoenix initiatives call:

Valley Coordinator: Bill Agee (623) 582-9227

Prayer: Bobby Capps: (623) 386-0300

Church Planting: Gary Dodrill (623) 936-4481

Evangelism: Jerry Martin (480) 835-9706

Urban; John Newson: (602) 841-1400

Youth: Brad Smith (602) 789-1111 x2

Church Strengthening: Michael Blankenship (602) 955-1544

Volunteers: Kimily Waldron (623) 582-9227

GLOSSARY OF TERMS

AAGR: Average Annual Growth Rate, a method of measuring the average annual growth of the Church for any number of years. (See Appendix "M" for further definition and description.)

Accountability Factor: The Church is accountable for acting upon the truth it knows, describing the situation in society as it actually exists in truth (fact, reality, light). Information precedes and breeds accountability.

Adaptive Deceptions: "Deceptive schemes adopted by the enemy to replace earlier strategies whose powers have waned. They may be viewed as necessary course corrections to the Adversary's strategies" (George Otis, Jr.).

algorithm: A defined process or step-by-step procedure that leads to and assures the desired output from a given input. Mathematical procedures, such as the procedure for calculating church growth in an area, are often described as algorithms.

alternative futures: A possible vision for a neighborhood, city or nation. A futurist does not predict the future, he develops possible alternative futures. These are modeled, simulated and studied. From these scenarios others can choose the future desired. When working with a city, for example, leaders may work together to explore various alternatives to define a common vision that all can agree to work toward.

amonie: A people, city or neighborhood without an identity. Durkheim, the great French sociologist, argues that people in the world were suffering from anomies, a condition of having no "name." God calls us by name to participate in His creative purpose, thus identifying us as unique (see Genesis 35:10, I Samuel 3:4, and Acts 9:4).

Animism: The belief that all natural elements (mountains, rivers, trees, thunder, fire, stars, animals and human beings) are endowed with and linked to a conscious spiritual life force.

anticipatory democracy: A process through which all groups can have the opportunity to influence the decisions that will determine their future (Toffler). This is in contrast to a theocracy in which leaders seek God for the Divine Initiative for their city and work toward that within their spiritual gifts.

Bethel Point: A point or gate from which God breaks through, usually to a spiritual or physical dimension. A gate to the heavenly kingdom (Genesis 28:16-19).

cartography: The art or process of making maps or charts. Mapping.

census group blocks: These are subdivisions of the census tracts, with each containing about 200-300 households, or a population of about 700.

census tract: Geographic areas defined by the U.S. Census Bureau for tracking population. Each has an approximate population of 4000 people.

channel: A link used to transfer information or other form of energy between two nodes. An information service provider (ISP) is a channel to the Internet.

charismatic power: A Christian tradition with an emphasis on the supernatural and miraculous. It addresses the desire to experience and express spiritual gifts.

charismatic tradition: A Christian tradition with emphasis on the Spirit-empowered life. It addresses the yearning for the immediacy of God's Presence among His people. It holds all of the spiritual gifts mentioned in the New Testament are operative today.

Church Growth: In the classic sense, it is the science of measuring, and determing the factors of, growth and non-growth of the Church, churches and denominations in peoples, cities and nations of the world. Dr. Donald McGavran helped establish and popularize the term when he inaugurated the Institute of Church Growth in Eugene, Oregon in the 60's which later moved to be adjunct to Fuller Seminary in Pasadena, California.

closure: A reference by researchers to completing the Great Commission by reaching every people group with the Gospel in this century.

complexity-consciousness: The basic tendency of the city, nation or neighborhood linking an increase in physical complexity in the area with a parallel increase in the knowledge of that area's part of God's Kingdom plan. The counter force to the Law of creating visual or mental images of the future that will motivate action.

contextualization: Literally meaning "weaving together." It implies the construction of an interpretive bridge into a culture such that the message being conveyed is acceptable and relevant to the culture. In missions and evangelism, it is the weaving together of the biblical message and the target culture. John Stott says effective contextualization requires double-listening: first listening to God, then listening to the target audience.

DAWN strategy: A process of mobilizing the whole Church in a city or nation to reach the whole city with the whole Gospel, and to see a gathering of outreaching believers within practical and cultural distance of every person in every class and kind of people (saturation church planting). There are several principles relating to the process that when applied have proven the process to be successful in a variety of nations, cities, cultures and circumstances (See *DAWN 2000: 7 Million Churches To Go* by Jim Montgomery).

ethnic group: an ethnic group is a group of people who share a common culture, think of themselves as sharing a common culture, or are defined by others as sharing a common culture. A racial group is supposedly a group of people who share a biological heritage that is specific to them and distinct from other groups. ("Supposedly" because not all biologists agree. - Luhman in *The Sociological Outlook.*)

excluded middle: A term used for the missing middle worldview layer of most of the Western world. The non-Western world has three layers: the cosmic or transcendent, the supernatural layer on earth, and the empirical world of our senses (George Otis, Jr.).

extrapolation: Extending of a variable into the future by assuming it will change at the same rate in the future as it has in the past. Also called trend analysis. For example, we can extrapolate church attendance in the future if we know the present rate of church growth and assume that rate will not change. Extrapolations are often made for a variety of other rates for "what if" projections.

feedback: The use of part of the output of a system as input to control the output and keep it within certain defined limits.

future shock: Stress and disorientation induced in individuals by subjecting them to too much change in too short a time.

futures research: A term used to describe the study of the future

(Ex: *Future Shock*, by Alvin Toeffler, and, *Global Paradox* by John Naisbitt).

futurism: A mood or movement that emphasizes the need to think seriously about the future.

futuristics: The discipline of study that deals with possible future developments.

futurology: The study of the future.

gate: A portal through which spiritual forces can act.

gatekeeper: A person who lives and acts at a spiritual portal in a city, church or region. This person is the node in the community for information in terms of a specific vision and controls or monitors access to information, discernment, wisdom, knowledge, healing and other spiritual gifts necessary for the vision to happen. In the Old Testament, a gatekeeper and watchman were not the same (2 Samuel 18:26).

gifts, spiritual: The unique part of our being that God gives us for His redemptive purposes. The equipment and enablement for life and ministry that is the portion for every born-again believer.

Harvest Field: The context in which the Church finds itself. All non-believers.

Harvest Field Data: Data that describes the non-true Church elements of the city and the various entities and societies that make up the city (See Appendix "G").

Harvest Force: All truly Christian organizations (institutions) and individuals actively involved in the Great Commission enterprise, either directly or indirectly. In a broad sense, the true Church.

Harvest Force Data: Data that describes, locates, and/or statuses the true Church in any of its variety of expressions (See Appendix "F").

holiness tradition: A Christian tradition that places emphasis on the virtuous life. It addresses the need to affirm a stronger moral fiber in the contemporary Church.

holistic: Pertaining to the whole of the Biblical Gospel. Emphasizing the interrelatedness or wholeness of a complex system in contrast with focusing on a portion of the system. The healing of a city, for example, is a holistic process. Spiritual healing is related to economic, social, emotional and political healing.

human secularism: A type of religion in which the person is elevated in importance and viewed as able to become perfect within his or her own resources. Human secularism evolved from early Roman and Greek philosophy, eventually reaching most of southern Europe (See Schaeffer, Francis, *How Should We Then Live?*).

information: Data that has been processed to some level or order by the human mind. Messages that change our world view, however trivial.

intentional communities: A community, city, or neighborhood that has definite visions, purposes and goals toward which energy and resources are mobilized. With churches, the term is used in contrast with storekeeper communities with little direction or overall goals.

intercessory prayer: Petitions, entreaties and thanksgivings made on behalf of another. Intercession involves the act of standing between the object of prayer and negative spiritual forces. Where God is involved, the positioning is taken in order to submit requests. In the case of Satan, it is to deflect his attacks.

inward journey: That part of our spiritual pilgrimage that is in dialogue with ourselves, God and others. Living a life of contemplation, meditation and a growing awareness about life and its relationship with God's work in the world (in contrast with the outward journey).

John Knoxer: A visionary leader for a city or neighborhood that has compassion for the city and can mobilize key leaders who in turn can mobilize the larger Church in the area for carrying forth the Great Commission in the city, toward seeing significant transformation take place. John Knox declared, *"Give me Scotland lest I die!"*

kairos: The essential period, the decisive period in time, the God-given moment. It is an opportunity imposed on us by God. We can know what it is, but fail to act on it. Kairos is not our own time that we choose and arrange for ourselves, but is the commanded opportunity, a definite step in God's previously conceived plan of salvation for mankind.

Law of Entropy: The second law of thermodynamics that, in terms of the city, relates to the city and its neighborhoods "running down" to an abased level of chaos and disorder. God alone stands outside of this dynamic, and man only to the extent he is in cooperation with God.

link: A communications path between two nodes, a channel. (see network, node).

linkage: A passive system of nodes and links. A city linkage is a community of people with resources and needs. A linkage (unlike a network) remains passive unless it is pushed. It has no common objective or goal, and responds to link needs and resources as it is pushed. Another example of a linkage is the Internet. Although highly organic and dynamic, it is passive until it is pushed in terms of needs.

logos: A word that denotes more than the name of an object, but an expression of thought, such as God's Divine Initiative given in revelation (See John 1:1).

meme: "The basic unit of cultural evolution. Examples of memes are musical tunes, certain phrases and words, ideas, clothing fashions, architectural models, etc." (Richard Dawkins).

mission statement: A statement that expresses the mission and purpose upon which we are embarking. It often includes: who we are, what we do, who we serve, and why we exist. Individuals, organizations, churches, neighborhoods and even cities often hold mission statements.

modeling: The use of algorithms, mathematical equations or games to simulate the real world processes or behavior. This also applies when strategies that are working in one city are applied effectively to another city. (However, it is usually the principles and not the forms which are expressed that are transferable.)

MSA: Metropolitan Statistical Area, a specific regional area used by the U.S. Census Bureau to define an urban complex.

multifold trend: A many-faceted trend in which many variables change that are interrelated with each other. Ex: Church growth in an area is related to a variety of internal and external factors.

Nehemiah Factor: The Nehemiah Factor deals with getting the right information, in the right form, into the right hands, at the right time. Nehemiah was the right person to receive information relating to the state of the children of Israel. In partnership with God, he applied the information to rally the people and restore Jerusalem and the nation of Israel to God.

network: An integrated system of nodes and links to accomplish a specified objective. A human network is a collection of people that are interlinked and share a common goal. Networking is the best method for bringing a variety of resources together to meet a need.

node: A specified connect point in a network for creating, editing, receiving or retransmitting messages.

outward journey: The part of our spiritual pilgrimage that is in dialogue with the world: the city, neighborhood or nation. Living into our calling, uniqueness, mission and destiny in a risk-style life.

paradigm: A pattern, example or model. paradigm shift - a change in the accepted cultural paradigm on the part of a large portion of the culture. In the late eighteenth century there was a paradigm shift from an agricultural age to an industrial age. Today, another paradigm shift is occurring.

people group: A significantly large group of people who have a common affinity because of their shared language, religion, ethnicity, residence, occupation, class, caste, situation, or a combination of these things.

Power Points: "Specific natural or man-made locations that are widely regarded as bridges or crossover points to the supernatural world. Such sites are often made numinous by the investments of faith offered over time by large numbers of people" (George Otis, Jr.).

Prayer expeditions: Long-distance, trans-territorial prayerwalks along strategically developed routes. Intercession is offered for entire countries and regions.

Prayer journeys: Intentional prayerwalking in cities other than one's own. Sites often include capitals and ideological export centers.

Prayer-walking: The practice of on-site, street-level community intercession. Prayers offered by participants are in response to immediate observations and researched targets.

prediction: A statement that something will happen in the future. Implies more certainty than forecasting or conjecturing.

rhema: The specific and spoken word of God that the Spirit brings to mind for use in a time of need. It is distiguished from *logos* -- it implies power or dunamis, in the speaking (See Eph. 6:17).

sacramental tradition: A Christian tradition that places emphasis on ceremonial worship and receiving the sacraments.

scenario: An interrelated sequence of events (script) that might possibly occur in the future. A projected model or simulation.

SCP: Saturation Church Planting (see *DAWN Strategy*).

Discovering Your City

Second Law of Thermodynamics: A basic and fundamental law of science that says the universe is "running down", or returning to the chaos from which it was created. An organism can only evolve to a higher form if energy is applied from outside the system. This law contradicts Darwin's concepts of evolution.

social justice tradition: A Christian tradition which places an emphasis on the compassionate life.

softspace: The information boundary of an individual or organization. The boundaries of a softspace are like membranes, admitting certain information and blocking other types. The acceptance and rejection of information is based on certain keys, which are in turn defined by our specific needs.

Spiritual Mapping: The discipline of diagnosing and responding to the spiritual dynamics at work in a given community. Otis: "The process of superimposing our understanding of forces and events in the spiritual domain onto places and circumstances in the material world." Victor Lorenzo: "The sum of divine revelation, plus research, plus proven facts, whose objective is to provide complete and accurate information about the identity of spiritual powers that rule over a region, their size of operation, and the forms and methods they use to influence the people and church of that region."

Spiritual Quest Sites: Any natural or man-made location that facilitates spiritual investigation, ritual or worship. Examples include temples, mosques, sacred mountains and metaphysical bookstores.

stewardship: A level of accountability with respect to resources. "Now all of Christianity is agreeing that they were wrong about something so basic as God's first instruction to the human race on how people should behave and act here in the earthly world. They are saying they were wrong for two thousand years and that now dominion has to be redefined in terms of stewardship. This is a revolution, a theological revolution. It's a profound transformation" (Jeremy Rifkin).

strategy: A general or inclusive plan for reaching a specific goal. Carrying forth a strategy will usually include a variety of tactics, or sub-plans. Example: the strategy to win a battle may be to employ air, land and sea forces. Tactics in this scenario would be the individual, detailed plans of each arm of the service for how they would carry out their role in the overall strategy.

stronghold: "A mindset impregnated with hopelessness or evil that causes us to accept as unchangeable situations that we know are contrary to the will of God" (from Victor Lorenzo). "Ideological fortresses that exist in the mind and objective territorial locations. They repel light and export darkness" (Otis).

subculture: Those specific objects, skills, ideas, beliefs and patterns of behavior that are unique to individual segments of an overall population and that differ from the larger culture.

synergy: The action of a number of parts working together so that the result is greater than the sum total of the separate actions of the parts. The Church, as the Body of Christ, is designed to be a synergistic institution. (Synergy based upon unity in diversity is the challenge.)

symbiosis: The relationship of two or more different organisms in a close association that may be, but are not necessarily, of benefit to each other. (From "companionship"- Gr.)

tactics: See description under "strategy."

target area (TA): A segment of the city, large or small, which becomes the focus for a particular purpose.

target people (TP): A segment of society targeted for ministry. A people grouping based on a criteria independent of geopolitical description, such as an ethnic or socio-economic group.

technicism: A world view or philosophy of life in which security is placed in human reason and rational or logical thinking. Obedience is to the mystification of social and technical tools. The individual is reduced to a machine, with rational explanations for all behavior.

telecommuting: The use of telecommunications, information technology and electronic cottages to replace or reduce travel to a work space.

teleconferencing: Any type of conferencing system using electronic communication media.

theocracy: A method of governing in which leaders see God as the Divine Initiative for their city and work toward vision that lies within their spiritual gifts.

time horizon: The greatest distance into the future to which an organization, church or individual plans.

topology: The geometric arrangement of nodes and links in a network. The primary topologies are the bus, star and ring.

Discovering Your City

Toynbee Crisis: Internal destruction of a community or culture, in part from its failure to learn from similar patterns of the past. So-called from Arnold Toynbee's observation that nineteen of twenty-two great civilizations have been destroyed from within.

transformation: A changing of form, shape or consciousness. Futurists use it to refer to a basic cultural paradigm change. For a Christian, it refers to the changed life, church, neighborhood or city through the dunamis of the Holy Spirit.

trend: The change in a variable over a period of time.

vision statement: A picture of a preferable future. It is more specific, focused and detailed than a mission statement.

vision walking: Visioning on site with insight. Walking a neighborhood to gain a vision of what God wants to do there.

watchman: A person who is uniquely sensitive to how God is working in a particular region, city or church (Isaiah 62:6). He/she sees the vision of what God is doing and can prophetically pray that vision into existence (see Numbers 11:10ff). The watchman has the responsibility of communicating the vision to the gatekeeper (2 Samuel 18:26).

weavers: "Those people who can take new ideas as they are introduced and link them with existing concepts and approaches" (Robert Theobald).

win-win strategy: A game strategy in which both players win, producing synergy so that both are richer. Strategies for a city or neighborhood should aim for win-win models.

world view: A perception of reality by an individual, church, organization, neighborhood or city. *"A set of presuppositions (or assumptions) which we hold (consciously or unconsciously) about the basic makeup of our world"* (James Sire in *The Universe Next Door*). It is our essential intellectual framework or system of beliefs through which we correlate and make sense of all our experiences in this world. It is the lens through which we view our various contexts, near and far, simple and complex. Sire sets forth that a well-rounded worldview includes basic answers to at least five questions:

1. What is real, or what is ultimate reality? (What is the nature and character of God and the universe?)
2. Who are human beings? (What is the nature and character of

    humans?)
3. What happens to people at death?
4. What is the basis for morality and ethics?
5. What is the meaning of human history?

zeitgestalt (or gestalt): A time-phase or plan in which an organism forms or evolves. "All living things have this in common: they begin to live as an organism at a definite moment, they develop according to a very definite plan, acting and reacting to their environment, and finally as an organism they vanish. The permanent factor in the process - that which actually forms the personality - is not the matter out of which the organism is made; for this changes constantly during life. Far more characteristic of a particular organism and the constant factor in its life is the plan according to which it is formed and evolves - its time-phase or zeitgestalt. Each living being has its own time-formation " (Theodor Bovet). Cities, neighborhoods and nations all have a unique zeitgestalt.

Bibliography

* Anderson, Leith. *A Church for the 21st Century* (Minneapolis, MN: Bethany House Publishers, 1992)
* Barker, Irwin & Posterski, Donald C., *Where's a Good Church?* (Winfield, BC: Wood Lake Books Inc., 1993)
* Barna, George. *Generation Next* (Ventura, CA: Regal Books, 1995)
  -- *The Index of Leading Spiritual Indicators* (Dallas, TX: Word Books, 1996)
  -- *Turning Vision Into Action* (Ventura, CA: Regal Books,
  -- *The Second Coming of the Church* (Nashville: Word Publishing, 1998)
* Butt, Howard E. Jr. *Renewing America's Soul* (New York, NY: Continuum, 1996)
* Dawson, John. *Healing America's Wounds* (Ventura, CA: Regal Books, 1994)
  -- *Taking Our Cities for God: How to Break Spiritual Strongholds* (Lake Mary, FL: Creation House, 1989)
* Dennison, Jack. *City Reaching: On The Road to Community Transformation* (Pasadena, CA: William Carey Library, 1999)
* Hewitt, Hugh. *Searching for God in America* (Dallas: Word Books, 1996)
* Hunter, George. *How To Reach Secular People* (Nashville: Abingdon Press, 1992)
* Malphursm Aubrey. *Vision America: A Strategy For Reaching a Nation* (Grand Rapids, MI: Baker Books, 1994)
* Montgomery, *Jim. DAWN 2000: 7 Million Churches to Go* (Pasadena, CA: William Carey Library, 1989)
  -- *Then The End Will Come* (Pasadena, CA: William Carey Library, 1989)
* Murren, Doug. *The Baby Boomerang: Catching Baby Boomers as They Return to Church* (Ventura, CA: Regal Books, 1990)
* Otis, George, Jr. *The Last of the Giants* (Tarrytown: Chosen Books, 1991)

Discovering Your City

-- *Spiritual Mapping Field Guide: North American Edition*
(Lynnwood, WA: The Sentinel Group, 1993)
-- *The Twilight Labyrinth* (Grand Rapids: Chosen Books, 1997)
-- *Informed Intercession* (Ventura: Renew Books, 1999)
• Regele, Mike. *Death of the Church* (Grand Rapids: Zondervan
Publishing House, 1995)
• Silvoso, Ed. *Biblical Principles for Reaching Our Cities for
Christ* (San Jose, CA: Harvest Evangelism, 1993)
• Stringer, Doug. *The Fatherless Generation* (Shippensburg:
Destiny Image Publishers, 1995)
• Tapia, Andres. *Reaching the First Post-Christian* (Wheaton, IL:
Christianity Today. September 12, 1994, pp. 18-23)
• Wagner, C. Peter. *The Third Wave of the Holy Spirit: Encoun-
tering the Power of Signs and Wonders Today* (Ann Arbor:
Vine Books, 1988)
• Wagner, C. Peter and Donald McGavran. *Understanding Church
Growth* (Grand Rapids: William B. Eerdmans Publishing
Company, 1970)
• Wagner, C. Peter. *The New Apostolic Churches* (Ventura: Regal
Books, 1998)
• Waymire, Bob and C. Peter Wagner, *The Church Growth Survey
Handbook* (Colorado Springs, CO: OC International, 1981,
1994)
• Waymire, Bob. *The Information Strategy Manual* (Etna, CA:
Light International, 1995)
-- *The National Research Mobilization Handbook* (Etna, CA:
Light International, 1994)
-- *The City Survey Data Guide* (Etna, CA: LIGHT International,
1999)
• Weiss, Michael J. *The Clustering of America* (New York: Harper
& Row, 1988)
• Wingerd, Roy A.. *DAWN Research Handbook: Principles and
Process of Research for a DAWN Project* (Colorado
Springs: DAWN Ministries, 1992)

Prayer Bibliography:

• Aldrich, Joe. *Prayer Summits: Seeking God's Agenda for Your Community* (Portland, OR: Multnomah Press, 1992)

• Beckett, Bob. *Commitment to Conquer* (Grand Rapids: Chosen, 1997)

• Duewel, Wesley L. *Touch The World Through Prayer* (Grand Rapids, MI: Asbury Press, 1986)

• Hawthorne, Steve and Kendrick, Graham. *Prayerwalking: Praying On Site With Insight* (Orlando, FL: Creation House, 1993)

• Johnstone, Patrick. *Operation World* (Grand Rapids, MI: Zondervan, 1993)

• Otis, George Jr. *Informed Intercession* (Ventura: Renew Books, 1999)

• Sheets, Dutch. *Intercessory Prayer: How God Can Use Your Prayers to Move Heaven and Earth* (Ventura, CA: Regal Books, 1996)

• Silvoso, Ed. *That None Should Perish: How to Reach Entire Cities for Christ Through Prayer Evangelism* (Ventura: Regal Books, 1994)

• Wagner, C. Peter. *Churches That Pray* (Ventura: Regal Books, 1993)

-- *Prayer Shield* (Ventura: Regal Books, 1992)

-- *Breaking the Strongholds in Your City* (Ventura, CA: Regal Books, 1993)

-- *Engaging the Enemy* (Ventura, CA: Regal Books, 1991)

-- *Praying with Power: How to Pray Effectively and Hear Clearly from God* (Ventura: Regal Books, 1997)

• White, Tom. *The Believer's Guide To Spiritual Warfare* (Ann Arbor: Servant Publications, 1990)

-- *Breaking Strongholds: How Spiritual Warfare Sets Captives Free* (Ann Arbor: Servant Publications, 1993)